DEFAMILIARIZATION
IN LANGUAGE AND LITERATURE

DEFAMILIARIZATION IN LANGUAGE AND LITERATURE

R. H. Stacy

SYRACUSE UNIVERSITY PRESS
1977

First Edition

Library of Congress Cataloging in Publication Data

Stacy, Robert H.   1919–
    Defamiliarization in language and literature.

    Includes index.
    1. Style, Literary. 2. Figures of speech.
I. Title.
PN227.S7   801'.95   77-8536
ISBN 0-8156-2184-1

Виктору Борисовичу Шкловскому

R. H. Stacy is associate professor of Russian Literature at Syracuse University and the author of *Russian Literary Criticism: A Short History* (1974).

Die Sprache ist die einzige Chimäre,
deren Trughaft ohne Ende ist.

Karl Kraus

PREFACE

AN ARTIST illustrates a bird-identification guide, a technical writer
prepares a description of a new computer for prospective buyers,
a language instructor teaches his students the rudiments of Japanese,
a satellite takes the first photographs of the dark side of the moon, an
agency is engaged to advertise a new product—in all these situations
something unfamiliar is being made familiar. But a sculptor depicts a
human figure in the form of cubes, an artist paints a picture with re-
verse perspective, a composer presents a composition of serial music,
a writer describes love-making in the language of cricket, a cipher
clerk puts a message into code, a friend tells you that he has finally
managed to purchase a crembalum, your wife informs you that she
intends to serve an *épigramme* for Sunday dinner—in all these cases
something familiar is being made unfamiliar. The Russian critic Viktor
Shklovsky coined the word *ostranenie* (which is often rendered as
"making strange" in English but which I shall translate as "defamiliarization") to refer, especially in literature, to situations analogous or
similar to the latter group of examples. Shklovsky believed that it is
the function of art to make the familiar unfamiliar; that "art exists to
make one feel things, to make the stone *stony*. The purpose of art is
to impart the sensations of things as they are perceived and not as they
are known."

This book is both an introduction to Shklovsky's theory of *ostranenie* and an attempt to show, on the basis of numerous examples, how
this concept is applicable to a wide range of human activity in general
and to language and literature in particular. The only license that I
have allowed myself is to interpret Shklovsky's theory in a broad sense

ix

by following up his explicit statements as well as implicit corollaries. That is, so far as literature is concerned, I have included under the term "defamiliarization" not only a large area of traditional metaphor and periphrasis but also such devices, for example, as parody, hyperbaton, and anacoluthon, as well as movements like *gongorismo*, surrealism, and *chosisme*. Shklovsky's term may also be applied to such matters as the creative manipulation, radical upsetting, and distortion of familiar traditions or the "foregrounding" of certain artifices formerly employed less manneristically. Regarding those cases of defamiliarization outside of literature which I refer to, careful consideration of these by the reader will, I believe, convince him that no sophistic reasoning is involved and that the common denominator in all such examples is, in fact, a process whereby something familiar is made unfamiliar or seen in a new and different light. I do, however, mention several typical areas in which defamiliarization is generally not encountered, and I call the reader's attention to certain ambiguous cases as well as the "familiarization/defamiliarization paradox."

The first chapter is a general introduction to the concept of defamiliarization with examples drawn from a number of areas. In the second chapter there is a more detailed account of what Shklovsky meant by defamiliarization, some discussion of the background, and a brief review of how the theory has been received and of comments by other scholars and critics concerning the phenomena that interested Shklovsky. In the third and fourth chapters I cite and discuss many representative examples of types of defamiliarization in several languages and literatures. The first four sections of the last chapter briefly survey those periods in various literatures during which defamiliarization appears to be most prominent; and in the final section I offer some conclusions. Although there has been a constant temptation to cite further relevant material and to comment on provocative associations, I have tried to keep the scholarly apparatus at a minimum; I trust, however, that some of my notes may be of interest to students.

Syracuse, New York   R. H. Stacy
Spring 1977

CONTENTS

INTRODUCTION

1

CAREFUL READERS of Tolstoy—not to mention numerous scholars and critics—have noted a particular ironic device in this writer's fiction. Let me cite, for the sake of illustration, one of the most familiar and typical examples, part of a lengthy passage occurring in *War and Peace* and concerning a visit to an operatic performance in Moscow, during which the scenes on the stage are viewed through the "innocent" eyes of Natasha Rostov:

> In the second act there were cardboard monuments on the stage, and a round hole in the backdrop representing the moon. Shades had been put over the footlights and deep notes were played on the horns and contrabass as a number of people appeared from both sides of the stage wearing black cloaks and flourishing what looked like daggers. Then some other men ran onto the stage and began dragging away the maiden who had been in white and was now in pale blue. They did not take her away at once, but spent a long time singing with her, until at last they dragged her off, and behind the scenes something metallic was struck three times, and everyone knelt down and sang a prayer. All these actions were repeatedly interrupted by the enthusiastic shouts of the audience.[1]

1. *War and Peace,* Part Five, 9. I have used the translation by Ann Dunnigan in the Signet Classics series (New York: New American Library, 1968), pp. 680–81. There is another excellent but more malevolent passage in *Resurrection* (Book I, chapter 39) in which the mass is defamiliarized. But one need not go to literature to find such a technique: the American comic, Andy Griffith, has an act in which he describes the reaction of a "hill-billy" as he watches his first football game.

Here Tolstoy has Natasha view the actions on the operatic stage through the eyes of (in Greek) an *eirōn* (i.e., one who *eirōneuetai* or "feigns ignorance"). She—or, we should say, the author—sees and considers, but as if through the eyes of a naive and almost primitive onlooker, something which is traditionally viewed not only as a beautiful and elaborate synaesthetic art form but also as a conventionally recognized feature of a cultured and sophisticated society. Tolstoy "takes apart" this complex phenomenon, "deromanticizes" and "debunks" it, and clearly, here as elsewhere, makes a very apparent and unequivocal judgment. In effect, Tolstoy "intends the reader to *see through* the device, to make some kind of judgment on the basis of the 'innocent' vision with which he has been presented."[2] In brief, this method of Tolstoyan irony involves "never calling complex things by their accepted name, but always disintegrating a complex action or object into its indivisible components. The method strips the world of the labels attached to it by habit and by social convention, and gives it a 'discivilized' appearance, as it might have appeared to Adam on the day of creation."[3]

Various modern critics have devised a number of interesting terms and phrases in order to refer to this particular method of irony used by Tolstoy and other writers, past and present. Thus we have such attempts to generalize as "the accurate notation of phenomena without any concern for their meaning" (Jean-Paul Sartre), "negative allegory" (Dmitry Chizhevsky), "perception without apperception" (Leon Stilman), "perspective by incongruity" (Kenneth Burke), and "making strange" (Ezra Pound). But the name most often associated with this aspect of Tolstoy's fiction is that of the Russian Formalist critic, Viktor Shklovsky (b. 1893). Early in this century Shklovsky (whose contributions in this respect will be discussed in the following chapter) introduced the phrase *priem ostranenija* by which to refer to such instances of irony in Tolstoy and other writers. Usually the Russian phrase is translated as "the device of making strange," the word *priem* (device) being a key term in Shklovskian and Formalist literary theory which, in its most radical stage, viewed a literary work as the sum total of the

2. Elizabeth Beaujour, *The Invisible Land: A Study of the Artistic Imagination of Iurii Olesha* (New York: Columbia University Press, 1970), p. 23.

3. D. S. Mirsky, *A History of Russian Literature* (New York: Knopf, 1949), pp. 252–53. Cf. the comments of Elder Olson on the poetry of Dylan Thomas: "[Thomas] uses an odd form of periphrasis which makes a familiar thing unfamiliar by describing it accurately but in the manner of a primitive definition: thus 'shafted disk' for 'clock,' 'bow-and-arrow birds' for 'weathercocks.'" *The Poetry of Dylan Thomas* (Chicago: University of Chicago Press, 1961), p. 60. See also below on Golding's *The Inheritors*.

stylistic devices used in it. The word *ostranenie* (see p. 32) is also rendered in English as "estrangement," "alienation," and "defamiliarization."[4] The word "alienation" in English is already closely associated, however, with Marx (it translates his *Entfremdung* which is rendered in Russian as *otchuzhdenie*) and, to a lesser extent, with Berthold Brecht's concept of *Verfremdung* ("V-effect").[5] "Estrangement" is fairly suitable, although it too has rather well-established non-literary connotations. Least used, it seems, by scholars in the West is "defamiliarization" which, however, despite its clumsiness and novelty, is most appropriate as a *terminus technicus*. This word is the one I shall use throughout this study not only to translate Shklovsky's *ostranenie* but also to cover, as we shall see, a much broader range of metaphor.[6]

2

Some of the careful readers mentioned above will also have recalled by now that the method referred to in connection with Tolstoy as defamiliarization is by no means a new device; and that it especially has, like so much else in Tolstoy, eighteenth-century affiliations. Thus Voltaire describes soldiers playing their drums as "murderers six foot

4. Occasionally "dishabituation" is also used: see D. E. Berlyne, *Aesthetics and Psychobiology* (New York: Appleton-Century-Crofts, 1971), p. 140. James Kugel in his *The Techniques of Strangeness in Symbolist Poetry* (New Haven: Yale University Press, 1971) refers briefly to Shklovsky and the Russian Formalists and renders *ostranenie* as "strangifying."

5. Sometimes *Verfremdung* is used in the Shklovskian sense. See Wolfgang Kayser, *The Grotesque in Art and Literature*, translated U. Weisstein (New York: McGraw-Hill/Indiana University Press, 1966), p. 163: "I use the word 'alienation' (*Verfremdung*) with emphasis on its prefix: something that was familiar is made strange."

6. "Defamiliarization" is used, for example, in *Russian Formalist Criticism: Four Essays*, translated Lee Lemon and Marion Reis (Lincoln: University of Nebraska Press, 1965). Frederic Jameson also uses "defamiliarization" in his *The Prison-House of Language: A Critical Account of Structuralism and Russian Formalism* (Princeton: Princeton University Press, 1972).

See Gillo Dorflès, *Artificio e natura* (Torino: Einaudi, 1968), p. 235: "Questo concetto [i.e., Shklovsky's *ostranenie*] è indubbiamente utile e fertile per tutta la poesia, anche del passato: ma è tanto più applicabile all'arte dei nostri giorni dove si è fatto largo uso di queste espediente. Ma l'interesse maggiore che si ha di rivalutare il concetto di *ostranenie* deriva dalla possibilità di applicarlo . . . a tutte le arti e non solo alla poesia." Dorflès uses *estraneamento* to translate *ostranenie*. Cf. also Andras Hamori, *On the Art of Medieval Arabic Literature* (Princeton: Princeton University Press, 1974), p. 82: "The Russian critic V. Shklovsky . . . reminds his readers of Gogol's comparison of the sky with the clothes of God: an association with more power than analytic clarity in it. And we should not for a moment suppose that the simile that more or less obscures the simple object occurs only in modern literature [!]."

tall, dressed in scarlet and beating on the distended skins of asses," while Montesquieu in his *Lettres persanes* satirizes French customs and mores as seen through the "naive" eyes of a Persian traveler.[7] But I shall postpone for the time being a survey of the literary history involved here and cite, as further examples, several modern instances similar to the Tolstoyan variety. In *Point Counter Point* (1928) Aldous Huxley, who was as acerbic a debunker of sundry romantic notions as Tolstoy, describes the music of the violin as the result of one's drawing "rosined horsehair across the stretched intestines of lambs." In Frederick Buechner's highly mannered novel, *A Long Day's Dying* (1949), the following passage occurs:

> The mirror reflected what seemed at first a priest. A white robe, which fell from his thick shoulders in crescent folds, circumscribed with diminishing accuracy the ponderous art of his great head, and gave to his obesity the suggestion of vulnerability rather than strength as he sat face to face with the fact of himself. This effect was intensified by the resignation with which he suffered what might have been his acolyte, also dressed in white, either to anoint his flourishing, grey-brown hair as if in preparation for some imminent solemnity or to give it a tonsure.

Here the quite conventional and familiar scene of a man in a barber's chair getting his hair cut is defamiliarized almost to the point of obscurity.

William Golding's novel *The Inheritors* (1955) is a treasure-house of defamiliarization, and Shklovsky (who at this writing is still alive in Soviet Russia) would certainly take delight in reading this novel and analyzing it as a *tour de force* of *ostranenie*. In this case the author has very successfully used defamiliarization in coping with the problem of writing a piece of fiction concerned with the activities of prehistoric man; he has somewhat modified his language and style in so doing, but at the same time has managed—has been compelled, rather—to provide sufficient clues for the reader. Here is a representative passage:

7. Novalis refers to soldiers with their bright red uniforms as "oxides of the state"; see R. Tymms, *German Romantic Literature* (London: Methuen, 1955), p. 176.

    In his Foreword to *The Silent Traveller in Paris* (New York: Norton, 1956), Sir William Hayter says of the author Chiang Yee's verbal and graphic impressions of Paris that the charm lies "in seeing familiar, or generally familiar, objects from an unfamiliar angle."

The bushes twitched again. Lok steadied by the tree and gazed. A head and a chest faced him, half-hidden. There were white bone things behind the leaves and the hair. The man had white bone things above his eyes and under the mouth so that his face was longer than a face should be. The man turned sideways in the bushes and looked at Lok along his shoulder. A stick rose upright and there was a lump of bone in the middle. Lok peered at the stick and the lump of bone and the small eyes in the bone things over the face. Suddenly Lok understood that the man was holding the stick out to him but neither he nor Lok could reach across the river. He would have laughed if it were not for the echo of the screaming in his head. The stick began to grow shorter at both ends. Then it shot out to full length again.

The dead tree by Lok's ear acquired a voice.

"Clop!"

His ears twitched and he turned to the tree. By his face there had grown a twig: a twig that smelt of other, and of goose, and of the bitter berries that Lok's stomach told him he must not eat. This twig had a white bone at the end.[8]

Even out of context, a careful reading makes clear that one primitive man on one side of a river is being shot at with bow and poisoned arrow by another but quite different primitive man on the other side.

In the eighth chapter of Lawrence Durrell's *Mountolive* (1958) there is the following passage:

"Now" she said angrily, determined not to lose the piastres which in her imagination she had already spent, already owed, "now I will make you *La Veuve*" and he drew his breath in an exultant literary thrill to hear once more this wonderful slang expression stolen from the old nicknames of the French guillotine, with its fearful suggestion of teeth reflected in the concealed metaphor for the castration complex.

8. *The Inheritors* (New York: Harcourt, Brace & World, 1962), p. 106. See a stylistic study of this novel by M. Halliday, "Linguistic Function and Literary Style: An Inquiry Into the Language of William Golding's *The Inheritors*" in *Literary Style*, edited by Seymour Chatman (New York: Oxford University Press, 1971), pp. 330–65. See also the comments of Maurice Nadeau in *The French Novel Since the War* (New York: Grove Press, 1967), p. 139, on Claude Ollier's novel, *La Mise en Scène:* "In *La Mise en Scène*, which describes a tropical expedition, the world is a decor, man an insect whose behaviour belongs to entomology. With minute care for detail, the author describes the gestures, the actions, reports the speech, recounts the events that the reader needs to recreate the whole. It is not a puzzle, since all the constituents of the construction are already connected by the narrative. The author is no more present in this narrative than in what he presents to our view and records like a machine. He wishes to be and is, in fact, pure vision."

La Veuve! The shark-infested seas of love which closed over the doomed sailor's head in a voiceless paralysis of the dream, the deep-sea dream which dragged one slowly downwards, dismembered and dismembering . . . until with a vulgar snick the steel fell, the clumsy thinking head ("use your loaf") smacked dully into the basket to spurt and wriggle like a fish. . . . *"Mon coeur,"* he said hoarsely, *"mon ange . . ."*

Here, as has been done down through the centuries in the literatures of both the Occident and the Orient, the erotic—more exactly, a sexual act in this case—has been defamiliarized.[9] Again I suggest that Shklovsky would be especially interested in this example, since he once treated erotic defamiliarization in some detail in one of his best-known studies, *Iskusstvo kak priem* (Art as Device, 1917).

Finally, Vladimir Nabokov's novel *Ada* (1969) is replete with instances of defamiliarization, often erotic and occasionally, as in this excerpt, quaintly euphemistic: "They [Van and Ada] stopped for a moment under the shelter of an indulgent tree, where many a cigar-smoking guest had stopped after dinner. Tranquilly, innocently, side by side in their separately ordained attitudes, they added a trickle and a gush to the more professional sounds of the rain in the night, and then lingered, hand in hand, in a corner of the latticed gallery."[10]

I should like now to make several comments on the examples so far cited. First, it is extremely unusual to find, in the critical literature on writers who employ something like the Tolstoyan type of irony—i.e., on writers such as Huxley, Buechner, Golding, Durrell, or Nabokov, or in stylistic studies of their individual novels—references either to Shklovsky and *ostranenie* or even to defamiliarization in a more general sense, viz., enhancing the "effect by presenting ordinary things in an unusual form or in an unusual perspective."[11] In studies of Tolstoyan defamiliarization by Slavists, of course, the name of Shklovsky is always mentioned, and quite frequently such names as Voltaire, Montesquieu, and Swift—or even Kafka—are referred to.[12] True, one

9. A. Thibaudet notes, incidentally, in *"Langage, Littérature et sensualité"* (NRF 37, p. 716) that the eighteenth century was *"le siècle de la périphrase érotique."* There is also, in the woman's "technical" reference in the Durrell passage, an element of idiolect: this may also be used for defamiliarization: see p. 128.

10. *Ada* (New York: McGraw-Hill, 1969), p. 263. Other pertinent examples are on pp. 375, 410 ff., and 561.

11. Gleb Struve, *Russian Literature Under Lenin and Stalin, 1917–1953* (Norman: University of Oklahoma Press, 1971), p. 207.

12. See, e.g., John Bayley, *Tolstoy and the Novel* (New York: Viking Press, 1966), p. 103 ff. References to Shklovsky and *ostranenie* are occasionally encoun-

often encounters in studies of Aldous Huxley (or of novelists who practice similar modes of irony and satire) comments on "debunking," "disenchantment," "distancing," or "dehumanization"; and in studies of novelists such as Buechner, Durrell, and Nabokov there are frequent and appropriate references to "mannerism," "*fin de siècle* decadence," or *faisandage*. But specific references to defamiliarization are quite rare. Even in the otherwise excellent study of Golding's *The Inheritors* the closest approach to the concept of defamiliarization comes in the "Discussion of Halliday's Paper" where the editor writes: "Speaking particularly of Voltaire, Sartre noted that these [the philosophical tales] proceed by a decomposition of finalized acts in a time-span without finality, such that there appears a procession of external and partial aspects which become absurd precisely because finality is lacking. In this respect *The Inheritors* seems to have some link with *le conte philosophique*, and with literature like *L'Étranger* whose vision is innocent." But of course it is not unusual to encounter in contemporary criticism discussions of particular literary phenomena which Shklovsky and the Russian Formalists put their fingers on precisely and to which they gave technical terms. Thus in *Limits of the Novel* David Grossvogel writes: "Structural subtleties that would normally be hidden within the fictional weave of the novel Sterne deliberately exposes for the purpose of turning his book into yet another kind of parlor game which he plays with his reader."[13] This is exactly Shklovsky's *obnazhenie priema* or "laying bare the device."[14] However, many of the terms used by critics in America and Europe to refer to such passages as those quoted above, although they may not refer specifically to defamiliarization, are in many respects quite germane and in the chapters that follow most of these relevant allusions will be mentioned.

Second, the passages quoted above, including that from Tolstoy, show that the device of defamiliarization may appear in different varieties and may be used in a number of ways with various intentions and effects. The example from Voltaire, with its mixture of social satire and the "metonymic periphrases" so characteristic of the eighteenth-century pseudoclassical style, is most clearly similar to the Tolstoyan mode.[15] The example from Huxley is also characteristically

tered in books on aesthetics and the psychology of art, e.g., H. and S. Kreitler, *Psychology of the Arts* (Durham, N.C.: Duke University Press, 1972), and Berlyne, *Aesthetics and Psychobiology*.

13. *Limits of the Novel* (Ithaca: Cornell University Press, 1968), p. 148.

14. See Victor Erlich, *Russian Formalism* (The Hague: Mouton, 1969), p. 77.

15. The seventeenth century—and the baroque in general—also shows a

ironic, although the more direct social satire so frequent in this novelist is absent in this brief excerpt. The passages from Buechner and
Nabokov have a curious and somewhat affected manneristic quality
about them; here the defamiliarization seems to be aesthetically motivated and the language is fastidiously oblique. Durrell's erotic defamiliarization is more complex, with a surprisingly large number of
allusions packed into a single paragraph. Most interesting of all, from
a purely technical point of view, is the excerpt from *The Inheritors*.
This may be called an instance of defamiliarization *par excellence:*
the device here is almost wholly functionally motivated. There is
nothing here that we would call, in any traditional sense, "decadent,"
"manneristic," or "affected"; indeed, there is no irony here (excepting
that irony taken in the broadest sense and meaning "saying one thing
and meaning another") and certainly no satire. But what, without for
the time being using the term "defamiliarization" and assuming, of
course, that we are dealing with certain forms of tropes, or metaphor
(in the broadest sense of this word), is the element common to all
these passages? We can find in all but two of these excerpts examples
of metonymy or synecdoche (in Tolstoy "something metallic" = a
bell; in Voltaire "distended skins of asses" = drums; in Huxley "rosined horsehair" = a violin bow; in Nabokov "they added a trickle and
a gush" = they urinated). But in the passages from *Mountolive* and
A Long Day's Dying the technique relies more on antonomasia or
metaphor (in the narrower meaning of this word): thus "acolyte" in
Buechner = barber; while in Golding there are instances of both
metonymy and metaphor. Though the technique (especially in eighteenth-century examples) may often involve metonymic elements and
though, quite naturally, metaphor is present (as it is in all language—
Jean Paul Richter remarked that language is in fact "a graveyard of
dead metaphor"), on the basis of our examples, many more of which
will be cited, we can see that the essence of what we call defamiliarization involves, above and beyond specific stylistic devices and
tropes, something more general. And that general, distinguishing
feature is simply this: something ordinary, commonplace, or familiar
(an object, event, situation, or tradition) is, in one way or another,
made to appear unfamiliar. In the case of Tolstoy, a scene from an

---

predilection for defamiliarization in several areas. See, e.g., D. B. Wilson, *Descriptive Poetry in France from Blason to Baroque* (Manchester: Manchester
University Press, 1967), p. 209: "But then the seventeenth century as a whole
devotes much of its ingenuity to the art of disguise—one may say without over-
much exaggeration that the whole of the complicated and unreal structure built
up around Versailles depends on this."

opera is described, quite unfamiliarly, as something absurd. Buechner describes an ordinary, mundane event in hieratic terms and thus renders it strange. Golding cannot be said to have defamiliarized pre-historic life, since this is hardly familiar; what he has done, however, is, by exploiting specific linguistic resources, to defamiliarize a narrative tradition (had Edgar Rice Burroughs and H. G. Wells been truly creative artists, they might have done something similar). Through verbal artifice Durrell renders unfamiliar and slightly cryptic a familiar situation (familiar, at least, in certain circles) that would in any case be treated in quite explicit and familiar fashion by Henry Miller. So, too, Nabokov, whose artifices are more than familiar,[16] periphrases familiar acts.

3

It goes without saying that not all prose writers or, for that matter, not all poets have any desire or intention to defamiliarize their subject matter. A great mass of writers are rather intent on making what is unfamiliar familiar to their readers, and this is especially true of good expository nonfiction; it would hardly do for a good technical writer, for example, to indulge in stylistic eccentricities. Occasionally, however, literary critics, one of whose generally accepted key functions is to elucidate and to familiarize, do indulge in such pursuits, and their essays, however circumstantially and exquisitely expressed, tend to obfuscate. Here, for example, out of context, to be sure, is a brief excerpt from Empson's essay, "Marvell's Garden":

> But if they were simply called the same we would not so easily be satisfied by the tricks. What we feel is that though they are essentially unlike they are practically unlike in different degrees at different times; a supreme condition can therefore be imagined, though not attained, in which they are essentially like. (To put it like this is no doubt to evade a philosophical issue.) A hint of the supreme condition is thus found in the actual one (this makes the actual one include everything in itself), but this apparently exalted claim is essentially joined to humility; it is effective only through the admission that it is only a hint.

16. See Patricia Merivale, "The Flaunting of Artifice in Vladimir Nabokov and Jorge Luis Borges," in *Nabokov: The Man and His Work*, edited by L. S. Dembo (Madison: University of Wisconsin Press, 1967), and John Stark, *The Literature of Exhaustion* (Durham, N.C.: Duke University Press, 1974), on Borges, Nabokov, and Barth.

And there is little doubt that some of the contemporary literary scholars of various persuasions (whose key function, one would think, is also to elucidate) occasionally seem to be usurping the creative writer's penchant for "making strange":

> It is no coincidence, for example, that it is the phallic period during which children learn to master the rolled [r], a sound which presupposes a strong erection of the tongue. It seems as if we could take literally the metaphor of the English phonetician T. H. Pear which characterizes the non-apical pronunciation of /r/ as an "emasculation."
>
> Elise Richter has described the habit of a certain doctor of pronouncing /r/ with strong rolling when he addressed inferiors. The rolling became weaker according to the social status of his clients, vanishing completely in the presence of the Queen of Serbia.[17]

But many a novel contains passages like this, from Salinger's *The Catcher in the Rye*: "It was still pretty early. I'm not sure what time it was, but it wasn't too late. The one thing I hate to do is to go to bed when I'm not even tired. So I opened my suitcases and took out a clean shirt, and then I went in the bathroom and washed and changed my shirt. What I thought I'd do, I thought I'd go downstairs and see what the hell was going on in the Lavender Room. They had this night club, the Lavender Room, in the hotel." Nor are similar passages found only in such poor stuff; even the so-called symbolic and "art" novels are often replete with explanatory matter—witness the technical cetological passages in *Moby Dick*. And poetry—or perhaps I should in this case say verse—is frequently a mere lineation of prosaic banalities—or worse. In this connection consider the opening lines of a Soviet poem by Pavel Radimov, appropriately entitled "Slop" (*Pojlo*):

> All kinds of garbage was shoved during the day into the big bucket;
> Here is a cucumber peel, crumbs, moldy bread;
> In the yellow slop made from the cabbage soup and soapy water
> There floats, roots up, a limp and beslobbered onion.[18]

17. From "The Functions of Vocal Style" by Ivan Fónagy in *Literary Style*, edited by Chatman, p. 161. I can hardly refrain from quoting in English translation two lines by the French surrealist Gui Rosey: "The eternal erection of poets' tongues/Traces a vaginal sign on the horizon's thighs." Cited in J. H. Matthews, *Surrealist Poetry in France* (Syracuse: Syracuse University Press, 1969), p. 129.

18. Russian text in *Modern Russian Poetry*, ed. Vladimir Markov and Merrill Sparks (Indianapolis: Bobbs-Merrill, 1967), p. 702. This is a classic of adoxog-

Though a writer may defamiliarize his subject matter or his content, real or imaginary, without modifying his language in any significant way, i.e., without using a radically unconventional language (and this is true of the examples so far given), that same subject matter may be rendered by another writer in a language that is itself strange, unconventional, highly allusive and metaphorical, even enigmatic; in a language that is, in effect, non-realistic. To take a specific instance, a writer may refer to a certain aspect of reality in, as we say, so many words, using a language that is mainly denotative and eminently clear; or he may refer to the same thing by using a term or phrase drawn either from the colloquial language or from a learned, technical lexicon; or, going further, he may use a Shakespearian tag ("lock," "et cetera," "plum," "wound," etc.) or a foreign word (*le sadinet, Bellamaunz*); or he may employ a mock-serious euphemism drawn from any number of languages; or he may proceed even further afield by using metaphorical periphrases of ever-increasing complexity—*la figue fendue, le canapé couleur de feu*—and so on.

If we assume that there is a difference between form and content, despite the manifold and clever attempts to do away with this difference (a difference which is inherent in language with its Janus-faced *signifiant/signifié* aspect),[19] there are, as I see it, four possibilities which simply represent the four possible combinations of either the realistic or non-realistic treatment of either realistic or non-realistic subject matter:

1. realistic language and realistic content,
2. realistic language and non-realistic content,
3. non-realistic language and realistic content,
4. non-realistic language and non-realistic content.

The great bulk of prose fiction (including the passages cited in the previous two sections) in the Western literatures falls into category 1. Category 2 also includes a large mass of fiction—folk literature dealing with the supernatural, science fiction, utopias, etc. For example, early

---

raphy and, in its own way, an example of defamiliarization. See Helga de la Motte-Haber, *Das Triviale in Literatur, Musik und Bildender Kunst* (Frankfurt a. M.: Klostermann, 1972).

19. One of the most delightful statements is that of De Sanctis: "In poesia non ci è propriamente né contenuto, né forma, ma che, come in natura, l'uno e l'altro. Il gran poeta è colui che uccide la forma, di modo che questa sia esso medesimo il contenuto." The frequently quite foolish statements by linguists as to the non-existence of content stand in marked contrast with René Wellek's observation: "The mere fact that great poets and writers . . . have exercised an enormous influence often in poor and loose translations which hardly convey even an inkling of the peculiarities of their verbal style should demonstrate the comparative independence of literature from language."

in *The War of the Worlds* H. G. Wells describes the appearance of a Martian, but his language is anything but unconventional; it is, in fact, essentially the same language that might be used to describe a rose garden. Category 3 might well be represented by Joyce's *Ulysses*. Here the subject matter (certain happenings in the city of Dublin during the twenty-four hours of a single day, June 16, 1904) is realistic but the language—in the sense explained above—is not. Many other literary products of what we loosely call "modernism" also fall into this category. As for category 4, this obviously offers the most difficulties for the reader, who must first work his way through the language only to encounter subject matter or content that is also nonrealistic. As an example of this category, we might cite a passage from William Burroughs' *Nova Express:*

> "They are giving me a short necessary process"—Screaming crowds entered the corridors the audience and the patios—The feeling and proclivities of connection with officials invaded with inexorable limestone and cousins twice removed—Virus and drugs plaintiff and defendant—Heavy Metal People of Uranus in a thousand languages live robes that grow on them blue and hideous diseases—The little high-fi junk note shrieking for compensation—Spine frozen on the nod color flashes the heavy blue mist of bank notes.[20]

But even in certain areas of folk literature examples close to the fourth category may be found. Thus some Russian *byliny* or "folk epics" have as their subject matter fantastic characters in fantastic situations, and the language is defamiliarized to a considerable extent: for example, prepositional phrases are broken up and the preposition repeated before each element of the phrase (polyprotheticism), diminutive endings are added to infinitives, and other forms modified in other ways in order to secure dactylic clausulae.

There are close—"graphic"—parallels to these categories in painting: thus in category 1 we have again the great bulk of realistic depiction with an extreme form in *trompe l'oeil;* in category 2 the paintings of the Decadents (e.g., Séon, Moreau, Delville)—including the meticulous, realistic portrayal of monsters;[21] in category 3 the

---

20. On Burroughs' juxtapositional or montage technique, see an interview with this writer in *Paris Review* (Fall 1965): 13–49.

21. I have in mind especially Séon's painting, *Le Désespoir de la Chimère;* see color plate 70 in Philippe Jullian, *Dreamers of Decadence* (New York: Praeger, 1971).

paintings of the Cubists; and in category 4 the paintings of some of the so-called Symbolists (e.g., Vrubel or Čiurlionis[22]). If we use the "window and scene" analogy (where window = form, scene = content[23]), in category 1 we look through a clear window and see something familiar; in category 2 we look through the window and see something strange; in category 3 we find it difficult to see through the window, but if we do, we see something quite familiar; and in category 4 we again have a rather opaque window and, if we manage to peer through it, we again see something strange and unreal.[24]

In the passages cited earlier, then, as examples of defamiliarization, the language is fairly conventional. In the case of the Tolstoyan passage where the author's particular mode of defamiliarization is ironically motivated and where, here as elsewhere, he is intent on debunking certain aspects of genteel upper-class Russian society or tsarist secular and ecclesiastical functions, category 1 is mandatory. Irony requires that the "window" be transparent and that we see clearly what is being "taken apart" and made to look absurd. The "scene" in the Tolstoyan passage is realistic, but this *need* not be the case: in Dostoevsky's *The Brothers Karamazov*, for instance, there is a long dialogue between Ivan and the Devil, a scene in which the particularly Dostoevskian irony is put wholly into the mouth of Satan who is radically defamiliarized as a "bourgeois" Devil:[25]

> My dear friend, above all things I want to behave like a gentleman and to be recognized as such. . . . I really love mankind. . . . I love the realism of earth. Here with you everything is circumscribed,

22. Specimens may be seen in Edward Lucie-Smith, *Symbolist Art* (New York: Praeger, 1972), illustrations 125 and 138.

23. See the use of this imagery by Ortega y Gasset in "The Dehumanization of Art" in *Literary Modernism*, edited by Irving Howe (New York: Fawcett, 1967), pp. 84–85. Beaujour also makes use of this image in *The Invisible Land*, pp. 79–80.

24. Perhaps it would be better to say that in categories 3 and 4 our vision stops at the surface of the window and that what we see on this surface (as "in" a painting by Mondrian) *is* the work of art. If, incidentally, there is an objection to the scheme of the four categories, if, for instance, it is objected that the realistic/non-realistic dichotomy in language is hardly on the same ontological footing as the realistic/non-realistic dichotomy applied to content, we may look at the situation in another way. We may simply assume, for example, that the writer, whether his "scene" is realistic or non-realistic, has at his disposal a range of language from the most conventional to the most unconventional.

25. That is, as compared with the Devil in Mann's *Doctor Faustus* who is a traditionally august figure, speaking MHG, making a "deal" for Leverkühn's soul, etc., or even the Devil in Bulgakov's *The Master and Margarita*.

here all is formulated and geometrical, while we have nothing but
indeterminate equations! . . . I like going to the public baths, would
you believe it? I go and steam myself with merchants and priests. . . .
I like going to the doctor too; in the spring there was an outbreak of
smallpox, and I went and was vaccinated. . . . I have the same philosophy as you. That is true. "I think, therefore I am," I know that for a
fact. All the rest, all these worlds, God and even Satan—all that is not
proved, to my mind.[26]

Although the modes of defamiliarization are different in the cases of
Tolstoy and Dostoevsky, the motivation—irony—is the same, and in
both cases the language is conventional.

The passage from Buechner's novel, on the other hand, is hardly
ironic (unless, out of context, we take it as a parody of a manneristic,
oblique style) and it appears to be aesthetically motivated;[27] the same
holds true for the Nabokov passage. In these cases, too, the "window"
must at least be translucent, since the two activities (or "scenes")
being described are after all to be understood. The "scenes" are
realistic, even commonplace; in such passages it would not do to have
a non-realistic scene, since the very purpose of such passages is, first,
to display the writer's cleverness and, second, to offer the reader an
everyday event but clothed in a language that is, while conventional,
periphrastic and allusive. How absurd would be the results if H. G.
Wells had described his Martian in the language of Buechner!

The passage from Durrell, an example of erotic defamiliarization,
relies for its effect on the man's and the woman's (i.e., the author's)
knowledge of certain esoteric erotic terminology which the reader, in
order to "explicate" the passage fully, must either himself be familiar
with or must research. (In actual fact, however, most novel readers
would merely skim over the passage without understanding, much
less appreciating, the allusion; in a novel, as in "real" life, one may
ignore many phenomena, something that is not quite so easy to do in
a poem.) This passage is not ironic and the "scene," at least in the
world of Durrell, is quite conventional; the language, too, is quite con-

26. It should be noted that the whole scene with the devil is given verisimilitude by being explained (although one is apt to overlook this) as a hallucination
on the part of Ivan due to "brain fever" (Constance Garnett translation).

27. See the comments of Walter Allen (who quotes this passage from Buechner) in *The Modern Novel* (New York: Dutton, 1965), pp. 304–305: "The style,
as Ihab Hassan observes, 'attempts to mythicize Tristram by establishing connections between the sacred and the profane, the priestly and the lay qualities of
existence.' But the connections seem to be stylistic only."

ventional, although somewhat pretentious.[28] The difficulty of the passage—its defamiliarization—is simply due to the doubly metaphoric (or metaleptic) use of the term "*La Veuve.*"

The defamiliarization we encounter in the passage from Golding's novel is of particular interest. The "scene" is realistic (as realistic as that of any historical novel), and there is no irony or manneristic affectations; the language here is on the whole conventional but slanted in the direction of simplicity and not (as in the Buechner, Nabokov, and Durrell passages) in the direction of archness. The author has tried to suggest a primitive level of human development and has (in addition to employing here the monosyllabic name "Lok"[29]) brought certain linguistic features to the foreground: a preponderance of short words, mainly of Teutonic origin; an avoidance of abstract terms of Greco-Latin origin; personified constructions ("a stick rose upright," "the dead tree acquired a voice"). Had the author gone much further in defamiliarizing the language of his narrative (by avoiding modalities such as "would have laughed," by replacing "stomach" with a periphrasis, even by supplying a partial glossary of invented "Neanderthal language" accompanied by footnotes), the "window" would have been even more darkened and the difficulties for the reader increased to a point of unacceptable obscurity.

Let me cite here another passage from a short story by Adolf Muschg where there is a similarly motivated defamiliarization. The narrator here, a farmer, is telling a court of law about his incestuous relations with his two daughters (Lina and Barbara) and the reasons for these; the language reflects both the narrator's rather low mentality as well as a certain reluctance or inability to be precise:

> So when Lina had gone to the road house with the milk, I took Barbara a jug of milk warm from the cow to her bedroom, since I had to take everything up to her, which became troublesome, and it was March 23rd. She grabbed hold of my hand at once so that I could feel if there wasn't a swelling there, and when I felt her she started that cruel screaming again, as well as spasms which ran visibly across her whole body, and I felt so sorry for her that I couldn't help myself but allowed what followed to occur. Then she got up quite amiable and

28. Anthony Burgess, summing up his discussion of Durrell in *The Novel Now,* says of the *fin de siècle* atmosphere of the *Alexandria Quartet* that the "decadence smells of stale incense."

29. Lok is a variant of Loki and one thinks of his adoption by the Aesir in Teutonic mythology; but this is very likely irrelevant.

smiled like a rogue, but I was too fond of my daughter to bear her any grudge, only begged her sincerely never to let it happen again. Whereupon she quite easily drank the milk which she had pushed far away from her before, then went quite sensibly to the kitchen and prepared an evening meal, which she hadn't done for a long time, indeed started cooking and frying so much that I got alarmed and we fed well that evening, in great obliviousness even drank brandy till it gave rise to new acts, and I was even the instigator, which I would beg to have taken into account today in my daughter's favour. That was March 23rd. For I must add that because of constant physical labour I am still full of sap, quite unexpectedly, nor knew any remedy for it till Lina took the matter into her hands, but this occurred with good will on both sides, like the relations with my younger daughter, which I did not need any more, as you will understand.[30]

Here the "scene" is realistic but defamiliarized by being described in a language that is, while conventional, strongly colored by the presence of many imitations of a substandard colloquial speech with characteristic anacolutha and synesis and an occasional stilted expression—a rambling, mostly paratactic narration that frequently seems a kind of stream of consciousness. (Though we have the passage from Muschg in translation, it might very well have been written in English and it will serve our purpose in this case as well as the original.) The effect is intensified by the striking disparity between the nature of the activities being suggested and the baldness, the commonplaceness, and the ingenuousness of the narrator's language. It is an effect comparable to that achieved by Isaac Babel in his *Red Cavalry* tales where the most cruel and wanton acts are described in an offhand sort of way (and frequently by characters much like Muschg's narrator). It is, incidentally, interesting that Babel employs what the Russians call *skaz* (i.e., idiolect technique, see p. 128) in his exposition. In effect (although Babel radically distorts the language of his characters), this is also the manner of Muschg's narration.

4

It might be useful at this point to consider briefly, as a background for viewing the linguistic and literary phenomena under discussion, some analogical forms of defamiliarization in the world

30. From "The Scythe Hand," translated by Michael Hamburger, in *Encounter* (November 1975): 3–10.

around us. There is, first of all, the defamiliarization that puzzles us in dreams, a phenomenon that has been noted from ancient times and which has often been utilized in literary works for various purposes. Dream defamiliarization has been of particular interest to psychiatrists such as Freud. Then there is defamiliarization in nature—the so-called celative coloration or other forms of concealment, notably among insects (*Palophus titan* or the "walking straw" of Australia is one of the most remarkable examples). Such phenomena in nature suggest various techniques of camouflage used by men, not only military camouflage but also methods of concealment used by hunters from very early times to the present. We also think of disguises of different kinds, from those of the spy or criminal (including plastic surgery) to a father's dressing himself in a Santa Claus costume at Christmas, or masquerades and the whole subject of masques and masks, screens and facades, including the employment of "screenladies" in Dante's *Vita Nuova* and the troubadours. There is the dissimulation practiced by members of oppressed or persecuted races, cults, sects, or parties, this often involving "secret languages," and there is ritually motivated defamiliarization (e.g., the precautions taken in connection with taboos). Games of various kinds, involving people or objects or both, are occasionally based on forms of defamiliarization—charades and jigsaw puzzles.[31] Riddles and enigmas are quintessentially forms of defamiliarization, and the word "enigmatography" might well be used of a large number of poems and, especially, of many modern novels.

From the earliest times men and women have done various things to their bodies to defamiliarize themselves: they have deformed heads and feet, elongated and pierced lips and ears, painted their faces (as well as the bodies of the dead), tattooed their skin, straightened, curled, and dyed their hair, and have employed various preparations to conceal or modify odors. Ovid's *Medicamina faciei femineae* is a cosmetics text and preserves in its hundred lines or so a number of Roman beauty recipes, including one for a mudpack. Roman ladies liked to alter the color of their hair after bleaching it with "Mattiac balls," and Ovid admonishes his mistress about the practice:

> Did I not tell you to leave off dyeing your hair? Now you have no hair left to dye. And yet nothing was handsomer than your locks. They came down to your knees and were so fine you were afraid to

31. See Johan Huizinga, *Homo Ludens* (Boston: Beacon, 1955), pp. 43 and 134–35.

comb them. Your own hand has been the cause of the loss you deplore.
You poured the poison on your own head. Now Germany will send you
slave's hair and a vanquished nation will supply your wig. How many
times, when you hear people praising the beauty of your hair, you will
blush and say to yourself: "It is a bought thing to which I owe my
beauty, and I know not what Sicamber virgin they are admiring in me.
And yet there was a time when I deserved all those compliments."[32]

In Europe, depending on the time and fashion, women have depilated
different areas of the body, heightened their foreheads by retracting
the hairline, narrowed or eliminated eyebrows, used beauty spots,
and have applied a multitude of pastes, pigments, and perfumes.
They have variously disguised or emphasized buttocks and breasts
with clothing and have piled their hair in fantastic coiffures. "There
are," writes Sir Max Beerbohm in "A Defence of Cosmetics," "many
such husbands as he who, suddenly realising that his wife was painted,
bad her sternly, 'Go up and take it all off,' and, on her reappearance,
bad her with increasing sternness, 'Go up and put it all on again.' "
      There are many instances in history of ethnic defamiliarization,
one of the best examples being the *Saqaliba* or Arabized Slavs of
medieval Spain. Brought originally into Spain as captives taken along
the eastern marches of Germany, the *Saqaliba* were first mercenaries
under the Moorish emirs and then, like the Mamelukes of Egypt, rose
to independent power among the so-called "party kingdoms" or
taifa-states in the eleventh century. Harold Livermore writes: "Another group of *taifas* was formed by the palace Slavs: one Khayran
and his successor Zuhayr held Almeria and Murcia; al-Mujahid took
Denia and the Balearics, and Nabil Tortosa. In the midst of these
Arabised Russians, a grandson of Almanzor set himself up in Valen-
cia."[33] It is interesting, too, that a Count Iosif Kornilievich O'Rurk
(died 1849) served as a cavalry general in the Russian Army during
the Napoleonic wars. He was the son of Cornelius O'Rourke, who
came to Russia under Peter the Great, and the grandson of Brian
O'Rourke, a descendant of the kings of Connaught who had settled in
France in the seventeenth century. In this case we have a real-life
instance of onomastic defamiliarization; were a Russian by the name
of O'Rurk to appear in fiction, the effect would certainly, like the
strange names in the works of Gogol, be defamiliarizing.

      32. Quoted in Aytoun Ellis, *The Essence of Beauty* (New York: Collier,
1962), pp. 68–69.
      33. *A History of Spain* (New York: Grove, 1960), p. 120.

The graphic arts (especially painting) and sculpture offer a rich field of exploration. To a considerable extent much modern, non-objective art involves defamiliarization (it is a commonplace to note the close affiliations between Shklovsky and the Russian Formalists, Russian futurism, and cubism) and from early times the practice of adding "strangeness to beauty" has frequently been advocated and commented on.[34] Marcel Proust once summed up the impact of the great painters (particularly the modernists) as *une métamorphose des choses,* and Emerson (one of Proust's favorite writers, as Harry Levin notes) defined the whole poetic process in almost identical terms.[35] Wolfgang Kayser, commenting on defamiliarization in surrealism, observes that occasionally a "super-clarity" makes the world "doubly strange."[36] In this particular connection, there have been many relevant and provocative statements on the nature and effect of "close-ups," both in nature and in art. Aldous Huxley remarks: "Nature at the middle distance is familiar—so familiar that we are deluded into believing that we really know what it is all about. Seen very close at hand . . . it seems disquietingly strange, wonderful beyond all comprehension."[37] And René Huyghe had this to say in the *New York Times,* January 17, 1960: "Take one of the modern works that claim to be non-figurative, a product of Abstract Expressionism, for example, and compare it with a scientific photograph, which, through the use of the electronic microscope or Wilson chamber, enables us to perceive the structure and motion of matter. We are immediately aware of disturbing coincidences. The normal appearance of reality is no longer there." The Russian writer Evgeny Zamyatin makes a similar observation:

Have you ever had occasion to examine a tiny piece of your own skin under a microscope? If you ever do, you will probably be startled at first: instead of your pink, delicate, smooth skin, you will see clefts,

34. See Wylie Sypher, *Rococo to Cubism in Art and Literature* (New York: Vintage Books, 1963), Part Three, Chapter II.

35. Harry Levin, *Refractions* (New York: Oxford University Press, 1966), p. 275.

36. *The Grotesque in Art and Literature,* p. 163. Anna Balakian, discussing the origins of surrealism, refers to Ortega y Gasset's comments on the new "infrarealism"—the evasion of traditional reality through the overemphasis of details which tend to distort familiar perceptions; see *The Literary Origins of Surrealism* (New York: New York University Press, 1947), p. 58. See p. 100 on infrarealism in the *nouveau roman.*

37. *Collected Essays by Aldous Huxley* (New York: Bantam, 1960), p. 170 ("Landscape Painting as a Vision-Inducing Art").

enormous bumps, pits; from the pits something rises, as thick as a young lime tree—a hair; next to it is a huge boulder—a speck of dust.

What you see will bear little resemblance to the usual appearance of skin; it will seem incredible, like a nightmare. Now ask yourselves: which is more real—this smooth, pink skin, or that one, with the bumps and clefts? After some thought, you will have to say: the real thing is that incredible skin we see under a microscope.[38]

So far as painting is concerned, this is interesting, since very often analogies are drawn between certain features of art and literature: thus one might claim that literary super-realism (i.e., extremely detailed literary realism) is to a radically defamiliarized style what *trompe l'oeil* is to a radically non-objective art. But in point of fact, extreme aniconic literary realism (*le réalisme écrit*) may produce the same effects of strangeness as do numerous examples of *trompe l'oeil*.[39] It is in connection with surrealism that one occasionally encounters remarks suggesting—but only suggesting—what Shklovsky meant by defamiliarization, even though, again, the name of Shklovsky is seldom mentioned.[40] Nor is defamiliarization as such ever mentioned in connection with *art nouveau*, although various other descriptive terms are employed suggesting a comparable kind of treatment. Thus Allan Janik and Stephen Toulmin in their study of Wittgenstein's Vienna write the following (discussing *Jugendstil*): "Under no circumstances should an object reveal its purpose by its shape—if, indeed, the object served any function at all. Ornament thus became a way of distorting things, an end in itself rather than an embellishment."[41]

In the area of communications, various techniques of "scrambling" messages are forms of defamiliarization, the Spartan scytale being one

38. Quoted in *A Soviet Heretic: Essays by Yevgeny Zamyatin*, edited and translated by Mirra Ginsburg (Chicago: University of Chicago Press, 1970), pp. 41–42. See also a brief notice by John Canaday, "Art: Enlarged Detail as Picture," in *The New York Times*, December 9, 1972, on a new interest in "close-up" painting.

39. See Nadeau, *The French Novel Since the War*, p. 139 (discussing the novels of Claude Ollier): "That meticulous, even fanatical description of reality can plunge, like dreams, into unreality." Photography, too, can defamiliarize: much art photography of the present, by using unusual camera angles, filters, and other devices, renders quite strange ordinary scenes of life. See also a brief article by Hilton Kramer, "The Dubious Art of Fashion Photography," in *The New York Times*, December 28, 1975, p. 28.

40. See, for example, Balakian, *The Literary Origins of Surrealism*, p. 9, where the author implies defamiliarization on the part of the surrealists when she refers to the "mania" of their romantic predecessors "which consists in reducing the unknown entity to the level of the known."

41. *Wittgenstein's Vienna* (New York: Simon and Schuster, 1973), p. 97.

of the earliest examples. Ciphers, codes, and other forms of secret messages, secret languages, argots, jargons, and cants must also be included.[42] Defamiliarization in typography is quite frequent, both in literary and commercial contexts. Many of the modernists, especially novelists, have resorted to sometimes significant, sometimes merely disturbing typographical oddities of one kind or another; thus Trotsky ironically suggests that one of the early Soviet writers, Boris Pilnyak, who occasionally toyed with the typography of his fiction, was in effect saying to his readers: "Please do not forget—I am a romanticist!" Amongst many examples closer to home, we could mention a number of writers, from Laurence Sterne to "e. e. cummings" in this connection, and there is a good deal more of this sort of typographical experimentation in avant-garde circles today.[43] Occasionally, in reading old European codices, the untrained eye is puzzled by not only the script and the ductus of individual letters but especially by the highly ornate (frequently historiated) initial capitals. Today, too, many of us can recall having seen examples of commercial advertising typography where certain words or phrases are difficult to make out because familiar elements are omitted or distorted, presumably to attract the reader's attention—or, as Shklovsky would say, for the purpose of "defacilitation" (*zatrudnenie*). There is to my knowledge no other script that has afforded such freedom to defamiliarize as the Arabic, with its wide range of ornamental and decorative styles—"beautiful," as I. J. Gelb remarks, "but difficult to read."[44]

In the field of music, aside from such particular defamiliarizing techniques as *themata cancrizantia* or "cancrizans" (i.e., retrograde) movement[45] or syncopation, there is the more general feature of juxtaposition in modern music (e.g., serial music), often likened to similar developments in literature and the other arts.[46] Certainly the

42. On the French *javanais, loucherbème*, and *contrepéterie*, etc., see p. 54.

43. See Emmett Williams, ed., *An Anthology of Concrete Poetry* (New York: Something Else, 1967), and Eugene Wildman, ed., *Experiments in Prose* (Chicago: Swallow, 1969).

44. *A Study of Writing* (Chicago: University of Chicago Press, 1963), p. 229. Arabic decorative script often struck foreigners as mere decoration and was imitated as such. See Kurt Erdmann, *Arabische Schriftzeichen als Ornamente in der abendländischen Kunst* (Wiesbaden, 1953).

45. There is also retrograde inversion: "In Hindemith's *Ludus Tonalis* the Postlude is the retrograde inversion of the Prelude which can be played by turning the pages upside down" (*Harvard Brief Dictionary of Music*). Cf. the palindrome and such things as inverted perspective in painting and Dylan Thomas' "inverted sonnets."

46. See Roger Shattuck, *The Banquet Years* (New York: Anchor Books, 1958), Chapter II.

radical departures that we find in Stravinsky and Schönberg provide striking examples of the defamiliarization of traditional and accepted musical canons if not of "reality" in any ordinary or literary sense. It might also be noted here that in music as well as in literature and painting we have an extreme form of defamiliarization (although other terms might be used to describe this particular development): I refer to such things as John Cage's *Four Minutes, Thirty-three Seconds,* an opus of total silence, analogous to Malevich's painting *White on White* or A. Gnedov's "Poem of the End" (*Poèma kontsa*) which is actually a blank page.[47]

I cannot close these remarks without referring to another area in which defamiliarization is of considerable importance—cookery. The art of altering the appearance and the taste of food, although it is sometimes done as an economical or emergency measure, is often intended to surprise and delight the appetite and of course to vary dishes that might become routine. Thus in a bilingual edition of Apicius' *Ars magirica* (or *De re coquinaria*) one of the editors writes in the Introduction that "the Romans abhorred the taste of any meat, fish, or vegetable in pure form. There is hardly a single recipe which does not add a sauce to the main ingredient, a sauce which changes the original taste radically. . . . Petronius' feast of Trimalchio offers grotesque examples of the Roman passion for the disguise of food."[48] In more recent times French cuisine especially has a similar reputation. But many of us can recall, after having eaten a dish prepared by an excellent and resourceful cook, being surprised to learn that it was, in fact, something quite ordinary, that the defamiliarization resulted from the skillful and innovational manipulation of the raw material by an expert. The achievements of a good cook, like those of a good writer, are no mean things: "to coax mouths that never open but in a simper, to beguile vapourish women, to give a *papier mâché* stomach occupation and rouse unsubstantial forms whose appetites are but the shadow of desire, requires more genius, penetration, and sheer hard work than the solution of one of the most difficult problems in the geometry of the infinite."[49]

47. The Russian "text" of this work together with its "translation" may be found in *Modern Russian Poetry*, edited by Markov and Sparks, pp. 362–63.

48. *The Roman Cookery Book*, edited by Barbara Flower and Elisabeth Rosenbaum (London: Peter Nevill, 1958), p. 20. At the end of one of his recipes, Apicius adds that, after tasting the dish, no one will know what he is eating!

49. Jean Brillat-Savarin, *The Physiology of Taste* (New York: Dover, 1960), p. 223.

5

Whereas the great majority of instances of defamiliarization in the history of human activities—especially in art and literature—clearly indicate purposeful employment and recognizable motivation, there are occasions when defamiliarization is accidental. If one examines the coinage of Mercia, for example, down to the reign of Offa II (eighth century A.D.), one can observe a steady deterioration in form from crude but adequate copies of Roman coins to coins which bear a mere jumble of lines and masses and with no resemblance at all to the original models. Although the later Mercian coins have a certain stylized and abstract quality about them, the defamiliarization in this case is simply the result of poorer and poorer copies made by a succession of less and less skilled die-makers over a period of years.[50] Although a rough linguistic parallel to this would be something like the history of a term such as "forlorn hope" (a hobson-jobson in English), there is a comparable effect of defamiliarization in literature when once familiar domains of reference cease, for one reason or another, to be meaningful even to a relatively small portion of educated persons or when these domains no longer provide common points of reference for both writers and readers. These phenomena have often been pointed out in connection with various literatures and literary periods, and I quote a relevant passage on this topic from George Steiner:

> As footnotes lengthen, as glossaries become more elementary (right now it might still be "Troilus: Trojan hero in love with Cressida, daughter of Calchas, and betrayed by her," but in a few years the *Iliad* itself may require identification), the poetry loses immediate impact. It moves out of any direct line of vision into a place of special learning. This fact marks a very large change in the consensus assumed between poet and public. The world of classical mythology, of historical reference, of scriptural allusion, on which a preponderant part of English and European literature is built from Chaucer to Milton and Dryden, from Tennyson to Eliot's *Sweeney Agonistes*, is receding from our natural reach.[51]

50. This offers a good example of what Bernard Berenson called "the originality of incompetence" in his *Aesthetics and History* (Garden City: Anchor, 1953), pp. 176, 186 ff. Cf. also Havet's *"la loi des banalités progressives."* There is a quaint reversal of the Mercian coin phenomenon in Lavater's "metamorphic sketches" entitled "From the Frog to Apollo"; see *Art News* (September 1957), p. 34.

51. *Language and Silence* (New York: Atheneum, 1970), p. 59.

Usually any study of the problem of obscurity in literature must concern itself with the obscurity that arises not in this case from the purposeful employment of modes of defamiliarization but rather from the loss of a common cultural heritage. Thus in his excellent study of this problem John Press writes:

> It will not have escaped notice that Yeats, Eliot, Charles Williams, Empson, and Auden, all highly educated men living between the two wars in the same country, have no common background of reference, and cannot count on their readers' being able to follow their train of thought. In Shakespeare's day, even in Johnson's day, all men with any pretensions to culture shared a common heritage, a fund of traditional myths, sacred books, accumulated knowledge, and canons of taste which, however limited, were clearly defined.[52]

But something quite similar to the Mercian coinage phenomenon has also happened—and is happening—in language, whether we refer to these changes as "corruption" or as the normal result of sound changes due to specific causes and following more or less regular patterns with occasional graphic tampering. Indeed, the view has been expressed that language itself originated as a device of deception: "All real intentions and emotions got themselves expressed involuntarily. . . . So voluntary communnication can scarcely have been called upon except to deceive; language must have been invented for the purpose of lying."[53] But alongside such changes as Latin *lis* from Old Latin *stlis* or English *loaf* from Anglo-Saxon *hlaf* or French *manger* from Vulgar Latin *manducare,* or words like *sweetheart* (from *sweet-ard*) and the often more radical changes and distortions that occur when a word of one language is borrowed by another language—especially of a different linguistic group—(e.g., Latin *caduceus* from Greek *kērukeion,* Arabic *funduq* from Greek *pandokeion,* German *Pferd* from Latin *veredus,* Russian *verbljud* from Gothic *ulbandus*) or words resulting from metanalysis (*fausse coupe*),[54] there is

52. *The Chequer'd Shade* (London: Oxford University Press, 1963), p. 66.

53. E. H. Sturtevant, *An Introduction to Linguistic Science* (New Haven: Yale University Press, 1947), p. 48. Cf. Sartre's remark: "As always in art, one must lie to tell the truth."

54. An especially interesting class of borrowed words and phrases is the so-called hobson-jobson. This is the name given to a word or phrase borrowed from another language but subjected to certain adaptive sound changes which often radically defamiliarize the original (e.g., "forlorn hope" in English). See Henry Yule and A. C. Burnell, *Hobson-Jobson: A Glossary of Colloquial Anglo-Indian*

another large area of verbal defamiliarization, including neologisms, nonce-words, and portmanteau words, as well as other types of very frequently purposefully modified forms such as apocopated, syncopated, and metathesized words, ananyms, cledonisms, euphemistic defamiliarization ("Drats!" "Cripes!"), etc., which are of more interest to the literary scholar. In this study we shall, for the most part, ignore accidental modifications and begin (in Chapter III) with various types of intentional verbal and phrasal defamiliarization as the basis for considering more complex varieties.

If we limit ourselves to literature and, further, to the Indo-European area, the writer has, depending on the literary-cultural milieu in which he is working as well as the age, a range of terms (not mere synonyms) at his disposal for referring, say, to *Equus caballus*. In English this range runs from "horse" downwards to such words as "nag" and "jade" and upwards to the more literary and "aureate" terms such as "steed" and "Pegasus." But beyond this normal range there is a wider one, limited only by the imagination and erudition of the poet and (in some cases) by the traditions and conventions of his age. Within this range the reference to a person, animal, thing, action, place, and other aspects of reality or phenomena may vary from mere, easily comprehensible metaphor or metonymy, hyponyms, and the use of obsolete, archaic, or rare words, and neologisms, through various antonomasias to "kennings," metalepses, *décalages d'expression*,[55] and other learned periphrases until we occasionally reach such an extreme stage as that represented, for instance, by the language of Lycophron's *Alexandra*. Generally speaking, the more abstract is the term subjected to defamiliarization, the wider the range of possibilities (e.g., the word and concept of "love" in world literature); the more specific the term (especially in a technical sense), the narrower the range. But even in the latter case, words such as "ladder" (*innumerosque gradus, gemina latus arbore clusos,/ aerium sibi portat iter*[56]), "com-

---

Words and Phrases (Delhi: Munshiram Manoharlal, 1968). Sanskrit words in Chinese and Japanese are severely modified (e.g., Japanese *zen* from Chinese *ch'an* from Pali, *jhana* from Sanskrit *dhyana*); but some of the most radical modifications occur in American English words and place names of American Indian origin (cf. the presumed origin of "Chicago").

55. The expression is J. Marouzeau's in his *Traité de Stylistique Latine* (Paris: Les Belles Lettres, 1954), p. 254 ff.

56. "Innumerable steps, enclosed between twin trees, an airy road" (Statius), quoted in Ernst Robert Curtius, *European Literature and the Latin Middle Ages*, translated by Willard Trask (New York: Harper, 1963), p. 276.

pass" (*del norte amante dura*—Góngora), or "telescope" ("sight-invigorating tube"[57]) may be defamiliarized, i.e., replaced by elaborate and, at times, absurd periphrases.

6

A word or two must be said about another area in which defamiliarization is used, not as a literary device, but merely for dissimulation or obfuscation: I refer to the very often purposefully (but sometimes accidentally) deceptive use of language by governments and by business organizations. Some governments (such as the Soviet Union) and some business concerns have been more guilty than others in this respect, but the phenomenon is widespread, and there is probably no other aspect of language that, at least in the West, has been commented on so often in newspapers and magazines. It was Representative Maury Maverick (d. 1954) who first used the word "gobbledygook" to refer to that peculiarly obscure, pompous, and tortuous form of verbiage so favored by officialdom, and examples of "Pentagonese" are frequently called to our attention today. Though a worse example than the late President Eisenhower might easily have been chosen, George Steiner makes his point well when he writes (in *Language and Silence*): "The English spoken by Mr. Eisenhower during his press conferences, like that used to sell a new detergent, was intended neither to communicate the critical truths of national life nor to quicken the mind of the hearer. It was designed to evade or gloss over the demands of meaning. The language of a community has reached a perilous state when a study of radioactive fall-out can be entitled 'Operation Sunshine.'"

The British magazine *Encounter*, which often concerns itself with language usage both in Britain and the United States, listed some further examples of gobbledygook in its May 1975 issue. Thus Turkey referred to its invasion of Cyprus as a "peace operation"; a U.S. secretary of Health, Education and Welfare described substantial cuts in social services as "advance downward adjustments"; a BBC executive announced the closing down of a switchboard "because of the very high non-utilization factor"; and a complaint to the British postal service concerning delays in mail delivery was answered with the following statement: "After a thorough investigation, we are able to establish that the late arrival of your mail was due to delay in transit."

57. This example is taken from *The Stuffed Owl: An Anthology of Bad Verse*, edited by D. B. Wyndham-Lewis and Charles Less (New York: Capricorn Books, 1962), p. 250 (Robert Blair).

Soviet Russia has its own problems with what is called *kantseljarit* ("chancelleritis" or bureaucratic jargon) and Korney Chukovsky devotes a chapter in one of his books (*Zhivoj kak zhizn'*, 1962) to this subject.

As for the use of deceptive language by business, especially in advertising, Daniel Defoe noted the following in the eighteenth century:

> Our shop-rhetorick is a strange kind of speech. . . . 'Tis composed of a mass of rattling flattery to the buyer, and that fill'd with hypocrisy, self-praises, falsehood, and in short, a complication of wickedness; it is a corrupt means to a vicious end. . . . The shopkeeper ought indeed to have a good tongue, but he should not make a common whore of his tongue. . . . Tradesmen ought no more to lie behind the counter, than parsons ought to talk treason in the pulpit.[58]

There are also varieties of medical and legal language which, to the layman at least, appear to be examples of defamiliarization. I refer not only to such things as the symbols and Latin abbreviations in doctors' prescriptions (q.v., t.i.d.) but also to such technical medical terms as "circumorbital haematoma" (black eye), epistaxis (nosebleed), and singultus (hiccoughs). But of course we can find in almost every technical or professional area a jargon which is often, purposefully or not, quite incomprehensible to the layman. It is interesting, by the way, that in the early editions of R. von Krafft-Ebing's *Psychopathia Sexualis* in English translation certain descriptive passages on various "perversions" were retained—and thus modestly veiled—in Latin. Indeed, there is an entire lexicon of anatomical, sexual, and scatological terminology that exists in dual form in English: the Latin and Greek "technical" terms and the Anglo-Saxon counterparts (the "four-letter words"). Some technical terms of erotology occasionally encountered in English are French rather than Latin (*l'épée de Charlemagne*), while the specifically French erotological lexicon—especially that of prostitutes—is quite extensive and, on occasion, positively poetic—e.g., *le papillon d'amour* (the crab-louse).[59] However, I daresay much the same thing may be claimed of other languages as well, notably those of India and the Middle East.[60]

58. Quoted in Miriam Beard, *A History of Business* (Ann Arbor: University of Michigan Press, 1962), Vol. I, p. 443.

59. See other examples in Dr. Jean Lacassagne and Pierre Devaux, *L'Argot du Milieu* (Paris: Albin Michel, 1948). If I am not mistaken, it was Goethe who called the spirochaete of syphilis *"der Wurm der Liebe."*

60. See, e.g., Allen Edwardes, *The Jewel in the Lotus: A Historical Survey of the Sexual Culture of the East* (New York: Julian, 1959).

Legal language is notorious for its denseness and occasional impenetrability (even to lawyers) and, in particular, for its "legal tautologies" (e.g., "to have and to hold"); although these latter are not clear-cut examples of defamiliarization, they are very close to a literary figure known as hendiadys which occasionally serves "to make strange."[61] In general, however, the attempt in legal language (in statutes, briefs, and other documents) to encompass a situation, define an action, or set forth the law as fully and as unequivocally as possible frequently leads to a feeling—again on the part of the layman—of bewilderment and estrangement.[62] Certainly this is the way in which the language of the law and of lawyers (as in the case of medical jargon and physicians) has been treated again and again in literature. Tolstoy, for example, had a special contempt—as he did for most professionals— for physicians and lawyers, and he takes every opportunity to mock, satirize, and debunk such characters in his fiction.

In all fairness we should not neglect to mention the occasions when the language of historians and scholars in other fields also seems more confusing than enlightening. Many examples could be cited from a mass of articles in the "learned journals."[63] But classical examples of such language occur in the writings of the late Arnold Toynbee, a man of vast learning. Here is one specimen:

> In the field of encounters in the Time-dimension an Antaean rebound that wins from Necromancy an anticipatory communion with the Future has its antithesis in an Atlantean stance in which a Necromancer who has yielded to the legendary Epimethean impulse of Lot's wife is petrified by the hypnotic stare of a resuscitated corpse's Medusan countenance into the rigidity of a pillar of salt pinned down by the incubus of the Past.[64]

The language of Thucydides, the difficulties of which were proverbial even in ancient times, has elicited over the centuries some interesting comments. Thus Marcellinus (fifth century A.D.) supposed

61. E.g., in English "the law and heraldry" for "heraldic law"; or, in Russian, *sud i delo* ("court and action") for *sudebnoe delo* ("court action").

62. Any loopholes in the law or in legal language might allow the employment of the "devices of Cepola," a term which covers just about all the technical strategies for circumventing the law.

63. See Edmund Wilson, *The Fruits of the MLA* (New York: New York Review Book, 1968).

64. Quoted in *Toynbee and History,* edited by A. Montague (Boston: Sargent, 1956), p. 109.

that the historian purposefully wrote in an obscure fashion lest he become too accessible to the masses and so that, on the other hand, he might be especially significant to intelligent readers who could interpret him correctly; and Quintilian very bluntly states that Thucydides employed unusual words and a multitude of figures for the specific purpose of avoiding monotony of narrative.

It is certainly a fact that, for every instance in literature of the parody and satirizing of physicians and lawyers, one can find the same treatment of *soi-disant* scholars as pedants and sciolists, speaking or writing an absurd and outlandish jargon. There are examples of these in ancient literature (e.g., Meton the astronomer in Aristophanes' *The Birds*) and numerous examples in later literatures. At the present time Vladimir Nabokov, for instance, quite obviously takes pleasure in poking fun at certain literary and linguistic scholars at every opportunity in both his fiction and non-fiction (see his *Strong Opinions*, 1973). And certainly there has been in recent years a notable proliferation of technical jargon in almost all areas of learning. Some of this is undoubtedly required for exactness of expression, but some of it appears, even to experts in the particular field, as mere verbiage (humorous examples of the language of educational and pedagogical theory are frequently called to our attention). It is interesting that some of the latest studies in the field of stylistics employ a highly technical language which draws heavily on the old Greek rhetorical terminology: merism, polyptoton, polymetochic, etc. This is especially true of structuralist studies: "In this respect structuralism has an august forbear whose historical role has generally been underestimated or discredited for ideological reasons: Rhetoric, that impressive attempt by a whole culture to analyse and classify the forms of speech, and to make the world of language intelligible."[65]

Aside from the (fortunately) rare cases of outright dishonesty and deception in scholarship, there are rather more numerous instances of cases in which a scholar or group of scholars "labor under misapprehensions" or fall into the trap of relying too strongly on secondary or tertiary sources or on other unreliable data. I recall, for example, the case of the Hebraist Gotthelf Bergsträsser who incorporated into his *Hebrew Grammar* the rules for setting *metheg*, which rules had been worked out by Heidenheim and Baer (and approved by the great Franz Delitzsch) on the basis of only late Hebrew biblical manuscripts. When Paul Kahle pointed out to Bergsträsser that none of

65. Roland Barthes in "Science Versus Literature" in *Introduction to Structuralism* (New York: Basic Books, 1970), p. 412.

these elaborate rules were observed in ancient Hebrew manuscripts, he was surprised and realized that what he had written in his grammar was *"Makulatur."*[66]

7

I should like, finally, to make a few brief comments on one more type of accidental defamiliarization—that which occurs in mistranslations. Gross errors or "howlers" in translation are frequent—more frequent, in fact, than one might suspect—and most of us engaged in language and comparative literature studies could cite numerous examples. On rare occasions such errors have, so to speak, been memorialized in lasting works of art, such as Michelangelo's *Moses* (whose horns are very likely due to a mistranslation by St. Jerome of *qāran* in Exodus 34:29[67]), but more often they are simply noted by knowledgeable readers or pointed out in reviews. Mistranslations in extended prose narratives (especially novels), even when serious and frequent, do not generally disturb or mislead the naive reader. Errors in poetry, however, are more grave; it is remarkable indeed that occasionally certain translations of a poem from one language into another are said to be "better than the original"—a statement that is at once a compliment and an accusation.[68]

There is a particular situation that presents a pitfall—and an occasion for accidental defamiliarization—for translators from the Russian. Russian, unlike the other European languages with their Latin alphabets, must frequently transliterate into Cyrillic non-Slavic words, especially personal names and place-names, and this is usually done phonetically rather than *literatim*. Let us say that the name of the

66. Paul Kahle, *The Cairo Geniza* (Oxford: Blackwell, 1959), pp. 113–14.

67. For the whole story, see Ruth Mellinkoff, *The Horned Moses in Medieval Art and Thought* (Berkeley: University of California Press, 1970). The University of Texas at Austin published six issues of a "Journal on and of Translation" entitled *Delos* (1968–71) containing many fine articles; the interruption in its publication is, I trust, temporary. Two excellent surveys of the problems of translation are: *On Translation,* edited by Reuben Brower (Cambridge: Harvard University Press, 1959); and *The Craft and Context of Translation,* edited by William Arrowsmith and Roger Shattuck (Garden City: Anchor, 1964). An elaborate study of the theory and problems of translation has recently been published: George Steiner, *After Babel: Aspects of Language and Translation* (New York: Oxford University Press, 1975).

68. I have in mind the Italian saying, *Traduttore-traditore.* The Russian poet Balmont's translation of Poe's *The Raven* is sometimes said to be better than the original.

Italian philosopher Vico is referred to in Russian; this must be transliterated *Viko*. When the translator encounters this, unless he or she knows (and you might think that most translators would know) who this is, he is liable to write "Viko" in his translation instead of restoring the Italian spelling.[69] Or take the painter Böcklin; this must be rendered in Cyrillic as *Beklin*, and again, in a translation, this name is apt to appear as "Beklin."[70] Translations from Russian works of both fiction and non-fiction are replete with such errors.

On occasion, translators (often anonymous) from language A into their own language B make an error which becomes part of language B's normal idiom. For example, some time in the seventeenth or eighteenth century a Russian translator of the French expression *Il n'est pas dans son assiette* ("He is out of sorts"), assuming that *assiette* meant only "plate" (instead of "disposition," as in this expression), translated the phrase into Russian as *On ne v svoej tarelke* (*tarelka* means only "plate" in Russian). This is a clear example of an erroneous calque and similar things may be found in all the major languages.

Lest I be accused of calling *all* (including linguistic and literary) phenomena examples of defamiliarization, let me mention briefly several random areas in which one *usually* does not encounter defamiliarization: the preparation of a corpse for ritual display in a funeral parlor, the introduction to books, "how-to-do-it" books, and bird, flower, plant, and rock identification guides, the directions accompanying various contraptions which must be assembled, dictionaries, etc. I say "usually," because of course any phenomenon *may* be defamiliarized, and in point of fact we can all recall having seen or heard defamiliarized versions of even the items listed above: parodies of "how-to-do-it" books, humorous skits on trying to follow the directions for assembling children's toys, etc. As for dictionaries, Ambrose Bierce's *Devil's Dictionary* is a good example of defamiliarization in this area, but to a great extent (with respect especially to certain entries) the *Encyclopédie* and Johnson's *Dictionary* are even better examples.

69. "Viko" appears in a translation of Trotsky's *Literature and Revolution* (Ann Arbor: University of Michigan Press, 1960), p. 27.

70. "Beklin" appears in a translation of Fedin's *Goroda i gody* ("Cities and Years") (New York: Dell, 1962), p. 211. A blatant example of such mistranslation occurs in a recent translation of Bely's *Serebrjanyj golub'* ("The Silver Dove") (New York: Grove Press, 1974), p. 109 ("Villamovitz-Mellendorf" instead of "Wilamowitz-Möllendorff"). Soviet translators often make errors, but on the whole the late Korney Chukovsky was right in deploring the frequency of mistranslations of Russian works in the West.

VIKTOR SHKLOVSKY
AND *OSTRANENIE*

1

IN THIS CHAPTER I should like to cite certain passages in Shklovsky that have to do with the concept of *ostranenie*[1] or defamiliarization, comment on these, and look at some recent developments in literary theory that stem from or may be associated with Shklovsky's writings. The major statements concerning defamiliarization occur in Shklovsky's essay, "Art as Device" (*Iskusstvo kak priem*), first published in 1919,[2] and it is from this work (in English translation) that I shall quote. "If we start to examine the general laws of perception," Shklovsky writes,

> we see that as perception becomes habitual, it becomes automatic. Thus, for example, all of our habits retreat into the area of the unconsciously automatic; if one remembers the sensations of holding a pen or of speaking in a foreign language for the first time and compares that with his feeling at performing the action for the ten thousandth time, he will agree with us. Such habituation explains the principles by

1. The word should properly be *ostrannenie*, i.e., with a double *n*. In an interview in 1967 Shklovsky explained that he had originally written the word as *ostranenie* and that he wanted it to remain in this form as a technical term. See Ignazio Ambrogio, *Formalismo e avanguardia in Russia* (Rome: Editori Riuniti, 1968), p. 129, note 4.

2. For further background on Formalism and Shklovsky's contributions, see Victor Erlich, *Russian Formalism: History & Doctrine* (The Hague: Mouton, 1969); Ewa Thompson, *Russian Formalism and Anglo-American New Criticism* (The Hague: Mouton, 1971); and Shklovsky's *Sentimental Journey: Memoirs, 1917–1922*, translated by Richard Sheldon (Ithaca: Cornell University Press, 1970).

which, in ordinary speech, we leave phrases unfinished and words half expressed.[3]

Stephen Heath, in his excellent study of the new French novel, referring to Shklovsky's *priem ostranenija* as defamiliarization, mentions another Shklovskian analogy: "One of his examples of habitual passiveness was drawn from the material presence of writing: reading the proofs of a book written in a language we know well it is only with difficulty that we can make ourselves *read* the words, and so pick out the misprints, instead of simply taking the text for granted in an unthinking and immediate recognition of the words expected."[4]

Aside from the reference to the well-known redundancy aspect of language, Shklovsky is pointing out here the tendency of language in general and words in particular to become (to use Malinowski's term) mere phatic formulas; and the same applies to literature which, from one point of view, may be seen in bulk as traditional commonplaces expressed in conventional forms. This tendency of language and literature to become habitualized, to settle into easy and familiar patterns, is a process which Russian and other critics have liked to associate with the concept of entropy.[5] In his definitive study of Russian Formalism, Victor Erlich writes: "It is this inexorable pull of routine, of habit, that the artist is called upon to counteract. By tearing the object out of its habitual context, by bringing together disparate notions, the poet gives a *coup de grâce* to the verbal cliché and to the stock responses attendant upon it and forces us into heightened awareness of things and their sensory texture. The act of creative deformation restores sharpness to our vision" (p. 177).

It need hardly be pointed out that criticism of habitualization, automatization, and triteness in literature is nothing new; such criticism, explicit or implicit, has been a marked feature especially of baroque-type poetics in many literary contexts of the past and we find it first in Aristotle (*Poetics*, 1458a): "The virtue of style is to be clear without being mean [*tapeinos*]. The clearest style is that which

3. *Russian Formalist Criticism: Four Essays*, translated by Lee T. Lemon and Marion J. Reis (Lincoln: University of Nebraska Press, 1965), p. 11.

4. Stephen Heath, *The Nouveau Roman* (Philadelphia: Temple University Press, 1972), p. 151.

5. See Evgeny Zamyatin, "On Literature, Revolution, and Entropy," in *Literary Modernism*, edited by Irving Howe (New York: Fawcett, 1967), p. 173 ff., and Tony Tanner, "The American Novelist as Entropologist," *The London Magazine* (October 1970): 5–18.

uses only proper words; but at the same time it is mean—witness the
poetry of Cleophon and Sthenelus. That diction, on the other hand,
is lofty and raised above the commonplace which employs strange
[*xenikos*] words. I mean strange, metaphorical, and lengthened
words—anything that differs from normal idiom."

A good deal of the linguistic and literary material to be presented
in the following two chapters will, in fact, serve as illustrations to
Aristotle's bald comment as well as to Shklovsky's "general theory" of
defamiliarization, while Chapter V will examine a number of literary
periods of the baroque type in which this practice is notably pre-
dominant. But Shklovsky continues:

> Habitualization devours works, clothes, furniture, one's wife, and
> the fear of war. "If the whole complex lives of many people go on un-
> consciously, then such lives are as if they had never been." And art
> exists that one may recover the sensation of life; it exists to make one
> feel things, to make the stone *stony*. The purpose of art is to impart
> the sensations of things as they are perceived and not as they are
> known. The technique of art is to make objects "unfamiliar," to make
> forms difficult, to increase the difficulty and length of perception be-
> cause the process of perception is an aesthetic end in itself and must be
> prolonged. *Art is a way of experiencing the artfulness of an object: the
> object is not important.*[6]

Both Shklovsky's emphasis here on *zatrudnenie* or "defacilitation" and
his brief reference to *zamedlenie* or "retardation" run counter, of
course, to such concepts as Herbert Spencer's "law of the economizing
of mental energy" (expounded in his *The Philosophy of Style*), notions
similar to which still abound today. The idea of "making difficult" in
literature, however this be referred to, is also of ancient vintage.
Earlier we mentioned (Chapter I, section 6), in connection with the
difficulties encountered in Thucydides, the remarks of Marcellinus and
Quintilian; and much counsel similar to that contained in these verses
by Geoffrey of Vinsauf could be cited:

> Longius ut sit opus ne ponas nomina rerum.
> Pone notas alias: nec plane detege, sed rem
> Innue per notulas, nec sermo perambulet in re,

6. *Russian Formalist Criticism*, p. 12.

Sed rem circuiens longis ambagibus ambi
Quod breviter dicturus eras . . .[7]

But perhaps most familiar is Mallarmé's admonition: "Il doit y avoir
toujours énigme en poésie: Nommer un objet c'est supprimer les trois
quarts de la puissance du poème qui est fait du bonheur de deviner
peu à peu; le suggérer, voilà le rêve."

That it is a function of poetry to concern itself with and to reveal
the haecceity, the quiddity of reality is also an idea that has often been
expressed not only by critics but by poets as well. Eliot, for example,
felt that it was his poetry that reflected the reality around him and that
his prose reflected his ideals.[8] And René Ghil once remarked (this is a
good example of defamiliarization in criticism) that it was Mallarmé
who was the realist and Zola the "poet." But we find the most radical
associations between poetry and the real, even the equating of these,
amongst the earlier German romantic poets and critics. Thus for
Novalis "Poetry is what is absolutely and genuinely real. That is the
kernel of my philosophy. The more poetic, the more real." It is, by the
way, in Novalis that we find a statement that comes nearest to being a
direct antecedent of Shklovsky's concept of *ostranenie:* "Die Kunst,
auf eine *angenehme* Art zu *befremden,* einen Gegenstand fremd zu
machen und doch bekannt und anziehend, das ist die romantische
Poetik."[9]

As for the reference to art making "the stone *stony*" and its purpose—"to impart the sensations of things as they are perceived and not
as they are known"—this reminds us not only of certain *dicta* of the
poets[10] but also of the Kantian rather than Schellingian aspect of

7. "To prolong a work you must avoid naming things by their names. Use
other designations; reveal not a thing entirely but suggest it by hints; nor let your
words course through your subject but rather take a long and circuitous route
around what you were going to say briefly." Quoted in Ernst Robert Curtius,
European Literature and the Latin Middle Ages (New York: Harper, 1963),
p. 277.

8. See W. Y. Tindall, *Forces in Modern British Literature* (New York:
Vintage, 1956), p. 91.

9. Fragment 2409, quoted in R. Tymms, *German Romantic Literature* (London: Methuen, 1955), p. 160. Cf. Victor Terras, *Belinskij and Russian Literary
Criticism* (Madison: University of Wisconsin Press, 1974), p. 171. This connection
is also pointed out in my *Russian Literary Criticism: A Short History* (Syracuse:
Syracuse University Press, 1974), p. 166.

10. Pasternak once remarked of two of his poems, "Venice" and "The Railway Station," that all he wanted "was that one poem should contain the city of
Venice and the other the Brest railway station."

Shklovsky's thinking. Schelling, the influence of whose "organic philosophy" was pervasive in Russia (especially, in the case of Dostoevsky,
via Apollon Grigoriev), held that art had a cognitive function: it could
reveal social, moral, and historical truths; but Kant, as we know, denied
art ("Zweckmässigkeit ohne Zwecke") this cognitive role. Studies of
Russian formalism occasionally point out this Kantian background as
well as certain general but nevertheless striking parallels between
Shklovsky's notion of *ostranenie* and statements made by Henri Bergson in his *Le Rire* (1900).[11] For example, Bergson writes the following:

> For a few moments at least, he [i.e., the artist] diverts us from
> the prejudices of form and colour that come between ourselves and
> reality. And thus he realises the loftiest ambition of art, which here con-
> sists in revealing to us nature. Others, again, retire within themselves.
> Beneath the thousand rudimentary actions which are the outward and
> visible signs of an emotion, behind the commonplace, conventional
> expression that both reveals and conceals an individual mental state, it
> is the emotion, the original mood, to which they attain in its undefiled
> essence. And then, to induce us to make the same effort ourselves, they
> contrive to make us see something of what they have seen: by
> rhythmical arrangement of words, which thus become organised and
> animated with a life of their own, they tell us—or rather suggest—
> things that speech was not calculated to express.[12]

There is another area in which one may also see some interesting
parallels with the Shklovskian concept of defamiliarization: this is Zen
Buddhism. Let me quote two passages from the writings of the late
D. T. Suzuki: "Satori may be defined as an intuitive looking into the
nature of things in contradistinction to the analytical or logical understanding of it. Practically, it means the unfolding of a new world
hitherto unperceived in the confusion of a dualistically trained mind.
Or we may say that with satori our entire surroundings are viewed
from quite an unexpected angle of perception." And Suzuki himself
quotes a Zen master, Seigen Ishin: "Before a man studies Zen, to him
mountains are mountains and waters are waters; after he gets an in-
sight into the truth of Zen through the instruction of a good master,
mountains to him are not mountains and waters are not waters; but

11. See Thompson, *Russian Formalism and Anglo-American New Criticism*,
pp. 54 ff. and 66–67.
12. From "Laughter" by Henri Bergson in *Comedy* (Garden City: Anchor,
1956), p. 161.

after this when he really attains to the abode of rest, mountains are once more mountains and waters are waters."[13]

I think we have in the Zen concept of satori (and I shall refer to this again in the following chapter) at least a good analogy to what happens to our perception when we encounter a striking simile, metaphor, or periphrasis. This is especially true where we have an effective defamiliarization or where, according to André Breton, we have a comparison between "deux objets aussi éloignés que possible l'un de l'autre" and when these are juxtaposed "d'une manière brusque et saisissante" as, for example, in the "Van Winkle" section of *The Bridge* when Hart Crane, imagining a schoolboy's picture of Cortes on horseback, speaks of the *conquistador* "reining tautly in— / Firmly as coffee grips the taste." Before we encounter this figure, "coffee is coffee," so to speak, and "reining a horse is reining a horse"; then, in juxtaposition, they are suddenly both defamiliarized (the familiar is made unfamiliar). Next, after we *remember* the peculiar effect of tasting a good cup of coffee, the picture is clarified: coffee is coffee once again and reining is reining, but in the process we have, in effect, been in a small way "enlightened."

Regarding the final sentence in the passage quoted last from Shklovsky, the statement that "the object is not important" is itself rather important. In the first place, this disparagement of the significance of content was, among other aspects of the Formalist approach, one of the reasons why Shklovsky and the Formalist movement as a whole came into conflict with Soviet and Party literary authorities in the years following the 1917 Revolution.[14] Second, it is again a restatement of a view that has often been expressed by both minor and major literary figures; perhaps the neatest formulation is that of Flaubert: "*Yvetot donc vaut Constantinople.*"

Now Shklovsky continues and touches upon the particular mode of defamiliarization found in Tolstoy: "After we see an object several times, we begin to recognize it. The object is in front of us and we know about it, but we do not see it—hence we cannot say anything significant about it. Art removes objects from the automatism of perception in several ways. Here I want to illustrate a way used repeatedly

---

13. *Zen Buddhism: Selected Writings of D. T. Suzuki*, ed. William Barrett (Garden City: Anchor Books, 1956), pp. 84 and 14. Satori (Chinese *wu*) is, according to Suzuki, another name for "enlightenment" (*anuttara-samyak-sambodhi*).

14. See Erlich, *Russian Formalism*, chapters VI–VIII.

by Leo Tolstoy."[15] He cites a number of characteristic examples from Tolstoy, including the passage from *War and Peace* quoted at the beginning of our Chapter I. "Tolstoy," he writes, "makes the familiar seem strange by not naming the familiar object. He describes an object as if he were seeing it for the first time, an event as if it were happening for the first time. In describing something he avoids the accepted names of its parts and instead names corresponding parts of other objects." Shklovsky then goes on to examples of erotic defamiliarization in literature (the *Decameron*, Gogol, Knut Hamsun) and in folktales.

In a basic study of the particular mode of ironic defamiliarization exemplified in Tolstoy, Dmitry Chizhevsky traces the history of this technique. The theme of the first part of *The Labyrinth of the World and the Paradise of the Heart* (1617) by the Czech writer Jan Comenius (Komensky) is, Chizhevsky notes, the senselessness of the world; and, in order to convey this senselessness, Comenius uses defamiliarization. For example, when the "wanderer" boards a vessel for a sea voyage, the ship is described as "a hut which was made of boards . . . it did not stand upon firm ground, but . . . on the water and rocked to and fro." The ship is a carriage "lying with its back upward, its shaft sticking up in the air." And when the wind starts blowing, some men "unrolled some sort of rolled-up cloths."

> Real things [writes Chizhevsky] are represented by certain "substitutes." The basic difference between allegory and this device is that it is the purpose of allegory to reveal the real meaning of the things (even though this meaning may sometimes have a negative value), while the device under discussion aims at exactly the opposite: things are to be shown in their plain physical existence, stripped and drained of any meaning. One could term this device negative allegory.[16]

Chizhevsky cites Xenophanes of Colophon (6th cent. B.C.) as the first practitioner of negative allegory in the surviving fragments of a poem on Nature in which he attacks religious anthropomorphism ("If the ox could paint a picture, his god would look like an ox"); and he then adduces a number of other ancient instances (in Plato, the Sophists, the Cynics, and the Stoics). Most interesting are the references to defamiliarization in Lucian (the *Anacharsis*) and Dio Chrysostom. But the "real flowering of the negative allegory," Chizhev-

15. *Russian Formalist Criticism*, p. 13.

16. "Comenius' *Labyrinth of the World*: Its Themes and Their Sources," *Harvard Slavic Studies* 1 (1953): 120. Subsequently in a note Chizhevsky points out that Shklovsky applied the term *ostranenie* to what he calls "negative allegory".

sky points out, "did not come until the Enlightenment"; and good examples are referred to in Voltaire (*Ingénue* and *Micromégas*).[17] No more modern instances are cited.

It should be emphasized that what Chizhevsky calls "negative allegory" is but one type of defamiliarization. Shklovsky himself, as we have seen, clearly implies that *ostranenie* includes all techniques whereby the artist portrays or describes—and thereby causes us to see—something familiar in a fresh, defamiliarized way. Indeed, he goes so far as to say: "I personally feel that defamiliarization is found almost everywhere an image is found."[18] In this very broad sense, defamiliarization is as old as literature, as old as metaphor, even as old as language itself and its history is in fact the history of these phenomena.

2

Three other aspects of Shklovsky's concept of defamiliarization should be mentioned. The first is his criticism of the view, long held in European and, particularly, Russian aesthetic theory, that all art is "thinking in images."

> Many still believe, then, that thinking in images . . . is the chief characteristic of poetry. Consequently, they should have expected the history of "imagistic art," as they call it, to consist of a history of changes in imagery. But we find that images change little; from century to century, from nation to nation, from poet to poet, they flow on without changing. . . . The more you understand an age, the more convinced you become that the images a given poet used and which you thought his own were taken almost unchanged from another poet. . . .
>
> Poetic imagery is a means of creating the strongest possible impression. As a method it is, depending upon its purpose, neither more nor less effective than ordinary or negative parallelism, comparison, repetition, balanced structure, hyperbole, the commonly accepted rhetorical figures, and all those methods which emphasize the emotional effect of an expression.[19]

In short, for Shklovsky poetic imagery is but *one* of the devices of poetic language, as indeed it is for prose as well.[20] Shklovsky and his

17. In note 94 Chizhevsky mentions the fact that Erich Auerbach in his *Mimesis,* discussing what we call defamiliarization in Voltaire, terms the method "*Scheinwerfertechnik.*" See *Mimesis* (Garden City: Anchor, 1957), pp. 353–55.

18. *Russian Formalist Criticism,* p. 18. I have changed "form" in the translation to "an image."

19. *Ibid.,* pp. 7, 8–9.

20. See Erlich, *Russian Formalism,* pp. 174–75. There are, of course, many

followers make much of the differences between the language of poetry and the language of prose, and they liked to note those linguistic phenomena which occur in prose but not in poetry, and vice versa. Thus Shklovsky lists a number of these, including Jakubinsky's conclusion that, because the "law of the dissimulation of liquids" does not apply in poetic language, poetry tolerates the admission of hard-to-pronounce clusters of such sounds; he calls Jakubinsky's paper on this subject "one of the first examples of scientific criticism."[21] In a similar way, I suppose, we might list those things we do in the kitchen that we do not do in the bathroom (and vice versa); but this would hardly be "scientific" and it would hardly in this case supplement our practical knowledge of the differences involved.

Shklovsky further distinguishes between two familiar aspects or functions of imagery: as a practical means of thinking or abstraction and as a means of reinforcing an impression. This is fine. But he suggests that the former function is characteristic of prose, the latter of poetry and such a differentiation is quite untenable unless further stipulations are made. The fact is that imagery, whether in poetry or prose, may function in both ways: in Lucretius' De rerum natura, for example, the imagery, while often striking and highly poetic, is necessarily didactic (in the peri physeōs tradition) and serves quite clearly "to put a point across" succinctly. It has frequently been observed that some of the great poetry contains no little prosaic material, while some of the great prose contains a good deal of poetry.

In any case, Shklovsky rightly contends that the purpose of the image (the good image, we might add) is not "to clarify the unknown by means of the known" but rather to defamiliarize the known: "An image is not a permanent referent for those mutable complexities of life which are revealed through it; its purpose is not to make us perceive meaning, but to create a special perception of the object—it creates a 'vision' of the object instead of serving as a means for knowing it."[22]

---

non-imagistic or non-figurative poems and Erlich cites Jakobson's reference to Pushkin's "I Loved You Once" as an outstanding example.

21. Russian Formalist Criticism, pp. 10–11. Jakobson later showed that Jakubinsky's conclusion was not valid.

22. Ibid., p. 18. Cf. Eliot's "objective correlative": "The only way of expressing emotion in the form of art is by finding an 'objective correlative'; in other words, a set of objects, a situation, a chain of events which shall be the formula of that particular emotion; such that when the external facts, which must terminate in sensory experience, are given, the emotion is immediately invoked" ("Hamlet and His Problems").

I might add that many critics amongst Shklovsky's contemporaries, did they know of his work, would certainly have utilized the concept of defamiliarization in their analyses of imagery. I think especially of Henry Wells's *Poetic Imagery: Illustrated from Elizabethan Literature* (1924). Although as an attempt at imagistic typology it is not too successful with its scheme of seven types, many of the comments on the three highest types (Sunken, Radical, and Expansive) seem to cry out for a term such as defamiliarization or estrangement. And Shklovsky would admire Wells' achronistic and descriptive approach.

The second feature of Shklovsky's concept is that elsewhere, in *O teorii prozy* (Moscow, 1929), he relates defamiliarization linguistically to what he calls a "semantic shift" (*semanticheskij sdvig*):

> The poet uses images—tropes and similes; he calls fire, let us say, a red flower or applies a new epithet to an old word or, like Baudelaire, he says that the carrion raised its legs as a woman does for shameful caresses. In this way the poet achieves a semantic shift: he takes a concept out of its former semantic setting and transfers it verbally (metaphorically) to another setting and we feel the novelty of the object in its new setting.

This seems an elaborate way of referring to metaphor (to say "semantic shift" instead of metaphor is like saying "pedal appendages" instead of legs) but the phrase is very popular in certain literary circles. Closely associated with the "semantic shift" or deviation from the norm is another idea which Shklovsky borrowed from the German aesthetician Broder Christiansen: this is the *Differenzqualität* or "quality of divergence."[23] On this subject Erlich writes:

> As spokesmen for the literary avant-garde, the Formalists were bound to set much store by the violation of artistic canons and by novelty in general. As estheticians they saw the core of esthetic perception and the source of artistic values in the "quality of divergence" (*Differenzqualität*). This concept seems to have meant to the Formalist theoreticians three different things: on the level of the representation of reality, *Differenzqualität* stood for the "divergence" from the actual, i.e., for creative deformation. On the level of language it meant a departure from current linguistic usage. Finally, on the plane of literary

23. *Die Philosophie der Kunst* (Hanau, 1909). Shklovsky uses the phrases *differentsial'nye oshchushchenija* and *differentsial'nye vpechatlenija* ("differential sensations" and "differential impressions"); see *O teorii prozy*, pp. 31–32.

dynamics, this catch-all term would imply a deviation from, or modification of, the prevailing artistic norm.[24]

The third aspect of Shklovsky's concept of defamiliarization I would like to mention is the fact that there is a certain ambiguity in the passages concerning *ostranenie*. This has occasionally been noticed and commented on and I quote here Jameson's statement regarding the nature of this ambiguity: "there is also about it [i.e., the concept of *ostranenie*] a profound ambiguity. . . . *Ostranenie* can apply either to the process of perception itself, or to the artistic mode of presentation of that perception. Even granting the nature of art as defamiliarization, it is never clear in Shklovsky's writings whether it is the content or the form itself which is defamiliarized."[25]

But of course such ambiguity is both understandable and excusable. Even for literary scholars much more linguistically oriented than Shklovsky a resolute attempt to confine oneself to the verbal surface of a text is, aside from the quaintness of such a performance, a difficult procedure and not always successful. Whether or not Shklovsky makes his position clear, then, as regards defamiliarization of form or content is not too important; the fact remains (as I have tried to show in Chapter I, section 3) that a writer may defamiliarize either his form or his content, or do neither, or do both.

3

I have already, in Chapter I both in the text and in the notes, mentioned a number of instances when contemporary literary scholars and critics have referred to Shklovsky's *ostranenie* theory, rendering the Russian term in various ways. Another set of terms that Shklovsky and the other Russian Formalists use in connection with defamiliarization is, as we have seen, automatization (habitualization) and disautomatization (or, as Shklovsky puts it in the third excerpt from "Art as Device" quoted above, the "removal of objects from automatism"). The term "disautomatization" caught on, and we find it in various modern (especially structuralist) studies in poetics. Thus Hans-Werner Ludwig in his study of Hopkins' sonnets writes: "In der Begrifflichkeit der russischen Formalisten und der Prager Schule ist solche Inversions-

24. Erlich, *Russian Formalism*, p. 252.
25. Frederic Jameson, *The Prison-House of Language* (Princeton: Princeton University Press, 1974), p. 75.

technik als Entautomatisierung oder Aktualisierung eingeschliffener sprachlicher Strukturen zu bestimmen. . . . Schliesslich wird man sagen müssen, dass auch und gerade bei Hopkins neben der Disautomatisation . . . durch Deformation der konventionellen Sprach-schemata."[26]

Ludwig's use of the word *"Deformation"* (cf. the phrase "creative deformation" used by Erlich in the excerpts from his book quoted above) reminds us that this concept, too, gained considerable popularity, especially amongst the literary scholars of both the Warsaw Literary Circle and the Prague Linguistic Circle. For example, René Wellek, discussing this latter group and one of its principal figures, Jan Mukařovský, has this to say:

> In agreement with the Russian Formalists, Mukařovský considers artistic form as having two main traits: deformation and organization. The term "deformation" has no derogatory implication: it simply means the changes imposed on the original materials, the novelty, for example, of poetic language in contrast to spoken language, the patterning imposed by meter, the tension of a plot, all "devices" (or possibly better "instruments" or "procedures") toward the aim of art which in Mukařovský, as in the Russian Formalists, is conceived as a shock to our ordinary indifference, as a heightening of awareness, as "making strange," *Verfremdung* in a wider sense than Brecht's.[27]

We also find mention of "style as deviation, that is infraction, transgression of a norm" as well as of Christiansen's "differential quality" and the Formalists in Tsvetan Todorov's article, "The Place of Style in the Structure of the Text,"[28] while Thomas McFarland in his paper, "Poetry and Poem: the Structure of Poetic Content," quotes another Czech scholar, B. Havránek: "By *foregrounding* . . . we mean the use of the devices of language in such a way that this use itself attracts attention and is perceived as uncommon, as deprived of automatization, as deautomatized, such as a live poetic metaphor (as opposed to a lexicalized one, which is automatized)." And Mukařovský is quoted: "The function of poetic language consists in the maximum of foregrounding of the utterance. Foregrounding is the opposite of automatization. . . . In poetic language foregrounding achieves maxi-

---

26. *Barbarous in Beauty: Studien zum Vers in Gerard Manley Hopkins' Sonetten* (München: Wilhelm Fin, 1972), pp. 244, 257.

27. René Wellek, "The Literary Theory and Aesthetics of the Prague School" in *Discriminations* (New Haven: Yale University Press, 1970), p. 281.

28. In *Literary Style*, edited by Seymour Chatman (New York: Oxford University Press, 1971), pp. 29–39.

mum intensity to the extent . . . of being used for its own sake; it is not used in the services of communication, but in order to place in the foreground the act of expression."[29]

Geoffrey Hartman, discussing dehumanization in the modern novel, speaks of writers who foster "techniques of perception which are dissociative rather than associative in nature. They do not make the strange familiar but rather estrange the familiar." In another essay Hartman refers to the history of literature as "a continual breach of style (high style being profaned, low style elevated), or a history of metaphorical transference (sacred attributes being secularized, and vice versa). . . . Great art is always flanked by its dark sisters, blasphemy and pornography"; and he adds a note in which he mentions the Formalists and their view that "in literary as distinguished from normative discourse language is 'deformed,' 'estranged,' 'rebarbarized.' "[30]

The idea of deforming, rupturing, and breaking is also present in modern French literary theory. Thus Roland Barthes has used the term "semioclastics" and other French novelists and critics occasionally use the words *briser* and *brisure* to refer to "breaking" linguistic and literary inertia (i.e., automatization). Julia Kristeva writes: "La pratique littéraire se révèle comme exploration et découverte des possibilités du langage; comme activité qui affranchit le sujet de certains réseaux linguistiques (psychiques, sociaux); comme dynamisme qui brise l'inertie des habitudes du langage."[31] And, commenting on the use of *brisure* by Philippe Sollers, Heath adds: "The 'brisure' is effected in the nouveau roman in its shattering of the passive readability of realist writing, consumed according to what McLuhan would call 'lineal decorum' . . . [it is a remedy] against the natural representation of linear writing, against the fixity of stereotype and repetition."[32]

Numerous introductions to structuralism and semiotics refer to Shklovsky's writings. For example, Johannes Anderegg cites the *Theory of Prose* in his *Fiktion und Kommunikation* and writes:

29. In *Literary Theory and Structure* (New Haven: Yale University Press, 1973), pp. 95–96. "Foregrounding" renders the Czech *aktualisace*. Halliday uses the term "foregrounding" in his study of Golding's *The Inheritors;* see above, Chapter I, note 8.

30. "The Heroics of Realism," *Beyond Formalism* (New Haven: Yale University Press, 1970), pp. 66, 23. Cf. also *The Theory of the Novel* (New York: Oxford University Press, 1974) and John Halperin's comments on Hardy's concept of "disproportioning" (p. 22).

31. *Semeiotiké: Recherches pour une sémanalyse* (Paris, 1969), pp. 178–79, quoted in Heath, *The Nouveau Roman*, p. 27.

32. *Ibid.*, p. 39.

Auch der Formalist Šklovskij begreift die Wirkung nicht nur der Fiktion, sondern des Kunstwerks überhaupt als Verfremdung. Meint er aber, es sei der Sinn der Kunst, "die Wahrnehmung des Lebens wiederherzustellen, die Dinge fühlbar, den Stein steinig zu machen," so unterscheidet sich sein Verfremdungsbegriff von dem hier gemeinten: Verfremdung scheint er gerade als Botschaft aufzufassen, als Hilfe zur Annäherung an objektive Erkenntnisse.[33]

But a critic need be neither a formalist nor a structuralist nor a semioticist in order to agree in general with Shklovsky's exposition of disautomatization and defamiliarization or to express similar ideas. I have already mentioned what Bergson wrote along these lines as well as a parallel in Zen philosophy; but many more such examples might be cited. For instance, Ortega y Gasset remarks in a note that repetition has a blunting and tiring effect and he refers approvingly to Heinrich Wölfflin's assertion that boredom has consistently mobilized art and compelled it to invent new forms. Such divergent figures as Max Eastman and T. S. Eliot have also expressed similar thoughts,[34] while statements by Shelley (in his *Defence of Poetry*) and Wordsworth are often cited in this connection.

4

Yury Lotman, the Soviet Russian structuralist, is a familiar name to many West European and American scholars. A number of his works are available here in reprint[35] and his name is occasionally mentioned in Western studies. His books are, in one respect at least, refreshingly different from earlier Soviet linguistic and literary studies in that the author fortunately has not felt it necessary to introduce those fulsome homages to Stalin (that "Coryphaeus of Philology," as Solzhenitsyn calls him) or to Lenin that were so familiar in the past. But such a work as *Lectures on Structural Poetics* (1964) is amusing. Shklovsky spoke disparagingly and ironically of Bely's "heroic effort to create a theory of art based on unverified facts from antiquated sources . . . and on Krayevich's high school physics text" and referred, as we have seen, to a paper by Jakubinsky as "one of the first examples of scientific criticism." Lotman, in turn, writes disparagingly of such

33. Johannes Anderegg, *Fiktion und Kommunikation* (Göttingen: Vandenhoeck & Ruprecht, 1973), pp. 137–38.

34. See Erlich, *Russian Formalism*, p. 179, note 39, for specific references.

35. E.g., *Lektsii po strukturaľnoj poètike* and *Struktura khudozhestvennogo teksta* in Brown University Slavic Reprints V and IX.

things as the use of terms from music and painting in literary studies as mere metaphor and not as "scientific definitions" (which of course is true and the point hardly need be pressed) and calls the Formalist term *priem* (device) a "metaphysical concept."[36] This concept, he informs us, is being replaced by the dialectical term, "the structural element and its function," which (though he does not use the adjective *nauchnyj* here[37]) he presumably believes to be "scientific." Further, Lotman likes, as many critics do in the West, to give a "scientifical" color to his text by throwing in now and then bits of data from the actual sciences. Thus, after stating that our "notion of the boundary between poetry and prose is beginning to be tied in not only with positive but also with negative structural elements," he suggests that the literary scholar concern himself with such things as the "holes" in space which, he says, astrophysicists call either "heavy" or "light," the mass of which occasionally has to be given in negative magnitudes. But here is an example of Lotman's own cold and objective approach. He cites these lines from Kamensky's poem, *Stepan Razin:*

> Po tsarevym mednym lbam.
> Bam!
> Bam!
> Bam!
> Batsk!
> > Butsk!

and then these from the same poem:

> > Bam!
> > Vam!
> > Dam!

and tells us that "the emotional content of the former excerpt is less than that of the latter, exactly because in the former there is less meaning."

So far as formalism is concerned, Lotman views it almost as if it were a movement spawned by Trotsky and he does not have much

---

36. *Lektsii po strukturaľnoj poètike* (Providence: Brown University Press Reprint, 1968), p. 57.

37. See the comments on the Russian use of *nauka* in James Billington, *The Icon and the Axe* (New York: Random House, 1970), pp. 182 and 696 (note 42).

good to say of it, as one might suspect. He makes this very (and officially) clear: "There cannot be anything in common between Formalism [on the one hand], which was based on the philosophical foundations of mechanistic materialism and positivism and which also shows the influence of Kantianism, and [on the other hand] the profoundly dialectical structural approach to the phenomena of spiritual culture."[38] But Lotman is right in criticizing poor Shklovsky for his later (1961) attempts to "semioticize" his theory by rephrasing it, viz., the artistic effect "is achieved by altering the signaling system, so to speak, by renewing the signal, which destroys the stereotype and makes us strain ourselves to perceive a thing." Here Shklovsky quite obviously is "the very same caterpillar" and Lotman—a little late, to be sure—catches him at it. As for defamiliarization and the other Formalist "devices," these are, according to Lotman, "empty concepts, outside the real historical context, outside an understanding of what is meant by the ideo-aesthetic unity of a work, the unity of the planes of content and expression."[39]

We find, I think, a more enlightened view of Shklovsky's contributions in a work by another Soviet structuralist, Boris Uspensky. In his *Poètika kompozitsii* (1970), a study of the structure of artistic texts, Uspensky writes, for instance:

> The external point of view, as a compositional device, draws its significance from its affiliation with the phenomenon of *ostranenie*, or estrangement. The essence of this phenomenon resides primarily in the use of a new or estranged viewpoint on a familiar thing, when the artist "does not refer to a thing by its name, but describes it as if it had been seen for the first time." . . . In the context of our approach, the device of estrangement may be understood as the adoption of a point of view of an outside observer, a position basically external to the things described.[40]

This occurs in Uspensky's Chapter 7, "The Structural Isomorphism of Verbal and Visual Art," in a discussion of internal and external points

38. Lotman is not telling the truth. See Erlich, *Russian Formalism,* p. 200, for a more valid assessment. See also Edmund Wilson's comments on the "dialectic" in *To the Finland Station* (Garden City: Doubleday, 1940), Part II, Chapter 11 ("The Myth of the Dialectic").

39. Lotman, *Lektsii po struktural'noy poètike,* pp. 156–57.

40. I quote from the English translation by Valentina Zavarin and Susan Wittig: *A Poetics of Composition* (Berkeley: University of California Press, 1973), p. 131.

of view both in literature and the graphic arts. In an earlier chapter, Uspensky makes reference to Lev Vygotsky's *Psikhologija iskusstva* (1968) which devotes an entire chapter to *ostranenie*.[41]

If references to Shklovsky and defamiliarization are not too common in the great mass of critical and analytical studies concerned with American, English, West European, and Oriental literatures, they do occur with greater frequency of course in articles and books by Western specialists concerned with Russian literature. Thus Hongor Oulanoff in *The Serapion Brothers: Theory and Practice* draws on Shklovsky's concept to explain the particular effect achieved by Zamyatin in a short story through the use of the "estranging mechanism of metonymic representation."[42] And Wolf Schmid in *Der Textaufbau in den Erzählungen Dostoevskijs* (1973) pays considerable (perhaps too much) attention to "text-interference" in the works of Dostoevsky and draws upon the Formalist concept of *ostranenie* together with its structuralist refinements.

5

We noted above several areas (there are many others) in which we do not ordinarily meet with defamiliarization, as well as a certain ambiguity in Shklovsky's application of *ostranenie;* the reader will also have noticed, in connection with the references to Zen and satori, an element of paradox. But there may also appear to be something paradoxical about Shklovsky's basic concept.[43] How, if art exists, as he puts it, "to make the stone *stony*," can we at the same time view the function of art as defamiliarization? Does not the poet, by somehow making us feel the anguish of love or actually hear the raucous voice of the raven, more accurately *familiarize* us with these sensations? I think, however, that the paradox is only apparent and that the problem may be resolved in several ways. In the first place, Shklovsky does not specifically equate the *existence* of art for the purpose of making us feel the sensations of things with the *function*

---

41. Vygotsky's study is also available in English translation: *The Psychology of Art* (Cambridge, Mass.: MIT Press, 1971). Chapter 3 is entitled "Art as Technique."

42. Hongor Oulanoff, *The Serapion Brothers* (The Hague: Mouton, 1966), pp. 120–21.

43. See Daniel Laferrière, "Potebnja, Šklovskij, and the Familiarity/Strangeness Paradox," *Russian Literature* 4 (1976): 175–98.

of art to defamiliarize any more than one need, for example, equate the existence of human sexuality viewed as a form of dalliance with its reproductive function. Furthermore, though a theologian might find it difficult to argue that the verb "to demythologize" (as used by Rudolf Bultmann) may in a certain sense mean "to mythologize," there are instances when something other than simple antonymy is involved in similar pairs of verbs or nouns. For example, I can quite easily conceive of situations in which at least the connotation of the word "de-emphasis" is very close to that of "emphasis." What I mean may be seen more clearly in a comment made by Christopher Isherwood concerning the "tea-tabling" manner of the novelist, E. M. Forster: "The whole of Forster's technique is based upon the tea-table: instead of trying to screw all his scenes to the highest possible pitch, he tones them down until they sound like mothers' meeting gossip. . . . In fact, there's actually *less* emphasis laid on the big scenes than on the unimportant ones. That's what's utterly terrific. It's the completely new kind of accentuation—like a person talking a different language."[44] And one is reminded here of such expressions, more rhetorical than paradoxical, as "He is conspicuous by his absence" or "Plus ça change, plus ça reste la même chose."

What I am saying, in effect (and this is precisely what Novalis says in the statement quoted on p. 35), is that the artist familiarizes by defamiliarizing, in the sense that, if successful, he brings to our recognition a new or different or more striking vision; he renews our familiarity, or even refamiliarizes us, with some more or less ordinary facet of reality, image, literary tradition, or resource of the language. But whether there is or is not any even apparent paradox here or whether we are rather involved in a matter of semantics, in the great majority of cases to be mentioned in the following chapters the meaning and effect of defamiliarization will be fairly clear: something familiar is, in one way or another, made to appear unfamiliar—new, fresh, or especially illuminating. This holds true whether it is a novelist reversing his chronology, a poet ironically theologizing (*Dieu me pardonnera, c'est son métier*—Heine), or a writer likening the delightful approach of somnolence to the aroma of the crocus sensed at a distance.[45]

44. Quoted in Walter Allen, *The Modern Novel* (New York: Dutton, 1965), p. 237.

45. *Namque ut crocus, ita somnus, priusquam prope adsit, longe praeolet, longe delectat* (Fronto).

FORMS AND VARIETIES

OF VERBAL AND

PHRASAL DEFAMILIARIZATION

1

A MONGST THE VARIOUS WAYS in which single words may be defamiliarized in literature there are two rather mechanical methods that
ought to be mentioned first. The letters in a word or name may simply
be reversed to produce an ananym—e.g., Los, the ananym for Sol, in
Blake; the character "Nosebag/G. Abeson" in Nabokov's *The Real
Life of Sebastian Knight;* or Llareggub in Dylan Thomas' *Under
Milkwood.* Samuel Butler's *Erewhon* is almost an ananym, but more
properly an anagram. Scrambling and rearranging the letters of words
(with occasionally a letter added or dropped) to produce anagrams
have been used from ancient times, often in conjunction with some
belief in the "magic of words" (we see the effects of such beliefs in
the doublet of "grammar"–"glamour") or to show that a certain word
has latent significance or simply as a conceit. Thus the Hellenistic
poet Lycophron cleverly anagrammatizes the name of Ptolemy's
queen, Arsinoë, as "(h)*eras ion,*" "Hera's Violet."[1] The Kabbalists
especially liked to explore the potentialities of words and names in
the biblical text—to draw the Hebrew word for "grace," for example,
from the name Noah. The practice was popular in the Middle Ages,
and this popularity persisted: Thomas Billon was appointed "Ana-
grammatist to the King" (Louis XIII) in seventeenth-century France.

Anagrams have been used primarily in connection with personal
names and very often to produce pseudonyms. The name Voltaire is
generally considered to be an anagram of "Arouet, l.j." (i.e., "Arouet

1. See the numerous examples of anagrams in C. C. Bombaugh, *Oddities
and Curiosities of Words and Literature,* edited and annotated by Martin
Gardner (New York: Dover, 1961), p. 49 ff.

the Younger"); François Rabelais used the anagrammatic pseudonym "Alcofrybas Nasier"; the Italian writer Renato Fucini called himself "Neri Tanfucio"; and the Russian writer Antiokh Kantemir used "Khariton Makentin." Many more examples could be cited. Occasionally a negative utopia (or dystopia) is referred to as "aipotu."[2]

Words may also (in some languages) be defamiliarized by being cut into two parts and another word or other words placed between these parts (tmesis), as in Ennius' *saxo cere comminuit brum*. We may also have aphaeresis (e.g., "He 'gan" in English or the name Pnin in Nabokov's novel of the same name[3]) or the word may be syncopated ("I'm good f'ler"—Stephen Crane), apocopated or abbreviated ("delish" for "delicious" or "guv" for "governor"), metathesized ("aks" for "ask" or "*E flir . . . e firl . . . ?*"—fumbling for the word *filtru*, in the Rumanian writer Ion Caragiale)[4] or, in some languages, a word may be revocalized (often for euphemistic reasons, as in the Hebrew Ashtoreth, a product of the consonants of Astarte/Ishtar, the Phoenician fertility goddess, and the vowels of *bosheth*, "shame").

A word may be defamiliarized by being rendered more or less phonetically in what is, or what appears to be, another language. Thus the Russian-born French caricaturist and illustrator Emmanuel Poiré (d. 1909), the grandson of one of Napoleon's officers who had settled in Russia, used the pseudonym *Caran d'Ache* (i.e., Russian *karandash*, "pencil"), which is essentially a pun or paronomasia.[5] This is somewhat different from a transliteration (e.g., the Arabic/Turkish *Maşala!* as used in a poem by the Rumanian poet Ion Barbu) or the *el-jamdul-lah* in Juan Goytisolo's *Count Julian*.

The so-called blend words or portmanteau words (e.g., Lewis Carroll's "chortle" and "slithy") may also be used both to defamiliarize

2. E.g., in the Afterword (in Russian) by V. Bondarenko to Zamyatin's *My* (New York: Inter-Language Literary Association, 1967).

3. Pnin, the name of an eighteenth-century Russian poet, is a truncated form of the name Repnin. See Andrew Field, *Nabokov: His Life in Art* (Boston: Little, Brown, 1967), p. 139. Field comments that *"Pnin* seethes with private Russian jokes, some of them esoteric enough to be understood by only a very select circle of Russians."

4. Such alterations are sometimes made *metris gratia* in poetry or for idiolect effect in prose. Aphaeresis, apocope, syncope, etc., are philological or lexicographical terms.

5. If the French for pun, *calembour*, derives (as Spitzer maintained) from "conundrum"; this points up well the at first puzzling effect of such devices. *Caran d'Ache* is in fact an intentional hobson-jobson.

and to combine, multiply, and associate meanings. In English, James Joyce's *Ulysses* and *Finnegan's Wake* are treasure houses of such usage ("chaosmos," "aiopen," "shemblable," etc.) and we find similar words in the fiction of the French novelist Raymond Queneau (*aiguesistance*, *représentasillon*), but the technique has been employed in many literatures.[6] In German such a word is called a *Schachtelwort*: an example would be the substandard Alsatian word for umbrella, *paraschirm* (a blending of *parapluie* and *Regenschirm*).[7] In Russian literature the use of portmanteau words, along with many other types of distortions and alterations, both humorous and ironic, is usually classed loosely under *skaz* (i.e., idiolect or "yarn" technique), Nikolay Leskov (d. 1895) being one of the best-known practitioners (e.g., *buremetry*, "storm-meters," instead of *barometry*, or *melkoskop*, "tinyscope," instead of *mikroskop*[8]). Such substitutions are also referred to in English as malapropisms (and the true malapropism should match, as in the examples from Leskov, the sound pattern and the rhythm of the word being altered); the European literatures supply many instances.[9]

Single words may be defamiliarized in many other ways. They may, for example, simply be distorted—occasionally beyond recognition: e.g., in Gogol's *Revizor* ("The Inspector General") Khlestakov's servant, Osip, refers to his master's rank as *elistratishka*, a radical mispronunciation of *kollezhskij registrator*, "collegiate registrar"; or the numerous examples in Dickens—for example, the "Wellerisms" in the *Pickwick Papers*. The introduction of foreigners speaking with varying degrees of incomprehensibility is a comic device that has been

6. See *transition* 21 (March 1932): 284–325, for an account of the linguistic experimentation of Joyce and others.

7. This is also a type of poecilonym or hybrid word; cf. such a word as "aeneolithic" (=chalcolithic) in English.

8. The Leskovian language, much like that of Gogol, presents more than usual problems for the translator. See, e.g., the Introduction to *Satirical Stories of Nikolai Leskov*, translated and edited by W. B. Edgerton (New York: Pegasus, 1969). The Russian Formalist critic, Boris Eykhenbaum, called Leskov a *slovesnyj izograf* (a "verbal iconpainter," but with the connotations of mimicry); see C. G. Schwencke, "Some Remarks on the Use of Structural and Linguistic Devices in Leskov's Prose," *The Slavonic and East European Review* 121 (October 1972): 546–57. On idiolect, see below, Chapter IV, p. 128.

9. The similarity between many of these formations and the language of children is striking. See Korney Chukovsky, *Ot dvukh do pjati* (Moscow, 1957) for many examples. This work is also available in English translation: *From Two to Five*, translated and edited by Miriam Morton (Berkeley: University of California Press, 1963).

used since the time of Aristophanes—e.g., the language of the Tribal-lian in *The Birds* and of Lampito in *Lysistrata,* of the Carthaginian in Plautus' *Poenulus,* of Scotsmen, Irishmen, and Welshmen coping with English, of various foreigners "murdering" French,[10] and of Germans or partially Russianized Germans in Russian literature trying to articu-late Russian (e.g., Vralman in Fonvizin's *Nedorosl'*).[11]

Further, defamiliarization may be effected through the coinage, for example, of absurdly long, polysyllabic monstrosities (such as the 170-letter-long word in Aristophanes' *Ecclesiazusae*) or other such neologisms.[12] Many great writers—and many more lesser figures—have felt that the lexicon available to them was inadequate and they have tried to remedy this situation by innovating, very often adding lasting coinages to their particular languages in the process. Indeed, it would be possible to cite a very long list of exemplary names from all the literatures of Europe and beyond, although the names of many mod-ernists are especially significant in this respect, notably the Futurists—including the Italian and Russian varieties—and the Surrealists. The neologisms in the Russian Symbolist, Andrey Bely (an immediate forerunner of the Futurists), and in Mayakovsky and Khlebnikov have been rather extensively studied.[13] Khlebnikov has a poem, *Zakljatie smekhom* ("Incantation by Laughter," 1910),[14] which is made up al-most entirely of words newly coined on the basis of the root *smekh,* "laughter"—an exercise that reminds one of the neologistic variations on the Spanish word *coño* in Part Three of Goytisolo's *Count Julian.* But there are interesting experiments along these lines in other than

10. Cf. the Spanish *vasconcear* and the French expression, "*parler* (e.g., *français*) *comme une vache espagnole* (where *une vache espagnole* was originally *un Basque espagnol*). In French, as in other languages, there are a number of terms used to refer to particular types of errors foreigners are especially liable to make—e.g., *le cuire* and *le pataquès*.

11. Solecisms (*soloikismos* originally meant the typical mispronunciations and abuses of Greek amongst the Athenian colonists at Soli in Cilicia) are often used as a device in idiolect passages.

12. Long (holophrastic) words are especially frequent in classical Sanskrit; see the compound made up of twenty components (113 letters in transliteration) cited by A. L. Basham in *The Wonder That Was India* (New York: Hawthorn, 1963), p. 392.

13. On the Russian Futurists, see Vladimir Markov, *Russian Futurism: A History* (Berkeley: University of California Press, 1968). On the Italian Futurists, see *Marinetti: Selected Writings,* edited by R. W. Flint (New York: Farrar, Straus and Giroux, 1971).

14. Russian and English texts in Vladimir Markov and Merrill Sparks, eds., *Modern Russian Poetry* (New York: Bobbs-Merrill, 1967), pp. 326–27.

the "major" literatures—in the writings of the Polish authors Witold
Gombrowicz and Stanislaw Witkiewicz, for instance.[15]

We may also have defamiliarization through the abuse of words
or metaphor (catachresis), again often in idiolect sequences reflecting
substandard or dialectical aberrations but often, too, with ironic
effect—e.g., Babel's "inveterate railway station" (*zakorenelaja stant-
sija:* the writer of the letter means something like *zakholustnaja,* "out-
of-the-way," "godforsaken"[16]) or the remark of Pnin in Nabokov's
novel of the same name that he will soon be an "Assistant Professor
Emeritus." (A special type of catachresis is the malapropism, as noted
earlier; another type is the so-called Hibernicism or "Irish Bull.")
But it is not at all unusual for poets often to expand (or narrow) the
meaning and application of words to an extreme degree: thus Mayakovsky, having in mind men with outstretched arms directing traffic,
refers to "policemen crucified (*raspjaty*) at street corners"; and Milton
in *Lycidas* refers to "blind mouthes," a usage that was attacked by
Johnson and defended by Ruskin.[17] There may also be a certain quaint
effect in the cases of words used in an *ad hoc* or "Pickwickian" sense
(often these border on a special "lingo"). Thus Durrell provides at
the end of *Balthazar* a glossary of Scobie's terms—e.g., "mauve" meaning "silly."

A particular type of verbal distortion or metathesis is heterophemy
(e.g., "calvary" for "cavalry"); and a more complex type is the Spoon-
erism ("roaring pain"/"pouring rain") or the marrowsky[18] or mar-
rowskying (sometimes called "Medical Greek" in England), the punning language—originally—of the students at London University
("poke a smipe" for "smoke a pipe"). There are similar modes of
defamiliarization in other languages—e.g., the French *contrepéterie*
(*"fouilles curieuses"/"couilles furieuses"*), *largonji, loucherbème,* and

---

15. See Northwestern University's *Tri-Quarterly* 9 (Spring 1967): "Tradition and Innovation in Eastern European Literature."

16. In *Sol'* (*Konarmija*), *ad init.*

17. "Blind mouthes," although often cited as an example of catachresis, is
very close to being an instance of *aisthēsis ant'aisthēseōs* or synaesthesia: "blind"
is to eyes (or vision) what "dumb" is to the mouth (or speech). An expression
such as "Children should be seen and not hurt," while being a kind of catachresis, is clearly an example of what Aristotle would have called a *para
prosdokian* pun. On catachreses in Aeschylus, see J. A. Schuursma, *De poetica
vocabulorum abusione apud Aeschylum* (Paris, 1932).

18. Nabokov refers to "marrowskies" in *Pale Fire* (in the commentary to
line 347) and provides a note in the Index. There are, of course, many similar
types of verbal distortion, such as "Pig Latin" and rhyming or back slang.

javanais.[19] An even more complicated technique is represented by the Hebrew Atbash (Athbash), an anagrammatic system (actually a form of cryptography) involving regular permutations of letters used by the Kabbalists.[20] Frequently words (especially foreign ones) may be distorted in a punning manner. Thus Castiglione in *Il Cortegiano,* discussing types of *facetiae,* writes: "Un altra sorte è ancor, che chiamiamo *bischizzi,* e questa consiste nel mutare ovvero accrescere o minuire una lettera o sillaba; come colui che disse: Tu dei esser più dotto nella lingua latrina che nella greca."[21]

Nonsense words and gibberish (or what appear to be such— often they are analyzable as ananyms or anagrams) are occasionally used in literature, such as the "Laputan" words and phrases in Swift's "A Voyage to Laputa" and the "Zemblan" expressions in Nabokov's *Pale Fire.*[22] The "Punic" passages referred to above in Plautus' *Poenulus* may originally have been an attempt to transliterate a Semitic language but they are more likely to have been merely a humorous, approximate mimicry. But the writer of fiction dealing with an alien world (e.g., in science fiction, utopias or dystopias), where, presumably, a language other than his own is spoken, must decide between two extremes: whether to defamiliarize completely (in which case his fiction would be incomprehensible unless accompanied by a glossary) or to use his own language and explain, somehow, the lack of verisimilitude. In actual fact, a compromise is usually reached in which there is, along with some defamiliarization, a fairly comprehensible narrative.[23] Some writers have experimented with invented languages:

19. In *javanais* (popular during the Second Empire) *av* or *va* is added to every consonant: thus *jeudi* becomes *javeudavi.* Cf. the expression, *C'est du javanais!*

20. On the Atbash and other systems, see the *Jewish Encyclopedia,* s.v. "Gematria," and Bernhard Pick, *The Cabala* (La Salle: Open Court, 1974), pp. 91–92.

21. Naturally this was picked up by Sir John Harington and alluded to in his *The Metamorphosis of Ajax;* see the edition edited by Elizabeth Donno (New York: Columbia University Press, 1962), p. 62.

22. See the interesting remarks by L. I. Timofeev on the so-called *"flon-flons"* and *"briolage"* as used in verse: *Ocherki teorii i istorii russkogo stikha* (Moscow, 1958), pp. 12–13. See also an article by Noel Perrin on the way animal cries are represented in different languages in *The New Yorker* (January 27, 1962): 28–29.

23. See, incidentally, *Le langage Martien* by the French philologist Victor Henry (d. 1909); this contains a discussion of some forty "Martian" phrases which a spiritualist learned while on a "voyage to Mars."

Stefan George used an invented language for workshop practice. Many people have invented private languages, usually as a secret means of communication or as a kind of personal cypher. In *The Lord of the Rings* J. R. R. Tolkien uses a number of invented languages and has included some fine poetry written in them. His is quite a different case; the language came first and everything else followed. Tolkien tells me that he long ago invented some languages out of pure philological enthusiasm; as they seemed to work, he thought it would be interesting to invent people who spoke them. The result was the whole thrilling world of dwarves, elves and hobbits which is already being exploited for Ph.D. theses by the academic machine, mainly in the United States.[24]

An effect akin to that of gibberish is often produced by the use of acronyms which frequently appear in modern literature as they do in modern cultures. The Russian writer Boris Pilnyak, referring to the grotesque appearance and sound of Soviet Russian acronyms (and the Soviet bureaucracy has produced myriads of them), once remarked that they seemed like the names of pagan Slavic deities come back to haunt us. Even the mnemonic word used by Newton for recalling the colors of the spectrum—vibgyor—has this alien effect.[25] I recall, in Peter Bamm's *Die unsichtbare Flagge*, the soldiers who referred to their evangelical chaplain as *Esak* (*Evangelische Sünden-Abwehr-Kanone*) and their Catholic chaplain as *Kasak* (*Katholische Sünden-Abwehr-Kanone*).[26]

The use of rare, archaic, and obsolete words frequently—but depending of course on the lexical sophistication of the reader—may have a defamiliarizing effect. I have already touched upon this in connection with the language of medicine and the law, but many writers come to mind. Lycophron's *Alexandra*, for instance, was renowned for its esoteric vocabulary even in antiquity and has, so I understand, the greatest number of *hapax legomena* of any other single work of ancient Greek literature. The introduction of rare and unusual words has been used since ancient times for various purposes, for the sake of humor and for the display of erudition being the most common.

24. Leonard Foster, *The Poet's Tongues: Multilingualism in Literature* (Cambridge: At the University Press, 1970), p. 88.

25. Nabokov uses "vibgyor" in *Ada* (New York: McGraw-Hill, 1969), p. 83.

26. Cf. also, in connection with nonsense words, the *chevilles* occasionally found in both prose and poetry; and the "ghost words" due, for instance, to metanalysis or some other error. The Russian writer Tynyanov has a story, *Podporuchik Kizhe* ("Lieutenant Kije"), dealing with the history of an officer whose very "existence" stems from a *fausse-coupe* error.

Whereas Cicero was content to say *latine loqui,* Apollinaris Sidonius in the fifth century wrote *latialiter insusurrare* (see Chapter V, p. 163); the stock figure of the pedant, spouting polysyllabic words and quoting learned authorities, is encountered in many literatures. But much more prominent are those poets and prose writers themselves who, either out of a predilection or because it is the fashion, puzzle and amuse readers with their recondite vocabulary. In the different European literatures—and in the Orient as well[27]—there were and are certain writers (often within contemporary or comparable movements) who are renowned for, among other things, a marked penchant for rare and curious words. Rabelais comes to mind, as well as Cervantes and Joyce, amongst the greats; or such men as Remizov and Nabokov—along with many, many others—amongst the not-so-greats. One of the pleasures in reading Nabokov is the purely philological one: along with his coinages (and one of the most striking is *ivanilich* in *Ada*[28]), there is a marvelous assortment of lexical rarities, but these are always used with the nice precision that the author's preoccupation with minute detail requires. Yet Nabokov frequently goes beyond, or is dissatisfied with, simple neologisms and the ordinary run of rare words and he will blithely introduce, in transliteration but without italicization, a Greek word that one can find only in Liddell and Scott—e.g., "skoramis" in *Pale Fire.*[29]

Writers will use rare words to express exact or very particular aspects of reality, in idiolect passages, or for a humorous or ironic effect. Such words may defamiliarize in much the same way as do antonomasia and other metaphors: thus one may substitute "crispisulcant" for "zigzag," "ephelides" for "freckles," "crembalum" for "jew's-harp," "cribriform" for "sievelike," "to fletcherize" for "to chew thoroughly," etc., almost without end. And when one includes here the use of foreign words and phrases (to refer, for example, to the

27. E.g., the Chinese *fu* poems, especially those by Ssu-ma Hsiang-ju (d. 117 B.C.). In Arabic literature, R. A. Nicholson, speaking of one poet (Abu 'l-'Atahiya), writes: "He showed for the first and perhaps for the last time in the history of classical Arabic literature that it was possible to use perfectly plain and ordinary language without ceasing to be a poet." *A Literary History of the Arabs* (Cambridge: At the University Press, 1956), p. 299.

28. *Ada,* p. 232. In Tolstoy's *The Death of Ivan Ilych* there is a rather strange passage concerning a *puf* (i.e., pouf or ottoman) that is rebellious and noisy. Nabokov uses the word "ivanilich" (which he italicizes) to refer to a kind of "sighing old hassock."

29. In commentary to line 172. The word is used by Aristophanes in the *Ecclesiazusae.* Cf. also his use of the Greek word *olisbos* (i.e., *penis coriaceus*) in the phrase "olisbos-like flashlight" in *Lolita* (New York: Putnam's, 1955), p. 96.

hair growing between the eyebrows with the French word *la taroupe*), the process, for all practical purposes, *is* endless.[30]

For the modern reader of the older poets and prose writers there is a real (although in some cases perhaps not originally intentional) defamiliarizing effect of words, the meanings of which have changed either in whole or in part. I refer to such things as Shakespeare's Elizabethan English, the various aspects of Milton's Latinate style ("elephants endorsed with towers") or, in the Russian domain, Kantemir's *Simfonija na psaltir'* (1727), i.e., "Concordance to the Psalter."[31] Many similar phenomena may be found in the other literatures. This effect is particularly true as well of certain older translations, such as Urquhart's version of Rabelais.

Specifically obsolete or obsolescent words, or words whose meanings have radically changed, are occasionally used, in addition to suggesting something archaic or forgotten, for an ironic effect. Thus in a fable by the Soviet poet Sergey Mikhalkov the word *piit* (from the Greek *poiētēs* with the Byzantine "itacistic" pronunciation), a doublet of *poèt* (from the French *poète*), is used in this way: *Komar piitom vozomnil sebja* ("The mosquito imagined himself a 'poet'"). If a modern British poet were to refer, say, to the "cruddy clouds," this usage would also have an ironic tone, especially for those who might know that Stephen Hawes in the sixteenth century spoke of the "cruddy firmament." An even more particular type occurs in utopian or science fiction set in the distant future when certain words for things of our present time are treated as vestiges of the past—e.g., the word "bread" (*khleb*) in Zamyatin's *We*.

In all the literary languages that I am acquainted with there are various linguistic resources, beyond those already mentioned, that can be drawn upon by a writer for the sake of defamiliarization. In English, for example, one may resort to Anglo-Saxon synonyms ("scopcraeft" instead of "poetry") or use certain obsolete or ordinarily non-productive forms—those with prefixes of the a- type for

30. In the various world languages, should Greek, Latin, and Sanskrit not suffice, one can find words for just about every minute aspect of man and nature (this is particularly true of the so-called primitive languages). Arabic, the lexicon of which is immense (the Arabic word for dictionary is *qāmūs*, from the Greek for "ocean"), has a word, *bulja*, for a clear space between the eyebrows, Greek has words for the hollow between the lower lip and the chin (*nympha*), the space between the thumb and forefinger (*likhas*), etc. Greek, Latin, and Sanskrit each have a term for the malacia or vitiated appetite that sometimes occurs during pregnancy (*kissa, pica, dohada*).

31. The Greek word *symphonia* also occurs in the Old Testament (*sūmpōnya*, Dan. 3:15) and means something like "bagpipes" (cf. Southern Italian *zampogna*).

instance (awriting, adown, addoom, etc.), paragogic forms, diastoles, "Addisonian terminations," etc., not to mention a wide range of provincialisms and dialecticisms. As English has a large number of pairs of either the Anglo-Saxon/Norman French (goat flesh/chevon), Anglo-Saxon/Scandinavian (shirt/skirt), or Anglo-Saxon/Greco-Latin (growing/crescent) varieties, so Russian, for instance, is rich in Old Church Slavonic/Russian doublets of the *zlato/zoloto* type as well as many other morphological and syntactical patterns that may be exploited for stylistic purposes and specifically for defamiliarization. But a French writer has his Old French forms to dally with, the Spanish writer his *arabismos*, the Arab his Persianisms, and so on.

Compound and hyphenated words may often defamiliarize, especially when they are oxymoronic and when they are fresh: even modifiers such as Sappho's *glykypikros* or Gerard Manley Hopkins' "lovely-dumb" tend to become clichés. But some compounds are often incongruous in appearance and sound and have certainly a defamiliarizing effect: e.g., Aristophanes' *krommyoksyregmia* ("a belch of onions and vinegar") or such oddities as the English "floccipaucinihilipilification" (OED). Of course some languages form more easily than others polysyllabic compounds which are frequently, in effect, holophrastic; this is especially true of the agglutinative languages. But the emotional effect of great poems is very often due to the poet's very skill in compounding (not to mention juxtaposing) words in unusual and striking ways—this is the effect called "synergical" by R. P. Blackmur and referred to in other terms by other critics. Such words may vary from merely clever and provocative combinations (such as Eustathius' *pyropipēs*, "oggler of red-heads") to more allusive ones such as the Russian epithet *nerukotvornyj*,[32] "not made by (human) hands" (a calque of the Byzantine Greek *akheiropoiētos*, applied originally to icons of miraculous origin), or Hölderlin's *gewittertrunken*.

Almost any individual word or formal linguistic element may be "foregrounded"—and thus made to appear strange—through repetition (Gertrude Stein, Samuel Beckett),[33] typographical emphasis (italics, letter spacing, different fonts—e.g., the occasional use of black letter in *Tristram Shandy*), or even through omission. Aside from the body

32. Pushkin uses *nerukotvornyj* in his *Pamjatnik* (1836), an adaptation of Horace's *Exegi monumentum*, as an epithet of *pamjatnik* (monument). Cf. Browning's "Builder and maker, thou, of houses not made with hands" (*Abt Vogler*).

33. See also the examples of Tolstoy's repetitions in R. F. Christian, *Tolstoy: A Critical Introduction* (Cambridge: At the University Press, 1969), pp. 139–40. The lyrical repetends that we find in some novels (such as Bely's *St. Petersburg*) also add to the non-realistic appearance of the prose.

of lipogrammatic works of prose and poetry, I would include here the rather widespread use of dots or dashes to replace words and of suspension points. The unidiomatic employment of, for instance, the English definite article is a regular feature of non-native or dialect speech; and G. Rostrevor Hamilton in his study of the English definite article also shows us how this word may be used to secure specific effects: how, for instance, in the poetry of Auden its use has a certain "snob" appeal.[34] Milton's frequent use of past participles without agent has been studied and interpreted, and Dostoevsky's unusually frequent employment of "adverbial verbs" was noted and parodied by Turgenev.[35]

Finally, although I do not claim to have exhausted all the possibilities of verbal defamiliarization, there is the stigmonym (i.e., a word or words replaced by dots), which is seldom used these days. But it was not too long ago that this, or a comparable device, was employed to lend either real or affected anonymity to persons and places or, euphemistically, to replace *praefanda*, and the practice is sometimes still observed. Thus Professor Shaw, in his Preface to his edition of Pushkin's letters in English translation, writes: "with some reluctance it has been decided to follow Russian editions and to consider as unprintable in English the equivalents of words considered unprintable in Russian, and to indicate them in the conventional manner" (in this case, by the initial letter of the word followed by a long dash). But authors in the past used the device extensively.

2

When more than one word or when phrases are involved, there are also some basic, rather mechanical devices of defamiliarization. There are, for example, various hyperbata, such as the numerous instances in Milton of a Latinate word order:

> Me lonely sitting, nor the glimmering Light
> Of Make-weight Candle, nor the joyous Talk
> Of loving Friends delights . . .

34. *The Tell-Tale Article* (London: Heinemann, 1949). See also Harald Weinrich, "The Textual Function of the French Article," in *Literary Style* (New York: Oxford University Press, 1971), pp. 221–34.

35. See Seymour Chatman, "Milton's Participial Style," *PMLA* 83 (1968): 1386–99. See P. M. Bitsilli, *K voprosu o vnutrennej forme romana Dostoevskogo*, in *O Dostoevskom: Stat'i*, Brown University Slavic Reprint IV (Providence: Brown University Press, 1966), pp. 49–50.

Though word order is freer in synthetic languages, the eighteenth-century Russian poet, Antiokh Kantemir, has hyperbata that are still radical in Russian—"*k kakomu vsjak u nego speet ovoshch' sroku*" (=*k kakomu sroku speet u nego vsjak ovoshch'*). But writers—especially poets—in several literatures (notably during baroque periods) have employed this and similar transpositions (e.g., Góngora). Particular types of unusual word order include those designated by such terms as chiasmus, hysteron proteron, prolepsis, and the interlocked arrangement or synchysis (e.g., *bonus filii pater boni*).

Intentional anacolutha (like unintentional ones) can, by disrupting the syntax, alert the reader or complicate or retard his perceptive processes and introduce an element of discontinuity. Many examples occur in ancient literature and, if some of the instances are unintentional or due to textual corruption, they are certainly not all accidental, the device having been employed with particular if subtle effectiveness by the Greek orators. Anacolutha have, in fact, been used frequently down through the ages (occurring in such diverse places as Tolstoy's novels and Claudel's poems) and are even more frequent phenomena in much contemporary prose and poetry.[36] Along with other devices, anacolutha constitute basic formal means not only in symbolist movements but in such particular techniques as the "stream of consciousness" as well.[37] Anacolutha often result from synesis, i.e., *constructio ad sensum,* when agreement and concord are based on logical or "internal" rather than formal grammatical or syntactical nexus (see below, Chapter IV, p. 148).

What might ordinarily be a single, self-enclosed statement is sometimes broken up, by the extraction of a phrase which is made to stand independently as a sentence fragment, into two separate elements: "At noon a knock on the door awakened Anna. A light but persistent knock." This is what the Russian syntacticians call *partsell-*

36. Anacolutha and other grammatical and syntactical aberrations in Tolstoy may very well be due to the author's aristocratic disdain of formal correctness: thus in a letter he once wrote: "I like what is called incorrectness—that is, what is characteristic." Cf. Plato's comment in the *Theaetetus:* "The careless handling as well as the imprecise arrangement of words are not only for the most part evidence of good breeding, but it is rather the opposite of this that smacks of servility." On Claudel's anacolutha, see Leo Spitzer, *Linguistics and Literary History* (Princeton: Princeton University Press, 1967), p. 227.

37. On symbolism, see William York Tindall, *The Literary Symbol* (Bloomington: Indiana University Press, 1960), p. 191 ff. On "stream of consciousness," see Shiv Kumar, *Bergson and the Stream of Consciousness Novel* (New York: New York University Press, 1963), pp. 33–35.

jatsija ("parcellation").[38] The Spanish version of Helmut Hatzfeld's study of Cervantes' language and style in *Don Quijote* uses a similar term—*dosificación*—to refer to examples, drawn from Cervantes and Flaubert, of something close to periodic construction, viz., the building up of anticipatory phrases or clauses in small "doses" ahead of the main verb or clause:

> Cependant/ au haut bout de la table/ seul parmi toutes ces femmes/ courbé sur son assiette remplie/ et la serviette nouée dans le dos/ comme un enfant/ un vieillard mangeait.[39]

This is a very obvious retarding device and one that might easily be carried to extreme limits.

Asyndeton, or lack of connectives, allowing as it does for the more direct juxtaposition of syntagmas (and consequently of "narremes"[40]), may also defamiliarize. The word "juxtaposition" (often associated with collage techniques in the graphic arts) is a key term in any significant discussion of much modern, non-objective art and is frequently used in studies of symbolism. Thus Roger Shattuck quotes the following poem by Guillaume Apollinaire as a good example of juxtaposition:

> Trois becs de gaz allumés
> La patronne est poitrinaire
> Quand tu auras fini nous jouerons une partie de jacquet
> Un chef d'orchestre qui a mal à la gorge
> Quand tu viendras à Tunis je te ferai fumer du kief
> Ça a l'air de rimer.[41]

38. See *Morfologija i sintaksis sovremennogo russkogo jazyka,* edited by M. Panov (Moscow: *Nauka,* 1968), Chapter IV, p. 277 ff.

39. Quoted in *El "Quijote" Como Obra de Arte del Linguaje* (Madrid, 1966), pp. 361–62. Hatzfeld writes: "Dosificación se llama el método de los pintores impresionistas de poner un rasgo de cepillo al lado de otro sin eliminar los contornos. En la literatura puede llamarse así los elementos aislados de una proposición que se ofrece en unidades rítmicas, conduciendo a un predicado psicológico atrasado."

40. The term is used, e.g., in Bruce Morrissette's article, "Games and Game Structures in Robbe-Grillet," in *Game, Play, Literature,* edited by Jacques Ehrmann (Boston: Beacon Press, 1971), p. 161.

41. Quoted in *The Banquet Years* (New York: Anchor, 1961), p. 333. On juxtaposition, see p. 332 ff. See also Monroe Spears, *Dionysus and the City* (New York: Oxford University Press, 1971), p. 20 ff., and Tindall, *The Literary Symbol,* p. 205 ff.

But Ezra Pound also provides a brief but excellent specimen:

> Spring . . .
> Too late . . .
> Gongula . . .[42]

Strangely enough, polysyndeton may also, especially when it occurs in a contrasting context, have a defamiliarizing effect. There is, for example, a passage in Tolstoy's *Family Happiness* which catches both the eye and the ear of the reader or listener because of the combination of polysyndeton and parataxis: "... *my podvigalis', i volshebnaja stena krasoty razdvigalas'* . . . , *i tam tozhe* . . . *byl nash* . . . *sad.* . . . *I my* . . . *khodili.* . . . *I èto* . . . *byl on* . . . , *i èto* . . . *byla Katja.* . . . *I, dolzhno byt'* . . ." Here Tolstoy is quite evidently supplementing structurally a picture of what he takes to be a basic, as yet uninvolved human relationship (and we must remember also that *Family Happiness* is written from the woman's point of view).[43]

Ezra Pound's *Papyrus*, quoted above, also reminds us of the frequent presence of fragmentariness or fragmentary art forms amongst romantic artists, something that has been commented on by numerous critics, while the general topic of *il non finito* has itself been the subject of scholarly study.[44] The whole of Pound's poem (or indeed of many other apparently "unfinished" works of art) is, in fact, a metaphor, viz., *pars pro toto* or synecdoche. Marcia Allentuck, in a finely written but all too brief a paper contributed to a memorial volume for the bicentennial of Laurence Sterne's death, calls our attention to the possibility that Sterne may have been acquainted with certain eighteenth-century adumbrations of *non finito* aesthetic theory, though he himself lived in a period (as the author puts it) "obsessed by closed

42. The poem is entitled *Papyrus;* see the commentary on it by Gilbert Highet in *The Classical Tradition* (New York: Oxford University Press, 1957), pp. 517–18.

43. See the remarks concerning asyndeton, polysyndeton, and anacolutha in Montaigne in R. A. Sayce, "The Style of Montaigne: Word-Pairs and Word-Groups," in *Literary Style*, pp. 383–402. In the Russian *byliny* or epic folksongs there is an interesting stylistic phenomenon known as polyprotheticism: here a prepositional phrase, such as *ko velikomu gradu Kievu* (to the great city of Kiev), is broken up and the preposition repeated before each word—*ko velikomu ko gradu ko Kievu.*

44. E.g., J. A. Schmoll gen. Eisenwerth, *Das Unvollendete als künstlerische Form* (Berne and Munich, 1959). See also Tindall, *The Literary Symbol*, p. 231.

forms and calculated regularities."[45] She quotes a passage from Henry James's preface to *Roderick Hudson* in which James attempts to cope with the age-old problem of closure, i.e., how the novelist may best circumscribe and delimit the immense complexities of reality. James's advice is for the artist, using a "geometry of his own," so to draw his line that the circle *appears* to be closed. But Professor Allentuck comments: "Yet never once . . . does James consider that *not* drawing the circle, *not* stopping the relations, in the sense of rounding them out, is at times an even more expert way of solving the problems, and affirming the potencies of the continuity of which he speaks." She then goes on to discuss Sterne; but it is interesting that her comments tie in well with Shklovsky's *ostranenie* theory as a form of "dishabituation," as noted in the preceding chapter: "If we start," writes Shklovsky, "to examine the general laws of perception, we see that as perception becomes habitual, it becomes automatic." To be given *pars pro toto* thus has the effect on the reader of defamiliarization and disautomatization.[46]

Oxymoron, best illustrated by phrases made up of two words (usually adjective + noun—e.g., "loud silence"), is another mode of defamiliarization through juxtaposition employed frequently in literature, although it is most characteristic of baroque or similar periods. It is a particular type of conceit that is also essentially a symbolist (that is to say, poetic) device, since it suggests its meaning implicitly rather than states it explicitly. The literatures of the world, especially their poetic forms, provide countless examples. In Greek literature (most notably in tragedy) the *mētēr amētōr* ("a mother who is no mother") type is frequently encountered (*polis apolis, nymphē anymphos*[47]) and a rather elaborate classification of other types might be made, ranging from such run-of-the-mill phrases as "cruel kindness" and what have in fact become clichés (e.g., in Russian poetry, *otrava sladkaja*, "sweet poison" = "love") to the much more clever and

45. "In Defense of an Unfinished Tristram Shandy: Laurence Sterne and the Non Finito," in *The Winged Skull* (Kent State University Press, 1971).

46. See the remarks by Maurice Merleau-Ponty on "unfinished" works of art in *The Prose of the World*, translated by John O'Neill (Evanston: Northwestern University Press, 1973), pp. 55–56.

47. These Greek examples are also "negative ploces" (ploce refers to the emphatic repetition of a word—"Here is a man who is a man!"). *Nymphē anymphos* (which occurs in Euripides' *Hecuba*) served, it seems, as the model (via a Byzantine Greek hymn known as an *akathistos*) for the Russian calque, *Nevesta nenevestnaja*, "a bride who is no bride," which in turn appears in the well-known Russian Orthodox hymn (or *akafist*) as the epithet of the Mother of God. The phrase is also used by the Russian Symbolist poet, Vyacheslav Ivanov.

allusive combinations that we find in Marino, Góngora, and Crashaw, in Zamyatin ("Tamerlane of happiness") and Babel ("passionate rags"). The oxymoron is a conspicuous feature of Baudelaire's poetry.[48] Anna Akhmatova's oxymora are exceptional and, according to Boris Eykhenbaum, they are this poet's favorite figure.[49]

Oxymoronic phrases, providing as they do succinct and striking verbal equivalents or symbols of certain situations, phenomena, or concepts that especially invite paradoxical treatment (such as "love" or "God"), have very frequently occurred in the prose and poetry of mystics and religious thinkers since the time of Heracleitus ("the way up is the way down") both in the West and in the East (e.g., in Zen Buddhism). One often encounters, in this connection, variations on the phrase *credo quia impossibile est,* which is itself an adaptation of Tertullian's *certum est quia impossibile est.*[50] In the vast literature of love, both sacred and profane, oxymora also appear frequently: such phrases are common, for instance, in Italian renaissance lyrics (e.g., love is an *affanno dilettoso* and a *dolce pena* in Guido Delle Colonne), in *trobar clus,* as well as in the modernists (e.g., Rilke's *dieser voreilige Vorteil eines nahen Verlusts* or Laforgue's *bonne blessure;* cf. Michelet's *"l'éternelle blessée"*). They are especially prominent in the poems of St. John of the Cross (*este saber no sabiendo, muero porque no muero*) and in the "metaphysical" poets—e.g., John Donne:

> yea thou art now
> Thy Makers maker, and thy Fathers mother.

The oxymora we find in the religious mystics and the metaphysicals, oxymora which are also *adynata* (see below), may be associated both

48. See Hugo Friedrich, *The Structure of Modern Poetry* (Evanston: Northwestern University Press, 1974), p. 28: "In Baudelaire, the oxymoron is used to a conspicuous degree. It is the key figure of his fundamental dissonance. And it was a good idea on the part of Baudelaire's friend H. Babou to employ an oxymoron in the title *Les Fleurs du mal.*"

49. See Victor Erlich, *Russian Formalism* (The Hague: Mouton, 1969), p. 195. Terms related to oxymoron, such as enantiosis and enantiadromia, are very rarely used; but see R. P. Blackmur, *Form and Value in Modern Poetry* (Garden City: Anchor, 1957), p. 76.

50. Cf. also Alain of Lille's "God is an intelligent sphere, whose center is everywhere and whose circumference is nowhere" and its long history. See Ernst Robert Curtius, *European Literature and the Latin Middle Ages* (New York: Harper and Row, 1963), p. 353, and J. L. Borges' essay, "Pascal's Sphere," in *Other Inquisitions* (New York: Washington Square Press, 1966), p. 5 ff.

with what is known as apophatic or "negative" theology (as we find it, for example, in Plotinus) and baroque poetics; but the boldness of imagery in St. John of the Cross seems to have its antecedents in an Arabic—in this case, Sufi—tradition.[51] The older historians, too, sometimes felt that the oxymoron could well express the spirit of an age: thus Gibbon quotes Mamertinus on the luxury of imperial Rome, concisely expressed in *aestivae nives, hibernae rosae.*[52]

It need hardly be said that, from a rigorously logical point of view, these and other paradoxical juxtapositions are merely *contradictiones in adjecto.* But in literature—especially in poetry—such inconsistencies (and the renowned Richard Bentley "corrected" many such expressions in his notorious "emendations" to Milton[53]) are the very stuff of verbal artistry; and what Doctor Johnson said of man applies equally well to poetry: "Inconsistencies cannot both be true, but, imputed to man, they may both be true."

Quite close to the oxymoron in effect are the so-called *adynata* (*impossibilia*) or "stringing together of impossibilities." One well-known *adynaton* is the "world upside down" topos, familiar both in literature and in Breughel's painting known as "Dutch Proverbs." Here is an example from Virgil's Eighth Eclogue as translated by C. Day Lewis:

> All is awry now. The wolf may fly from
>   the lamb, and oak trees bear fruit of gold;
> Alders surprise us with sweet narcissus,
>   and tears of amber down a tamarisk roll.
> Let screech-owl's flyting be more delightful
>   than swan-song.[54]

There is a rather detailed account of these in Ernst Robert Curtius' *European Literature and the Latin Middle Ages,* including some

---

51. See the note in Gerald Brenan, *The Literature of the Spanish People* (New York: Meridian Books, 1957), p. 107, referring to a recently discovered *diwan* of the Sufi poet Shushtari (d. 1269). Brenan remarks of Shushtari's poems, "Their boldness is remarkable, for in them the poet plays the passive role of the prostitute and God that of the lover, and no details of their intercourse are left out." See also Bernard Pick, *The Cabala,* pp. 34 and 67 on the *en soph* doctrine in the Kabbala.

52. *Decline and Fall,* II, xxii, note 56.

53. See A. E. Housman, *Selected Prose,* edited by John Carter (Cambridge: Cambridge University Press, 1961), p. 12 ff.

54. *The Eclogues and Georgics of Virgil* (Garden City: Anchor, 1964), pp. 59–61.

comments on Arnaut Daniel. In *Harvard Slavic Studies* 1 (1953), Chizhevsky also points out the "world upside down" topos in Comenius' *Labyrinth of the World* and cites some relevant literature.

Also closely related to the oxymoron is another kind of *callida junctura* (to use Horace's phrase) that is called synaesthesia. This term is used here not, of course, in the very broad sense of aesthetic theory which attempts to bring into play all areas of our sensorium (as in the case of Wagner and his notion of a *Gesamtkunstwerk* or Scriabine's musical fancies) but rather in the more limited sense of what the Greek rhetoricians called *aisthēsis ant'aisthēseōs* ("sensation in place of sensation"). The usual type again consists of adjective and noun, the noun relating to one sensation being modified by an adjective more properly relating to a different sensation ("loud color," "pink sound," "green taste"). Though employed most often in poetry, synaesthesia occurs also in highly mannered prose, such as that of Proust.[55] There is a beautiful example of synaesthesia in Quevedo:

> Vivo en conversación con los difuntos
> Y escucho con mis ojos a los muertos,

and Zamyatin, who uses a great deal of algebraic and geometrical imagery in his novel *We,* has: "I saw the resonant curve of this laughter" (*zvonkuju krivuju ètogo smekha*).[56] Synaesthesia occurs in the Old Testament, e.g., Exodus 20:18 where "the people saw the voices" (*ro'ïm eth-haqqōloth*, Latin: *populus videbat voces*), and this passage is cited in a humorous context in Rabelais dealing with the "seeing of sounds."[57]

Still another very effective type of juxtaposition is the combination of abstract and concrete—e.g., Wallace Stevens' "complacencies of the peignoirs," the many examples in Laforgue (*traintrain pavoisé d'estime et de chiffons*) and the other French Symbolists, and—perhaps most familiar of all—the instances in Eliot.[58]

55. See David Grossvogel, *Limits of the Novel* (Ithaca: Cornell University Press, 1971), p. 192 ff.

56. Cf. also *audition colorée.* In an interview in *The Listener,* November 22, 1962, Nabokov claims that he has the gift of *audition colorée,* granted, he tells us, to one in a thousand.

57. "Comment, en haute mer, Pantagruel ouit diverses paroles degelées." On this passage in Rabelais, see below, Chapter IV, p. 121.

58. On the mingling of the concrete and the abstract, see Anna Balakian, *The Literary Origins of Surrealism* (New York: New York University Press, 1947), p. 110 ff.

It is obviously possible to juxtapose—and thus suggest a connection between—almost any two words or phrases, whether this connection be based on real or apparent etymological relationships, contrarieties, correspondences, the "doctrine of signatures," or any other esoteric system, since there is, in fact, an entire symbolism of juxtaposition. But the collocation of words may also be used punningly: thus Nabokov in *Ada* inserts parenthetically after the words "whatever he be" the Russian words *"tvoyu mat'"* and thereby signifies quite clearly the *matershchina* or "mother oath."[59] In Heimito von Doderer's novel *Die Dämonen* the names of two women, Fella and Trix, which sound so cute and innocent separately, are obscene in juxtaposition.

Hypallage or transferred epithet, sometimes considered a type of catachresis, is a not uncommon feature in poetry. Although it is a metaphor (in the literal meaning of the Greek word) and a defamiliarizing device, it is usually hardly noticeable as such. Thus Lermontov speaks of air imbued *dykhan'em chistym aromata,* "with the pure breath of fragrance" (= with the breath of pure fragrance), while Annensky mentions *solntsa pozdnij pyl,* "the Sun's tardy heat" (= the heat of the tardy Sun). But to "correct" the concord is obviously to eliminate much of the poetry there is in such phrases. The transferred epithet comes easily in certain languages (even, as we see above, in some highly inflected languages) and it occurs frequently in English, even in colloquial speech where it is a kind of prolepsis: "a quick desire for victory," "the royal seat of power." Such a verbal trajection is roughly comparable to an "inverted" temporal clause ("A week went by, when he came again") in much the same way a syncopated word is comparable to an elliptical sentence or brachylogy—"He acts as (he would act) if he were drunk."

What might ordinarily in prose be a phrase consisting, usually, of adjective and noun is sometimes analyzed in poetry into two nouns: this is called hendiadys ("one through two"). Virgil (*Georgics,* 2.192) provides a classical example: *pateris libamus et auro,* "we pour from cups and gold" (= we pour from golden cups). But a more mundane example would be such a phrase as "bread and butter" (= buttered bread); and "buttered bread" is to "bread and butter" as

---

59. Elsewhere in *Ada* the author calls this the "Oedipean oath." One of the best puns in *Ada* occurs in Part Two, Chapter 5: "The night was oven-hot and we were stark naked . . . and she was a dream of white and black beauty, *pour cogner une fraise,* touched with fraise in four places, a symmetrical queen of hearts."

hypotaxis is to parataxis. Somewhat close to hendiadys is merism, i.e., indicating the whole by reference to two extremes within the whole (e.g., "rich and poor," "young and old," "thick and thin"). I have elsewhere used the term hendiadys to refer to a particular phenomenon in Russian, especially technical Russian, where one often encounters synonymous doublets, one word being of Slavic origin, the other a non-Slavic "gloss": e.g., *rezervy i zapasy, vidy i formy, ljufty i zazory*, and even such things as *dvukhmotornyj samolet s dvumja dvigateljami* ("a twin-engine aircraft with two motors").[60]

Some interesting effects are possible in inflected languages by exploiting the resources of case endings—by, for instance, repeating the same word several times but in different cases, e.g., *homo homini hominem*. This is known as polyptoton and there are examples in ancient literature where the device is used for various purposes such as emphasis or irony. Longinus uses the term rather loosely in *On the Sublime* to cover variations in number, person, tense, and gender. The Byzantine rhetoricians knew the term, and the practice occurs in early Russian literature.[61] Roman Jakobson also uses the term in some brief structural comments on Shakespeare.[62] But if, like Longinus, we include here other variations—for example, if we exploit fully all the syntactical possibilities of the word "that" in English, we come up with something that sounds like verbigeration but which does make sense: "It is true for all that, that that 'that' that that 'that' signifies is not the one to which I refer." Góngora's use of the so-called Greek (or synecdochical) accusative (. . . *la primavera/ Calçada Abriles y vestida Mayos* or *Desnuda el pecho anda ella*[63]) or other unusual grammatical and syntactical usages (such as the various schemata in ancient Greek[64]) are all, to a certain extent, defamiliarizing with respect to the traditional language of prose or poetry.

60. "A Note on a Type of Hendiadys in Technical Russian," *Slavic and East European Journal* (Winter 1960): 345–46.

61. See D. Chizhevsky, *History of Russian Literature from the Eleventh Century to the End of the Baroque* (The Hague: Mouton, 1960), p. 253.

62. "Closing Statement: Linguistics and Poetics" in *Style in Language*, edited by Thomas Sebeok (Cambridge: MIT Press, 1968), p. 375. See the extravagant examples from Quirinus Kuhlmann quoted by Robert Browning, *German Baroque Poetry* (University Park: Pennsylvania State University Press, 1971), p. 86.

63. Not much different from our English adverbial accusative ("conscience stricken"). See R. Lathuillère, *La Préciosité* (Geneva, 1966), p. 307.

64. E.g., the Theban or Pindaric (singular verb with plural subject), the Rhodian (*Kaleson tou anthrōpou* for K. *ton anthrōpon*), etc. There are eleven others mentioned in Lesbonax, *Peri skhematōn.*

There is a vast range of possibilities in various types of word coinages, word play, and *Worthäufung*, often asyndetic, such as the many examples in medieval literature (including *versus rapportati*), the numerous instances in Rabelais, e.g., his play on terms for his reactionary enemies at the Sorbonne (*sorbillans, sorbonages, sorboni-gènes, sobornicoles, sorboniformes*, etc.), the even more bewildering passages in Fischart, Pulci's variations on *crai* (*poscrai, poscrilla, posquacchera*), as well as more modern examples—Khlebnikov's variations on *smekh* or Goytisolo's on *coño* (both noted earlier). Raymond Roussel's *métagrammes* should also be mentioned and other forms of experimentation by the French Surrealists are also significant in this connection, e.g., Jean Arp:

> le papillon empaillé
> devient un papapillon empapaillé
> le papapillon empapaillé
> devient un grandpapapillon grandempapaillé.[65]

Zeugma ("yoking") is another grammatical figure of ancient lineage; an example occurs in a *paraklausithyron* by Horace (Odes 3.10):

> audis quo strepitu ianua, quo nemus
> inter pulchra satum tecta remugiat
> ventis, et positas ut glaciet nives
> puro numine Iuppiter?

Here the word *audis* is appropriate with *quo strepitu ianua, quo nemus . . . remugiat,* but only by extension (or synesis) with the *ut*-clause. One need not, of course, believe that this particular usage occurred here because Horace, in his creative enthusiasm, lost sight of his construction; it is much more likely due to the fact that in the Asclepiadic strophe great concision is required and, by giving bold scope to the verb *audis*, Horace achieves both this concision and a synaesthetic effect. And Luther does something similar in his *Die Augen des Herrn sehen auf die Gerechten und seine Ohren auf ihr Schreien.*

65. Quoted in J. H. Matthews, *Surrealist Poetry in France* (Syracuse: Syracuse University Press, 1969), p. 97.

Similar to zeugma is syllepsis, except that here one word is linked correctly (i.e., without any extended meaning) but in different ways with two or more words. Tzvetan Todorov cites a passage from Racine: *"Je souffre . . . brûlé de plus de feux que je n'en allumai."* Here Todorov points out that the word *feux* is taken in two different ways: as both metaphorical burning and as a fire that is said actually to be kindled. Sylleptical puns are common: "Or stain her honor—or her new brocade" (Pope), "She washed the clothes with joy and with Joy," "We raised the money and our hopes," etc.[66]

The so-called *apo koinou* construction, less common in the Indo-European languages, is a syntactical aberration, and the term covers a variety of usages. It occurs, for example, in pithy apothegms and proverbs (e.g., Seneca the Philosopher's *ducunt volentem fata nolentem trahunt*), in MHG literature, and occasionally in modern writers (e.g., Enzensberger's *die Tücher knattern im heissen Wind treibst du*), and in expressions which reflect a colloquial synesis: *Dijo la verdad y que no iría* or *Il croit à son étoile et que tout lui réussira.*[67]

3

Although all the modes of verbal and phrasal modification so far mentioned in this chapter as devices of defamiliarization are tropes, metaphors, or figures in the very broadest sense of these words (*paene quidquid loquimur figura est*—Quintilian), the vast horizon of

66. Tzvetan Todorov, "Language and Literature," in *The Structuralist Controversy,* edited by Richard Macksey and Eugenio Donato (Baltimore: Johns Hopkins Press, 1972), pp. 128–29. Todorov finds a narrative structural parallel to syllepsis in Boccaccio: "We are told that a monk was visiting his mistress, the wife of a village bourgeois. Unexpectedly the husband returns home. What is the couple going to do? The monk and the woman, who are hidden in the baby's room, pretend they are caring for the baby who, they say, is sick. The husband is content and thanks them warmly. The movement of the *récit,* as we see, follows exactly the same form as syllepsis. A single incident, the monk and the woman in the bedroom, acquires one interpretation in the first part of the *récit* and another interpretation in the part which follows." Occasionally a syllepsis in one language may be translated easily into another. Thus Dickens' "She fell into a chair and a fainting fit simultaneously" (*Nicholas Nickleby*) goes perfectly into Russian: *Ona odnovremenno upala v kreslo i v obmorok.* See *Tetradi perevodchika,* edited by L. Barkhudarov (Moscow, 1964), p. 20.

67. What is *apo koinou* in the Indo-European languages may, of course, be quite normal syntax in other languages—cf., e.g., the Arabic asyndetic relative clause. Cf. also the so-called squinting construction in English ("those who lie often are found out"), as well as the "pivot words" (*kenyogen*) in Japanese *No* drama.

defamiliarization only really becomes apparent when we begin to consider metaphor itself in particular. For even within the limited meaning of the word "metaphor" (or its Latin calque, *translatio/ tralatio*, "tralation"), i.e., when we distinguish, say, between metaphor and metonymy, a wide variety of linguistic phenomena is involved. This is made clear through Aristotle's definition in *Poetics*, 1457b: "Metaphor is the application [*epiphora*] of an alien name by transference either from genus [*genos*] to species [*eidos*], or from species to genus, or from species to species, or by analogy." But before we consider metaphor proper, a few comments on simile are called for.

Though disparaged somewhat by Aristotle, simile (*eikōn*) or explicit comparison has very often been—and continues to be—used with great effectiveness by good writers. Many striking examples (some of them quite familiar) might be cited from the various literatures, beginning with Homer's likening of the voluble Odysseus' words to "snowflakes in winter" (*Iliad*, III, 222) or the Old Testament's "Thy two breasts are like two fawns" (*Canticles* 4:5) and including Pushkin's lines from "The Bronze Horseman":

> I pered mladsheju stolitsej
> Pomerkla staraja Moskva,
> Kak pered novoju tsaritsej
> Porfironosnaja vdova,

("And old Moscow has paled before the younger capital, like a dowager clad in purple before a new empress") or Robert Frost's "And dead wings carried like a paper kite" ("Design").

But there is, of course, a range of "pedestrian" simile, from merely convenient and prosaic denotative prepositional phrases ("He looks like me" or "Her dark hair, like the hair of a Japanese") to those that have become clichés (*"plus léger qu'un bouchon"*).[68] The great mass of world literature is replete with this inferior range of similes (which can hardly be said to defamiliarize), beginning with Greek literature ("For quickly, like a thought, bright youth passes"—Theognis); even the works of the better writers contain a surprising amount of very commonplace similes (e.g., E. M. Forster: "New ideas had burst upon her like a thunder clap"). This is not so disturbing in prose, but when it occurs in poetry, unless compensated for by the musicality of the

---

68. Even a cliché may be used ironically and have, in certain contexts, a defamiliarizing effect. And many an item from Eric Partridge's *Dictionary of Clichés* (London: Routledge & Kegan Paul, 1950), such as the antonomasia "The Wizard of the North," would be quite unfamiliar to a wide circle of readers.

verse, it is quite debilitating. Thus Allen Ginsberg (of one flower) writes: "It had a/ brittle black stem and/ corolla of yellowish dirty/ spikes like Jesus' inchlong/ crown"; and, of another flower, a "corolla of bleary spikes pushed down and broken like a battered/ crown."[69]

There is a further range of simile that includes comparisons which, while not particularly striking, show at least a more perceptive imagination at work—e.g., "His face was profoundly wrinkled and black, like a mask of obsidian" (Aldous Huxley) or *"un bateau frêle comme un papillon de mai"* (Rimbaud). And now the similes seem to move in two directions. While both directions are towards "submerged simile," metaphor, and imagery ever more complex in form, one is the way of affectation and *conceptismo*, the other the way of apt connotative significance and control. All the similes in both areas are interesting, however; indeed, from the point of view of defamiliarization the gongoristic and the most esoteric are of special interest. As examples of the former direction we might cite, in prose, something like W. Somerset Maugham's "She was like a silvery flower of the night that only gave its perfume to the moonbeams" or, in poetry, Neruda's "y los roncos gatos que cruzan mi jardín en tinieblas/ como un collar de palpitantes ostras sexuales" ("Caballero Solo"; the *roncos gatos* are young men). Examples of the latter direction would be Melville's "The original iron entered nigh the tail, and, like a restless needle sojourning in the body of a man, travelled full forty feet, and at last was found embedded in the hump" or Rilke's "Frühling ist wiedergekommen. Die Erde/ ist wie ein Kind, das Gedichte weiss" ("Sonette an Orpheus," 21). The similes in Melville, by the way, are by no means limited to marine and cetological imagery; one, for example, from Chapter 119 of *Moby Dick*, is particularly remarkable: frightened by the appearance of a corposant (St. Elmo's fire), the seamen stood "In various enchanted attitudes, like the standing, or stepping, or running skeletons in Herculaneum."

A particular type of the simile is the "epic" simile or the *comparaison à longue queue* ("long-tailed simile"), so called because of its frequency in Homer. But Tolstoy (whose other "epic" features are often pointed out) also uses it, e.g., "Just as the foreman of a spinning mill, once he has set the hands to work, walks through the factory and when he notices any stoppage, any unaccustomed creak or rattle of a spindle, quickly checks its action or sets it going, so Anna Pavlovna

69. These specimens are from *Howl and Other Poems* (San Francisco: City Lights, 1959), pp. 28 and 44.

moved about her drawing room."[70] Gogol employs this "long-tailed simile" but carries it to comically absurd lengths in Chapter I of *Dead Souls*:

> Everything was flooded with light, and black frockcoats kept flashing by, singly and in clusters, like flies on a gleaming white sugar loaf on a sultry July day as an elderly housekeeper breaks it into shimmering splinters in front of an open window: the curious children gather to watch the movements of her roughened hands as they lift the mallet while the soaring squadrons of flies, riding in on the light air, land boldly as if they owned the place, and taking advantage of the old woman's poor sight and her being blinded still further by the sun, scatter over the tasty pieces, here singly, there in heaps. Sated during the opulent summer, which anyway offers them morsels at every turn, they come flying, not to eat really, but to show themselves, to swagger up and down over the sugary heap, to rub their front and back legs together or to scratch themselves under their wings, to stretch out their front legs and rub the tops of their heads with them— then they turn and take off, only to return again in new harassing squadrons.

Dante also uses the extended simile:

> E gia venia su per le torpid'onde
>   un fracasso d'un suon, pien di spavento,
>   per che tremavano amendue le sponde,
> non altrimenti fatto che d'un vento
>   impetuoso per li avversi ardori,
>   che fier la selva e sanz'alcun rattento
> li rami schianta, abbatte e porta fori;
>   dinanzi polveroso va superbo,
>   e fa fuggir le fiere e li pastori.
>   (*Inferno* IX, 64–72)

as does Milton:

> As when a Vultur on Imaus bred,
> Whose snowie ridge the roving Tartar bounds,
> Dislodging from a Region scarce of prey
> To gorge the flesh of Lambs or yeanling Kids

70. *War and Peace*, Book I, Chapter 2 (Ann Dunnigan's translation). Hugo von Hofmannsthal once remarked that he could not read Tolstoy's *The Cossacks* without thinking of Homer.

On Hills where Flocks are fed, flies towards the Springs
Of Ganges or Hydaspes, Indian streams;
But in his way lights on the barren plaines
Of Sericana, where Chineses drive
With Sails and Wind their canie Waggons light:
So on this windie Sea of Land, the Fiend. . . .
(Paradise Lost, III, 431–41)

and Spenser:

Like as a ship, that through the Ocean wyde
Directs her course unto one certaine cost,
Is met of many a counter winde and tyde,
With which her winged speed is let and crost,
And she herselfe in stormie surges tost;
Yet making many a borde, and many a bay,
Still winneth way, ne hath her compasse lost;
Right so it fares with me in this long way,
Whose course is often stayd, yet never is astray.
(Faerie Queene VI, 12, 1)

And Melville has "As in the hurricane that sweeps the plain, men fly the neighborhood of some lone, gigantic elm, whose very height and strength but render it so much the more unsafe, because so much the more a mark for thunderbolts; so at those last words of Ahab's many of the mariners did run from him in a terror of dismay" (*Moby Dick*, Chapter 119).

In the twelfth-century Russian epic, *The Lay of Igor's Campaign*, a kind of multiple, reinforced simile is used (Nabokov's translation):

For he, vatic Boyan,
if he wished to make a laud for one,
ranged in thought
[like the nightingale] over the tree;
like the gray wolf
across the land;
like the smoky eagle
up to the clouds.

It is interesting that Quintilian (*Institutio Oratoria*, 8.3.74), commenting on simile, anticipates both Marino ("To evoke astonishment is the task of the poet . . . he who cannot startle would do better to become a stable-boy") and Shklovsky when he writes: "The more remote the simile from the subject to which it is applied, the greater will be the impression of novelty and the unexpected that it produces." And Doctor Johnson states: "A simile may be compared to lines converging at a point, and is more excellent as the lines approach from a greater distance." Such remarks are more baroque than classical in their implications and are similar to numerous observations made by writers and critics of the eighteenth century; thus Mikhail Lomonosov advocates many baroque devices in his *Rhetoric* (1748), including "involved turns of phrase" (*vitievatye rechi*). Certainly Kierkegaard for example, uses a type of simile that illustrates Johnson's and Shklovsky's observations—e.g., "silent as a dagesh," "shrunken as a *shva*," "I feel like a letter printed backward in the line and as introverted as a *pronomen reflexivum*."[71]

Tolstoy's shorter similes are overwhelmingly (and surprisingly) faunal and "skeuomorphic," e.g., "On Vronsky's face . . . she saw that expression of submission and bewilderment . . . an expression like that of an intelligent dog when it feels guilty" and "their minds are like a driving wheel without a load." One might think that this type of simile, so earthy, so proletarian and technical, would characterize Soviet Russian usage, and, in fact, it is quite common (especially in something like Gorky's *The Mother*); but even more frequent are similes that are either naively incongruous, lending themselves readily to parody, or simply ridiculous such as the absurd assortment in the early version of Gladkov's "novel," *Cement*.[72] The similes in Dostoevsky are quite unlike those in Tolstoy and, as one might expect (*ex ungue leonem*), they very often involve pain, anguish, revulsion, or humiliation: "Stavrogin was like a man forcing himself to hold a red-hot iron bar" or "her face continued to twitch spasmodically as though she had touched some slimy creature" or "as revolting as a spider."

Similes may defamiliarize in two principal ways: they may either involve a comparison between two things seldom, if ever, thought of as being comparable; or the comparison may be recondite, cryptic, or occult. Thus Bely in his novel *St. Petersburg* says of a flight of stairs

71. Quoted in N. J. Jacobs, *Naming-Day in Eden* (New York: Macmillan, 1969), p. 76.

72. This may be read in an English translation of the 1925 edition (New York: Frederick Ungar Atlantic Books, n.d.). The 1950 version is considerably improved (if this is possible); but "Gladkov's fundamental indifference to his novel as a literary product is shown by the ease with which he altered both content and style as times and fashions changed" (Edward J. Brown).

that "its steps were soft, like the convolutions of the brain" (*kak mozgovye izviliny*) and Hart Crane has

> Forgetfulness is like a bird whose wings are reconciled,
> Outspread and motionless—
> A bird that coasts the wind unwearyingly,

and in a hunting-poem by Ibn al-Mu'tazz an alert bitch is said to be "like a pen's black *madda*" (*kamadda min kalam saudā*, the *madda* being a tilde-shaped diacritical sign used in Arabic). Such similes, for an instant at least, make the familiar (stairway steps, forgetfulness, a hunting dog) "unfamiliar" and thus bring the image into sharper focus: the dog is first a dog, then something else, then a dog again (in terms of the Zen paradox mentioned in the preceding chapter). But these similes do not require either explanatory notes or special knowledge as the following examples do. In one of his "Sonnets to Orpheus" Rilke refers to children who, "*wie das Lamm mit dem redenden Blatt,/ sprachen als schweigende*"; or Gumilev's "Ja proigral tebja kak Damajanti/ Kogda-to proigral bezumnyj Nal'" ("I have lost thee as once the senseless Nala lost Damayanti"), or in Carlyle's *Sartor Resartus:* "through the Clothes-screen, as through the magical *Pierre-Pertuis,* thou lookest." It is quite obvious that there is really no limit to the extent to which even simile may be carried in either of these directions. An essential difference, however, is that the former type requires primarily imagination and poetic vision, the latter primarily esoteric or at least uncommon learning. The former type is the forerunner of pure metaphor and imagery of the best kind, the latter is the model of what might often be called *Professorenpoesie.*

But absurd or grotesque similes (or sorites of these) may also, as the extended simile from Gogol quoted above shows, result in defamiliarization through a kind of "multifaceting." For example, in Thomas Nashe's picaresque *The Unfortunate Traveler* (1594) there are numerous passages such as this:

> I had my feather in my cap as big as a flag in the foretop; my French doublet gelt in the belly as though (like a pig ready to be spitted) all my guts had been plucked out; a pair of sidepaned hose that hung down like two scales filled with Holland cheeses; my long stock that sat close to my dock, and smothered not a scab or a leacherous hairy sinew on the calf of the leg; my rapier pendant like a round stick fastened in the tacklings for skippers the better to climb

by; my cape cloak of black cloth, overspreading my back like a thornback, or an elephant's ear, that hangs on his shoulders like a country housewife's banskin.

And one can find many similar passages in the other literatures; here is one from Vasily Maykov's mock epic, *Elisey or Bacchus Enraged* (1771):

Then every ray of hope for Bacchus was extinguished
And in despair, as in a sea, he wallowed;
He leaves the drinking establishment
Just like a beast flushed from its lair.
And no more there delaying than an hour,
He went with his uncle to the heavens;
He flies more swiftly than the Amazon empress
And surpassed the whirlwinds with the speed of a horse;
He flies on winged tigers, like the wind. (Canto I, 231–39)

and another from Gottfried Keller's *A Village Romeo and Juliet* (*Romeo und Juliet auf dem Dorfe*): "Actually he possessed a disproportionately large nose, which protruded from his lean, black face like a carpenter's square and which even more closely resembled a sizeable club or stick stuck onto his face. . . . All that could be seen of the fellow's eyes were their whites, since the pupils moved continuously and rapidly like two rabbits running along a zigzag course."[73] There is a certain element of *fatrasie* and a bambocciade effect in such passages, and it is interesting that C. S. Lewis, for example, has noted a similarity between Nashe and Bosch.[74]

So far as intentionally grotesque and bizarre (rather than simply humorous) similes are concerned, *Revelation* (9:7–9, Revised Standard Version) provides a good example:

In appearance the locusts were like horses arrayed for battle; on their heads were what looked like crowns of gold; their faces were like human faces; their hair like women's hair, and their teeth like lions' teeth; they had scales like iron breastplates, and the noise of

73. Quoted in Wolfgang Kayser, *The Grotesque in Art and Literature* (New York: McGraw-Hill, 1966), p. 107.

74. Quoted in John Berryman's Introduction to Nashe's *The Unfortunate Traveler* (New York: Putnam, 1960), p. 16. Kayser also uses the terms "Boschian" and "Breughelian" of the works of Keller and others.

their wings was like the noise of many chariots with horses rushing into battle.

Kayser also quotes Hans Arp:

> The tables are as soft as freshly baked bread
> And the loaves of bread on the table as hard as wood.
> This explains the large number of broken teeth
> That have been spat out and lie around the tables. (p. 165)

And here is Guillaume Apollinaire:

> *Du dicke Du* L'amour revient en boumerang
> L'amour revient à en vomir le revenant
> Ils ont demandé tant de ces bouteilles longues
> Comme les longs cyprès d'un grand jardin rhénan.

Even more extreme specimens may be found in the works of the Futurists and the Surrealists as well as amongst the strange experiments of writers in less familiar movements.

Similes are very frequently found in proverbs and apothegms (and some of the earliest of these are Sumerian[75]). Although proverbs generally reflect a markedly realistic view of the world and, in exemplifying some pithy truth, they do not defamiliarize, there are some proverbs (not necessarily containing similes) which are unusual—at times even cryptic—and which do defamiliarize. There is a Russian proverb, *Kuritsa ne ptitsa a baba ne chelovek* ("A chicken is not a bird and a woman is not a person"), which makes a malicious but perspicacious comparison, while the Hungarian proverb, *Az istenek halnak, az ember él* ("The gods die but man lives on"—also the title of a volume of poetry by Mihaly Babits), says something that many of us might think but seldom say aloud. The Arabic (Moroccan) proverb, "The lips are like sugar and the cheeks like ochre," is used of a person who speaks well and whose writing is as beautiful as the cheeks of a woman painted with ochre.[76] D. J. Enright, in *Encounter*, Novem-

75. See Edmund Gordon, *Sumerian Proverbs: Glimpses of Everyday Life in Ancient Mesopotamia* (New York: Greenwood Press, 1968); the proverbs are given in Sumerian and English.

76. See Edward Westermarck, *Wit and Wisdom in Morocco* (New York: Liveright, 1931), p. 291 (#1758).

ber 1975, calls our attention to two particularly enigmatic English proverbs: "An egg will be in three bellies in twenty-four hours" and "Everything hath an end, and a pudding hath two."

Much like the paroemiac simile is the type found in such "gustatory-literary" comparisons as Macaulay's "To read Seneca through is like dining exclusively on anchovy-sauce and *pâté de foie gras*" or Doctor Johnson's remark that Greek is like fine old lace and one should get as much of it as one can. Then there are the implied comparisons which point up literary qualities and evaluate writers, such as George Moore's disparaging comment on Dostoevsky (that he is "Gaboriau with psychological sauce"), Swift's well-known comparison between the classical writer and the bee, the romantic writer and the spider, and the frequent contrasts noted between Tolstoy, resembling the *plein-airistes*, and Dostoevsky with his Rembrandt-like *chiaroscuro*. Perhaps the most familiar (due to Lessing's *Laokoön*) simile in this area is the one usually quoted in Latin from Horace's *Ars Poetica* (but the idea of which goes back to Simonides of Ceos)—*Ut pictura, poesis*. But similar comparisons are encountered in all areas of thought and not solely in connection with literature and the arts. Thus Emerson writes, as I recall, "Money, which represents the prose of life, and which is hardly spoken of in parlors without an apology, is, in its effects and laws, as beautiful as roses"; and C. Northcote Parkinson likens *Das Kapital* to the Bible, the Koran, or the Analects ("it is only religious texts that never go out of date"). There may not be much "strangifying" in many such comparisons, but they are often provocative and help us to see various relationships with a fresh vision.

Finally, there is an especially learned type of simile in which the author (if he is writing in English or another Indo-European language) uses similative adjectives in -oid, -iform, -ine, and -eous, etc., which are ordinarily limited to technical usage. Thus Nabokov in the English version of *Dar* (*The Gift*) refers to a minor writer as one who "has left a scolopendrine trace in literature." In like manner such adjectives as "botryoid," "scobioform," and "psittaceous" may be used in this way.

4

With regard to metaphor or implied comparison, much has been written and much continues to be written on the subject.[77] One of the

77. A standard work in this area is Christine Brooke-Rose, *A Grammar of Metaphor* (London: Secker & Warburg, 1958).

more recent comments of note in this domain (aside from I. A. Richards' distinction between "tenor" and "vehicle"—see below) is Roman Jakobson's "binary" concept of the metaphoric and metonymic poles as an analytic and classificatory tool.[78] In this section I shall consider metaphorical language (excluding simile) in a broad sense and shall point out and illustrate different varieties.

I shall use Richards' "tenor" and "vehicle" terminology, the tenor being the subject of the comparison, the vehicle the word or phrase "transferred."[79] That is, in the metaphor "hoary old age," "old age" is the tenor, "hoary" the vehicle. It is quite obvious that in some cases the vehicle may be very complex and merely a means for elaborating on— or defamiliarizing—the image suggested by the tenor; in other cases, the tenor itself may be simply a *cheville* or expletive. In the simplest metaphors there is a rather apparent connection between the tenor and the vehicle (e.g., "whiteness" in the example above); but in more complex metaphor this relationship becomes tenuous and there may, in fact, be one or more intermediate steps between the tenor and vehicle. What was said, then, in the preceding section about simile (i.e., the development in the direction either of relevant significance or of mere conceit) holds true *a fortiori* for metaphor as well.[80] We can, for our present purposes, overlook here the simpler types (such as "caprice of the coppice" or "wisdom of time"), even though some of these may be extremely effective and evocative, and refer immediately to some of the more unusual varieties. A single metaphor may of course be polysemous—this goes without saying—but it may also "be" different things at the same time and function on several levels: phonetic, grammatical, syntactical, rhetorical, positional, etc. For example, "the deliquescent ductus of his hand heraldic" is a complex of metaphor, metonymy, synecdoche, alliteration, chiasmus, and anastrophe; and we might well find or imagine even more multifaceted examples.

If we replace the tenor of a metaphor with something other than a mere synonym—with a metonym, for example—we have more specifically a periphrasis which is a particular type of metaphor. For ex-

---

78. "The Metaphoric and Metonymic Poles" in *Fundamentals of Language* (The Hague: Mouton, 1956). See also James Boon, *From Symbolism to Structuralism* (New York: Harper, 1973), pp. 72 ff.

79. For a fuller explanation, see W. F. Thrall *et al.*, *A Handbook to Literature* (New York: Odyssey Press, 1960), s.v. "metaphor."

80. See the article, "Bluspels and Flalansferes: A Semantic Nightmare," by C. S. Lewis in *Science and Literature* (Garden City: Anchor Books, 1970), pp. 53–70. In his Introduction, the editor writes: "Lewis distinguishes inspired metaphors from pedestrian analogies; the former group trigger jolting insights while the latter are pedagogical devices."

ample, "winged ship" is a metaphor; but if we replace "ship" with the metonym "oak," we have Góngora's *alado roble*, "winged oak," and we are expressing ourselves periphrastically or, as the Latin expression has it, *per ambitum verborum*. Or take a metaphor such as "musical bird," i.e., "something musical that flies"; if we replace the tenor ("something musical") with "a violin," we get "a violin that flies"—Góngora's *aquel violín que vuela*. Whereas Isidore Ducasse ("Comte de Lautréamont") has metaphor when he writes *ton ventre de mercure contre ma poitrine d'aluminium*, Aeschylus is using a periphrasis when he refers to a rocky, dangerous coast as a "stepmother of ships" (*mētruia neōn*). We might assume—*did* we know that, out of context, the phrase refers to a coast—that this periphrasis resulted from an (hypothetically) original metaphor such as "cruel (sc. to ships) coast" in which the tenor is omitted. But the fact is that in this case (*Prometheus Bound, 727*) the periphrasis is simply epexegetic, i.e., it is essentially an explanatory, decorative epithet, used in much the same way as Garcia Lorca's gloss on *ranas* as "muezzins of the shadow" (*muecines de la sombra*) in the poem "El Concierto Interrumpido." When, however, the word to which the periphrasis stands in apposition is omitted; when, that is, the reader must guess the meaning of the circumlocution, difficulties arise. This is especially true of certain very "obscure" poets. Persius (whom Doctor Johnson referred to as that "crabbed coxcomb" has, for example, the lines "et tibi quae Samos diduxit littera ramos/ surgentem dextro monstravit limite callem" (Satire III, 56–57), which mean "and the letter that spread out into the Samian branches has shown you the path rising steeply on the right." But "the letter that spread out into the Samian branches" stands for the "Pythagorean letter" (Pythagoras was from Samos), viz., *ypsilon* which, as originally written with a straight stem and a curving cusp on the left, represented the steep path of virtue and the easy path of vice.[81]

We have something similar in what Marouzeau has called "*décalage d'expression*" (see note 55, Chapter I) and what is more generally called metalepsis,[82] or replacing one metaphor with another, e.g., "The Phrygians were being besieged by the tenth harvest" (Petronius) = "The Trojans were being besieged by the tenth year" =

81. It is remarkable that John Harington refers to the Pythagorean letter in a pun on "a shooting place written with the Pythagorean letter." See *The Metamorphosis of Ajax*, edited by Elizabeth Donno (New York: Columbia University Press, 1962), p. 56.

82. Rightly called "the far-fetched" in Shipley's *Dictionary of World Literature*. There are many examples of metalepsis in Lycophron's *Alexandra*.

"Troy was being besieged for the tenth year." In Chinese poetry, although metaphor in our sense may not be involved, a similar series of associations are often required. Thus the two-character phrase *chih hsüeh* means literally "wish (to) study"; but for the learned reader of Chinese poetry it suggests Kung Fu-tse's remark, "At fifteen I set my mind on studying," and may thus simply be used to mean "fifteen years of age." Though things like this make for many difficulties in fully understanding some of the more recondite Chinese poems and, as Professor James Liu says, they "set a constant trap for the unwary,"[83] we can find many similar usages in other literatures.

Just as there are poems about poems and poems which use the technical terms of prosody in their structure,[84] chapters about chapters, novels about novels or novels containing novels, and plays about plays, etc., so metaphorical terms themselves have at times been used as metaphor, both in the West and in the East. A number of interesting examples are given in Excursus III of Curtius' *European Literature and the Latin Middle Ages*. In Arabic poetry, too, grammatical features are used as metaphor; thus one of the greatest poets, al-Mutanabbi, has a line in an ode dedicated to Saif al-Dawla which reads in English: "When what you intend to be a future act/verb, it becomes perfective before any conditional particles can be attached to it."[85]

There are a number of ways to classify metaphor (aside, that is, from merely listing the technical names for the different tropes), one of the most common being classification according to the general or particular area of reality or knowledge which a writer draws upon for his imagery.[86] This is the method used in a multitude of studies of the imagery in various authors and it is also the method employed by Caroline Spurgeon in her well-known and revealing study of Shakespeare's imagery. It is quite possible to classify exhaustively the metaphor in a single author and it might be possible to classify, at least in general terms, the different domains which have been used as sources

83. *The Art of Chinese Poetry* (Chicago: University of Chicago Press, 1966), p. 7.

84. The Russian poet Mandelshtam, for instance, has a line "Kak by tsezuroju zijaet etot den' " ("This day yawns like a caesura"), and Pushkin has a sonnet on the history of the sonnet.

85. The word *fi'l* in Arabic means both "act" and "verb."

86. The very concept of classification may be defamiliarized. Borges mentions (citing Franz Kuhn) a division of animals in a Chinese "Celestial Emporium of Benevolent Knowledge" which begins: "a) those that belong to the Emperor, b) embalmed ones, c) those that are trained, d) suckling pigs, e) mermaids," etc. *Other Inquisitions*, p. 108.

of metaphor in literature; but it would be impossible to do so here. Therefore I shall mention a number of specimens drawn from several literatures, including some examples that are, more clearly than others, cases of defamiliarization.

Metaphor involving the sea and ships, for instance, is very old, and we find some of the first examples in Egyptian literature (where the sea is "w3d wr," the "Great Green") and in the literatures of the Semitic peoples of the eastern Mediterranean, including the Hebrews.[87] Such metaphor is especially frequent in Greek literature from the earliest period (Alcaeus appears to have been the first to use the "ship of state" metaphor and Pindar introduced the word "anchor"— *agkyra*—into literature[88]) to George Seferis in the twentieth century:

> Their souls became one with the oars and the rowlocks,
> With the grave figurehead at the prow,
> With the wake of the rudder,
> With the water that broke their images.[89]

Homer's "watery ways" (*hygra keleutha*) is the same metaphor we find in Psalms 8:9 (*ārhōth yammīm*, "sea paths"), a figure strikingly defamiliarized in the skaldic and Old Germanic *kenningar* and in Beowulf's *hronrád* ("riding place of the whale").[90] Marine and naval metaphors are employed in Greek tragedy, and even Aristophanes, in the *Thesmophoriazusae*, describes Agathon's poetry in terms of shipbuilding. According to Plutarch, Theseus' ship, which was preserved at Athens down to the time of Demetrius of Phalerum and which had been repeatedly repaired, was used by the philosophers as a stock instance in discussing the problem of continuous identity.

Many other examples of sea and ship metaphor might be cited

87. See Cyrus Gordon's attempts to find a common background to the Greek and Hebrew cultures (usually opposed, as in Lev Shestov's *Athens and Jerusalem*) in *The Common Background of Greek and Hebrew Civilizations* (New York: Norton, 1965), reminiscent of Zachary Bogan's *Homerus Hebraizon* (1658) claiming Solomon as the author of the *Iliad* and the *Odyssey;* or G. Croesus' *Homeros Hebraios* (1704) which explains the *Iliad* as an account of the conquest of Canaan and the *Odyssey* as the story of the wanderings of the children of Israel.

88. In Homer only *eunai* or "mooring-stones" are mentioned.

89. Greek text in *The Penguin Book of Greek Verse*, edited by C. A. Trypanis (Harmondsworth: Penguin Books, 1971), p. 608.

90. See C. Brady, "The Synonyms for 'Sea' in *Beowulf*," in *Studies in Honor of Albert Morey Sturtevant* (Lawrence: University of Kansas Press, 1952).

from classical Greek literature, but it is not until the Hellenistic period
that we begin to encounter a really "baroque" type. For example,
Callimachus, in an epigram dedicated to Arsinoë II Philadelphus, has
the nautilus say:

> I the nautilus that did sail the sea if windy,
>   stretching my sail on my own forestays; or,
> if Calm, the bright deity, prevailed, I rowed
>   with my feet, my actions matching my name.

The *Alexandra* by Lycophron, already mentioned, is replete with such
metaphor, but complicated by metalepsis and periphrasis: "And the
centipede fair-faced stork-hued daughters of Phalacra smote maiden-
slaying Thetis with their blades, over Calydnae showing their white
wings."[91] And later we have such affectations as Musaeus' reference to
Leander, as he drowns, swallowing the "useless drink" (*poton
akhrēiston*) of the sea.

The Romans were not originally a sea-people and their early
naval defeats were largely the result of trying to employ ground tactics
at sea. The sea and travel by sea became commonplaces in Latin
poetry for sheer danger and the infatuated search for new ways to die.
How well men lived *Saturno rege*, exclaims Tibullus: "nondum
caeruleas pinus contempserat undas,/ effusum ventis praebueratque
sinum" (I, 3). But over the centuries, especially under the influence
of Greek literary usage, Latin writers produced a large body of metaphor, although the Roman imagination is often disparaged as compared with that of the Greeks.[92] It is interesting, by the way, that it is
from much of their figurative language—their marine and naval metaphor, for example—that English derives many terms: nave (*navis*,
"ship"); the carina of a flower, carinate birds, carinate geological
formations (*carina*, "keel"[93]); governor and gubernatorial (*gubernator*,
"helmsman," from the Greek) as well as the gubernaculum of the
foetus; the physician's undine and the unda maris in organ-building
(*unda*, "wave"); the remiges of birds (*remiges*, "oarsmen"), etc. Be-

91. A. W. Mair's translation in the *Loeb Classical Library* edition. The
"centipede fair-faced stork-hued daughters of Phalacra" = the ships of Paris
made from wood from Phalacra in the Troad.

92. Thus the great variety of Greek given names contrasts with the rather
limited Roman assortment; indeed, in large Roman families it was not long before
children were numbered—Quintus, Sextus, Septimus, Octavus, etc.

93. Cf. also the *carina vaginae* as well as the British popular term for the
clitoris, "the little man in the boat."

sides numerous ship metaphors in the Latin language (*remis velisque, dare vela indignationi*, etc.), the literature contains some fine examples (without here including Virgil[94]), e.g., Propertius' "una ratis fati nostros portabit amores/ caerula ad infernos velificata lacus" (II, 28) (J. Wight Duff's translation is "Our loves must fare in Doom's one caravel,/ Dark blue, with sails set for the meres of hell"), or Cicero's "*quaerebam . . . utrum panderem vela orationis statim, an eam ante paululum dialecticorum remis propellerem*" (Tusc., 4.5.9). The tyro poet is a "*rudis nauta*," and poets must negociate dangerous waters. Quintilian (*prooemium* to Book XII) sees himself as a lone sailor on the high seas. Ausonius of Burdigala refers to the "oar-footed ducks" (*anates remipedes*).

Nautical metaphor, as Curtius notes, was "extraordinarily widespread throughout the Middle Ages," and Helen Waddell, quoting Aldhelm's *Per pelagi itinera/ Salsa spumabant aequora*, writes: "for the first time, unless indeed the *Seafarer* be older, an English poet has entered on his kingdom of the sea."[95] Dante begins the second book of the *Convivio* with nautical metaphor and speaks of the *artimone de la ragione* (where *artimone* is the "mizzensail," from the Greek *artemōn*). The *Purgatorio* begins "Per correr migliori acque alza le vele/ omai la navicella del mio ingegno," and Canto II of the Paradiso

> O voi che siete in picciolette barca,
> desiderosi d'ascoltar, seguiti
> dietro al mio legno che cantando varca,
> tornate a riveder li vostri liti:
> non vi mettete in pelago, chè, forse,
> perdendo me, rimarreste smarriti.

And at the end of the Middle Ages Denis the Carthusian remarked, after a busy life (he has left us forty-five quarto volumes): "*Ad securae taciturnitatis portum me transferre intendo.*"[96]

94. There is an interesting study by W. F. Jackson Knight, "Cumaean Gates," in *Virgil, Epic and Anthropology* (New York: Barnes & Noble, 1967) in which the author theorizes that the story of Palinurus in the *Aeneid*, who falls into the sea taking the rudder with him, is a Virgilian echo of a similar detail in the Babylonian Gilgamesh epic. Scott uses the Palinurus legend metaphorically as applied to Lord Nelson in *Patriotism*, Part 2. See also Cyril Connolly, *The Unquiet Grave* (New York: Viking, 1957), pp. 134 ff.

95. Helen Waddell, *The Wandering Scholars* (Garden City: Anchor Books, 1961), p. 41.

96. Quoted in J. Huizinga, *The Waning of the Middle Ages* (Garden City: Anchor Books, 1956), p. 189.

When we move on to the beginnings of the modern European literatures, we find not only a continuation but also a resurgence of such metaphor in connection with—and following—the great age of exploration. This period left its impress on the poetry of the sixteenth and seventeenth centuries, especially in Spain and more especially in the poetry of Góngora.[97] Góngora refers to the sea very often, and his metaphors in this domain—most often periphrases—are classics of *culteranismo:* e.g., *del norte amante dura* (the compass),[98] *nieto de la spuma* (Cupid), "Fábrica escrupulosa, y aunque incierta,/ siempre murada, pero siempre abierta" (i.e., a fishing net), etc. Góngora also applies sea metaphor to the countryside—e.g., *farol de una cabaña.* This gongoristic metaphor is echoed in Spanish America and in our own century in, for instance, the poetry of Neruda: a cat is a *conquistador sin patria,* a whale is *paz iracunda,* and a piano opens its *boca de ballena.*

Besides the many "buried" metaphors, nautical and other, in the English language (e.g., "to the bitter end"), English and American poetry down to the present offers many examples of metaphor drawn from the sea. Without including Shakespeare, who has many instances (they are especially effective in *Othello*[99]), we may note the following: Dryden's "Slack all thy sails, and fear to come,/ Alas, thou know'st not, thou art wreck'd at home!"; Thomas Love Peacock's "And our ballast is old wine/ And your ballast is old wine"; Matthew Arnold's

> Yes: in the sea of life enisled,
>> With echoing straits between us thrown.
> Dotting the shoreless watery wild,
>> We mortal millions live *alone;*

the imagery in Tennyson's *Crossing the Bar* ("I hope to see my Pilot face to face/ When I have crost the bar"); Dante Gabriel Rossetti's "And though thy soul sail leagues and leagues beyond,/ Still, leagues beyond those leagues, there is more sea"; or the imagery in Whitman's

97. See Eunice Joiner Gates, *The Metaphors of Luis de Góngora* (Philadelphia: University of Pennsylvania Press, 1933).

98. Cf. Kantemir's periphrastic reference to the compass needle in his Satire II; the passage is also quoted by Timofeev in *Ocherki . . . russkogo stikha,* p. 332.

99. One must take note, however, of the dilogies in Shakespeare—e.g., "to board a land carack" (*Othello* I.ii.51). See the further examples in connection with nautical metaphor in Eric Partridge, *Shakespeare's Bawdy* (New York: Dutton, 1960), p. 42.

O Captain! My Captain; Robinson Jeffers' "the tides are in our veins" and "A drop from the oceans: who would have dreamed this/ infinitely little too much?" Then, of course, there is the ridiculous: in Phineas Fletcher's *The Purple Island* (1633) there is a metaphorical tracking of food as it passes through the human body—e.g., we see

> . . . the victuals shipped at fittest tide:
> Which straight from thence with prosp'rous channel slide,
> And in Koilia's port with nimble oars glide.[100]

A great number of nautical metaphors might also be adduced from the prose literatures of Europe and the Orient. They may be found in ancient and medieval prose (not necessarily fiction), in *La Celestina* (fifteenth century), and in *Jou Pu Tuan*, a Chinese erotic novel of the seventeenth century by Li Yü. This latter work is of particular interest because of the combination of metaphor, periphrasis, and euphemism to produce a classical example of erotic defamiliarization:

> The junk was floating free—almost too free, he feared. Fearing that his ambassador might skid on the slippery path and miss the entrance, he requested his companion to guide him to the right spot with her tender little hand. She complied with some difficulty—it took all ten of her lotus shoots to hold the doughty ambassador. But soon, with her willing assistance, he had the difficult passage behind him and was presenting his credentials in her audience chamber.[101]

But one of the modern novels that is amongst the very first to come to mind in connection with the sea is Melville's *Moby Dick*, already quoted above, and one passage will be cited here (the first paragraph in Chapter 116):

> Not seldom in this life, when, on the right side, fortune's favorites sail close by us, we, though all adroop before, catch somewhat of the rushing breeze, and joyfully feel our bagging sails fill out. So it seemed with the Pequod. For next day after encountering the gay

100. Cf. Housman's ironic interpretation of the allegory in Poe's *The Haunted Palace* in *A. E. Housman: Selected Prose*, edited by John Carter (Cambridge: At the University Press, 1961), p. 187.

101. *Jou Pu Tuan* (New York: Grove Press, 1966), p. 218. This is a translation of the German version by Dr. Franz Kuhn.

Bachelor, whales were seen and four were slain; and one of them by
Ahab.

There is, finally, a whole range of peripheral domain which may
supply material for metaphor (still nautical), such as "monsters of the
deep," "mermaids," "voyages," "sea changes," etc.[102] If something
cannot be explained *litteratim*, it may be suggested *figuraliter*:

> The Russian who thinks Turgenev was a great writer, and bases
> his notion of Pushkin upon Chaikovsky's vile libretti, will merely
> paddle into the gentlest wavelets of Gogol's mysterious sea and limit
> his reaction to an enjoyment of what he takes to be whimsical humor
> and colorful quips. But the diver, the seeker for black pearls, the man
> who prefers the monsters of the deep to the sunshades on the beach,
> will find in *The Overcoat* shadows linking our state of existence to
> those other states and modes which we dimly apprehend in our rare
> moments of irrational perception.[103]

5

Though it might be worthwhile to trace, even in a similarly
sketchy fashion, other metaphors in other literatures which draw upon
such specific domains as war, love, and death, I shall turn now to a
brief survey of several more examples of metaphorical usage which,
in Shklovskian terms, also defamiliarize and disautomatize. The first
thing that strikes one who examines this aspect of world literature is
the correctness of Cicero's observation (*De Oratore* III.40.161):
"There is nothing in the world, the name or designation of which cannot be used in connection with other things." This is a rather bald
statement, as one might expect from Cicero; but we can see here, I
think, the influence of Stoic organicism with its concept of the "sympathy of the whole," a concept that was carried much further in

102. On mermaids and *homines marini* and their place in eighteenth-century
thought, see Arthur Lovejoy, *The Great Chain of Being* (New York: Harper,
1960), p. 184 and note 57, p. 566. On "voyages," see the brief but important
remarks by Wallace Fowlie in *Love and Literature* (Bloomington: Indiana University Press, 1965), p. 73 ff. and p. 128 ff.

103. Vladimir Nabokov, *Nikolai Gogol* (New York: New Directions, 1961),
p. 145.

medieval Christian thought. Thus St. Irenaeus writes: *"Nihil vacuum neque sine signo apud Deum."*[104]

A word or two might be said here concerning the use of metaphor in non-literary contexts—in philosophical, scientific, or political studies, for example. In such cases metaphor is generally employed for the sake of familiarization—to make clear something that might otherwise be difficult to see or understand, as though through an analogy. But, in the sense that quite often such metaphors in non-literary texts also cause us to see something anew or from a different, unusual point of view, they may well be examples of defamiliarization and disautomatization. Thus in a well-known and rather poetic statement Paolo Mantegazza metaphorizes the lowly condom: *una tela di ragno contro il pericolo, una corazza contro il piacere.* Norbert Wiener, expatiating on neoteny or pedomorphosis, writes: "Among the animals, man is a Peter Pan who never grows up."[105] A Nobel Laureate in Medicine, Sir Charles Sherrington, whose language is remarkable in several ways, frequently employs striking metaphors in his *Man on His Nature.* Philosophers, from Plato to contemporary figures, have been especially fond of metaphor, and I need hardly cite examples from George Santayana or Albert North Whitehead in whose writings there is more poetry than in many a professional bard.

Literary critics, too, find it difficult to avoid metaphor. This is particularly true of the autotelic critics; Oscar Wilde provides a good example:

> Criticism can recreate the past for us from the very smallest fragment of language or art, just as surely as the man of science can from some tiny bone, or the mere impress of a foot upon a rock, recreate for us the winged dragon or Titan lizard that once made the earth shake beneath its tread, can call Behemoth out of his cave, and make Leviathan swim once more across the startled sea.[106]

Even Roman Jakobson, in arguing that the study of poetry should be taken from the literary critics and turned over to linguists, employs a most engaging figure: he likens the methods of traditional literary

104. Quoted in Huizinga, *Waning of the Middle Ages,* p. 202. This foreshadowing of symbolism and the "doctrine of signatures" cannot, however, concern us any further in this study.

105. Norbert Wiener, *The Human Use of Human Beings* (Garden City: Anchor, 1954), p. 58.

106. *The Artist as Critic: Critical Writings of Oscar Wilde,* edited by Richard Ellmann (New York: Vintage, 1970), p. 404.

scholarship to those of the police who, after a crime has been committed, eagerly arrest everyone in the culprit's apartment as well as passers-by on the street.[107] From time immemorial critics have employed a kind of antonomasia in commenting on the significance or insignificance of certain writers: I mean the use of "equivalent authors"—calling Lucian, for example, the "Voltaire of antiquity" or Belinsky the "Russian Lessing" (Turgenev). Most such comparisons are unenlightening, to say the least. Even when the figures being compared are drawn from societies which have certain historical and cultural similarities—such as Russia and Spain—the result is apt to be absurd, e.g., Salvador de Madariaga's statement that "Ortega y Gasset is our Turgenev and Unamuno our Dostoevsky."[108]

Genealogical or personal metaphors, involving the phrases "father of," "mother of," "son of," are frequently used in epithets and antonomasias (Father of His Country, Father of Comedy, Necessity, the Mother of Invention) and in technical expressions (*matres lectionis*). Aeschylus was fond of these and he has, in addition to the phrase "stepmother of ships" cited earlier, *mētēr eupraxias* ("mother of success" = obedience) and *kasis pēlou* ("brother of dirt" = dust). Such expressions are frequent in the Old Testament as indeed they are in the Semitic languages in general (e.g., Arabic *abu 'l-hawl*, "father of terror" = the Sphinx, *bint al-warda*, "daughter of the rose" = cockroach). They were used in the Middle Ages (Matthew of Vendôme calls the cough "stepmother of the chest"), by Dante, and in subsequent periods of baroque mannerism (we have elsewhere cited Góngora's *nieto de la spuma* = Cupid), as well as in the verse of major poets, e.g., Keats: "Thou still unravish'd bride of quietness,/ Thou foster-child of silence and slow time."

It is always surprising—and defamiliarizing—to encounter in metaphor the association of things otherwise beautiful and tender with aspects of violence, although love and war have frequently been linked in this way (*militat omnis amans*—Ovid). I refer not so much to such simple conceits as D'Urfey's "Love steals artillery from her eyes" as to expressions like Khlebnikov's *zapakhov vesennikh pulemet* ("the machine-gun of spring aromas"), P. Vasiliev's *tvoe jarostnoe telo/ S jadrami grudej* ("thy fierce body/ With its cannonball breasts"), or Anaïs Nin's "The guitars and the singing opened fire." Owen's imagery in "The shrill, demented choirs of wailing shells" is not so striking

---

107. See Erlich, *op. cit.*, p. 71.
108. Introductory Essay to Unamuno's *Tragic Sense of Life* (New York: Dover, 1954), p. xxxi.

simply because the sharp contrast between choral music and gunfire is weakened and neutralized through the almost synonymous adjectives "demented" and "wailing."

The very presence of words of erotic, sexual, scatological, or blasphemous significance in metaphor is often quite enough to shock the sensibilities; though it is a facile technique, it has generally been (at least until the present day) effective. There is, to be sure, considerable variety in the imagery of the Surrealists, but some of their most striking figures are erotic and sexual. Thus Louis Aragon, one of "whose principal contributions to surrealism is his refusal to view the familiar world as others see it" (J. H. Matthews), defamiliarizes the Eiffel Tower:

> Mais le plus beau moment ce fut lorsqu'entre
> Ses jambes de fer écartées
> La Tour Eiffel fit voir un sexe féminin
> Qu'on ne lui soupçonnait guère,[109]

and Jean Arp has:

> Les étoiles ouvrent le lacet de leur corsage
> Et montrent leurs rosaces lascives.[110]

Mayakovsky likes occasional metaphor such as this:

> Uvazhaemye
> tovarishchi potomki!
> Rojas'
> v segodnjashnem gavne[111]

("Most respected comrade descendants! Excavating in today's petrified crap"), or this:

> Marija! . . .
> telo tvoe prosto proshu
> kak prosjat khristiane—
> "khleb nash nasushchnyj
> dazhd' nam dnes'."

109. Quoted in Matthews, *Surrealist Poetry in France*, p. 40.
110. *Ibid.*, p. 93.
111. The word *gavne* is usually printed "g . . . ."

("Maria! . . . I simply ask for your body as Christians pray: 'Give us this day our daily bread.'")

Let us take now the human head and facial features and see how (in this case) certain prose writers have chosen to "estrange" these features. The Russian author Nikolay Gogol, for instance, who had a marked predilection for either likening human beings—or parts thereof—to things or comparing things to humans, writes in Chapter 1 of *Dead Souls:* "In the corner store or, rather, in its window there was a vendor with a red brass samovar and a face just as red, so that, from afar, it looked as if there were two samovars, were it not for the fact that one of them had a pitch-black beard." And elsewhere Gogol sees two heads, a woman's and a man's, as, respectively, a cucumber with a bonnet on it and a calabash (or gourd). Gogol also shows a special interest in noses: one of his best-known stories is entitled *The Nose,* and commentators on Gogol frequently refer to the prevalence of "nosological" works in European literature of the early nineteenth century.[112] Earlier in this chapter we cited a "nose" passage from Gottfried Keller, and here is another from Ivan Goncharov in *Oblomov,* Part III, Chapter 4: "'They pawned their silver? Then they have no money either,' Oblomov thought, his eyes wandering over the walls in horror and then coming to rest on Anisya's nose, since there was nothing else in her face that one's eyes could fix on. Indeed, it seemed she had been saying everything with her nose and not with her mouth."[113]

Ears, which in any case appear to be grotesque appendages upon close inspection, have often evoked bizarre similes and metaphor. Andrey Bely, who regularly uses adjectives of color to defamiliarize, refers to the "green ears" of the elder Ableukhov in *St. Petersburg.* This Gogolian metaphoric tradition continues in the prose of Evgeny Zamyatin who, in *We,* entries 16 and 17, likens the thin lips of a physician to scissors and then refers to these "scissors," rather than lips, opening and closing; or he makes far-fetched comparisons ("eyes like the horns of a bull tossing the patients up") that remind one of the extreme type of metaphor found in a poet like Neruda.

Metaphors involving eyes are legion. But there is a particular type of eye defamiliarization in the romantic literature of the nineteenth century, especially in works containing a portrayal of the

112. See the comments on noses in Gogol and in Russian proverbs in Nabokov's *Nikolai Gogol,* Chapter 1.

113. Cf. Martial, *Epigrams,* 7.18.

Byronic *homme fatal.* The character Pechorin in Lermontov's *A Hero of Our Time* is such a figure, and the author writes the following of Pechorin's eyes in the Maxim Maximich chapter: "In the first place, they did not laugh when he laughed. Have you ever noticed an oddity like this in certain people? It is a sign either of an evil temper or else of constant melancholy. From behind his partly lowered eyelashes they shone with a certain phosphorescent brilliance [*fosforicheskim bleskom*], if one can so express it."

These "satanic" eyes became a commonplace feature of many of the macabre characters in the gothic novels and tales, and numerous references to such eyes, in both male and female characters, may be found in the strange assortment of prose and poetry in *The Romantic Agony* by Mario Praz. The French Decadents also liked to expatiate on such eyes, especially of women. Georges Rodenbach, for example, has this in *Le Voyage dans les yeux:*

> Ah les yeux! Tous les yeux! Tant de reflets posthumes
> Reliquaires du sang de tous les soirs tombants
> Chaires où toute noce a promulgué ses bans
> Sites où chaque automne a laissé de ses brumes.

An even more favorite aspect of the human form for romantic writers and, especially, for the Decadents, is women's hair. Loosened feminine hair has always been a symbol of woman's return, so to speak, to a state of nature, and it has been given all sorts of erotic— even fetishistic—overtones in prose and poetry. The same holds true in the oriental literatures (this is particularly noticeable in, for example, Yasunari Kawabata's *Snow Country*), and considerable attention is paid in Arabic poetry to defamiliarizing women's actions with their hair. Thus Professor Hamori quotes the following passage (attributed to Ibn al-Mu'tazz) which describes, in oblique metaphoric language, a woman quite literally letting her hair down: ". . . and she let down darkness over light,/ so that her morning vanished under night."[114]

Among modern writers there are now many in whom we can see a Gogolian tendency to reify human beings and human features (and, conversely, to personify things) in a bizarre yet artistically satisfying manner, as well as many more who show a preoccupation in general

114. Andras Hamori, *On the Art of Medieval Arabic Literature* (Princeton: Princeton University Press, 1974), p. 105.

with things. There are, for example, the new French novelists and their *chosisme*—most notably Alain Robbe-Grillet with his peculiar attention to things and the surfaces of things (referred to by François Mauriac as the *technique du cageot*) and Francis Ponge with his *le parti-pris des choses*.[115] And there is a German tradition in this connection as well: one thinks, for instance, of F. T. Vischer (see below, p. 101). But it is in the works of Günter Grass especially that we see another writer of genius experimenting with the German language and producing some startling but beautiful results. Critics frequently comment on his particular concern in describing men and things; thus Kurt Lothar Tank in his study of Grass writes the following (referring in turn to Peter Löffler's article, "Zum Thema Gegenstand und Mensch im Modernen Drama"):

> The magical object, Löffler says, is to be regarded as "a kind of secularized relic," like the furniture of the "new tenant" and the chairs in Eugène Ionesco's play *The New Tenant*. This alteration that is taking place with regard to the object and man in modern drama might be characterized as "a tendency to transform the human into the inorganic and a tendency to transform the objective into the organic." In the realm of metaphor, Löffler continues, there are, as we know, comparisons whereby something living is represented by means of something without life, and something lifeless by means of something living. In the objectification of living beings and the animating of dead things, it is as if these metaphoric forms were running rampant. The metaphor is not only used in words but is extended to the total represented reality.[116]

Grass himself, speaking through the mouth of Oskar in *Die Blechtrommel* (1968), says:

> Heute weiss ich, dass alles zuguckt, dass nichts unbesehen bleibt, dass selbst Tapeten ein besseres Gedächtnis als die Menschen haben. Es ist nicht etwa der liebe Gott, der alles sieht! Ein Küchenstuhl, Kleiderbügel, halbvoller Aschenbecher oder das hölzerne Abbild einer Frau, genannt Niobe, reichen aus, um jeder Tat den unvergesslichen Zeugen liefern zu können.

115. See Herbert Kohl, *The Age of Complexity* (New York: Mentor, 1965), Selection Six (an essay by Robbe-Grillet).

116. *Günter Grass* in "Modern Literature Monographs" (New York: Ungar, 1969), p. 56. See also the references here to Klaus Wagenbach's stylistic study of Grass, pp. 78 ff.

A good example of Grass's metaphor is his amplification of German tanks as *die Hengste aus den Gestüten der Krupp von Bohlen und Halbach, was Edleres ward nie geritten.* Rich in allusion and suggestiveness are also many of the seemingly absurd discursive comments on things—skirts, for example, which "are masculine by nature." There are quaint and ironic periphrases (e.g., *der Betthimmel der breiten Eheburg*) as well as many clever and vivid metaphorical phrases, such as the reference to Hitler's "rectangular salutes." The frequent mock-euphemistic allusions to sexual matters are also good examples of erotic defamiliarization (or "negative allegory"):

> Und nun erkannte ich sie sofort. Wut, Scham, Empörung, Enttäuschung und eine halb komisch, halb schmerzhaft beginnende Versteifung meines Giesskännchens unter dem Badeanzug, liessen mich Trommel und beide Trommelstöcke um des einen, mir neu gewachsenen Stockes willen vergessen.[117]

It will have been noticed that, among the examples of metaphor so far cited in the preceding sections of this chapter, a number are more specifically instances of metonymy and synecdoche. Though it has become customary to overlook the technical distinctions between these two tropes (the term metonymy often doing duty for the term synecdoche), both terms are frequently used with either specialized or expanded and generalized meanings. (I have already referred, in section 2, for example, to the so-called synecdochical accusative, i.e., the "Greek" or partitive accusative.) Occasionally critics will speak of the synecdochic descriptive technique of certain writers: thus Tolstoy, after introducing a character and pointing out some particular feature of his or her appearance, will thereafter refer to this character synecdochically, i.e., with reference to this one physical feature (the downy upper lip of the Princess Volkonsky, the heavy footstep of her sister-in-law, Princess Maria Volkonsky, the rotundity of Platon Karataev, etc.).

It is not unusual to encounter the notion of synecdoche applied to concepts such as microcosm/macrocosm or Leibniz's monadology; indeed, Kenneth Burke calls all artistic representation synecdochic.

---

117. There are other more explicit passages, such as those in the sculpture-class scene with its cubist allusions (pp. 560–61 in the German text of *Die Blechtrommel*), ending in the English translation by Ralph Manheim: "Priapus in terms of solid geometry."

Burke even includes the present/future and active/passive dichotomies: "At the opening of *The Ancient Mariner,* for instance, the Albatross is a *gerundive:* its nature when introduced is that of something *to be* murdered, and it implicitly contains the future that is to become explicit. In *Moby Dick,* Ahab as pursuer is pursued; his action is a passion."[118]

A reference to synecdoche occurred in an unusual context when, in 1967, the Inspector General of the Central Intelligence Agency wrote in an internal report, cited by Richard Lyons in the *New York Times,* November 21, 1975: "The point is that of frequent resort to synecdoche—the mention of a part when the whole is to be understood, or vice versa. Thus we encounter repeated references to phrases such as 'disposing of Castro,' which may be read in the narrow, literal sense of assassinating him, when it is intended that it be read in the broader figurative sense of dislodging the Castro regime."

As for the terms metonymy and metonymic, these are also used to cover a broad range of symbolic allusion, since, of the many forms of symbolism, there are clearly both metonymic and synecdochic symbols.[119] One can easily think of examples of these not only in prose and poetry but in music (snatches of Thomas of Celano's *Dies Irae* theme in a piece of music represent Death as specifically as the figure of a shoe outside a shop signals the presence of a cobbler) and painting as well (doorways, bridges, wheels, or wheel-like forms, etc., with their respective connotations). Kenneth Burke again writes that I. A. Richards is quite "metonymic" when he suggests that we should speak not of the emotions aroused in the reader but rather of the "commotions," and Lévi-Strauss uses the term metonymy in non-literary contexts.[120]

118. Kenneth Burke, *A Grammar of Motives and a Rhetoric of Motives* (Cleveland: Meridian, 1962), p. 509.

119. See the numerous examples of "metonymic devices" in Chekhov pointed out by Thomas Winner, *Chekhov and His Prose* (New York: Holt, Rinehart & Winston, 1966).

120. See James Boon, *From Symbolism to Structuralism* (New York: Harper, 1973), p. 104.

PROSE AND POETRY

1

THE VERY TITLES of prose works, especially novels, may defamiliarize. In the preface to his play, *La Galerie du palais*, Corneille says that authors must choose titles for their works which "excite the curiosity of their audience."[1] Of course, many titles of prose works are descriptive, being either the name of a principal character (*Pamela, Oblomov*) or merely short forms of the theme statement of the narrative (*Fathers and Sons*); others may indicate a particular time (*1984*), place (*Howards End*), or situation (*La Peste*) in the novel; still others may be in some sense symbolic or allegorical (*Die Schlafwandler*) or allusive (*For Whom the Bell Tolls*). A great mass of descriptive novel titles, in English and in certain other languages, begin with the definite article, very often simply definite article plus noun or noun phrase, and this practice seems to be increasing in popularity: *The Time Machine, The Gallery, The Pistol, The Caine Mutiny*. But there is a defamiliarized quality about a novel title such as Michael Zack's *Oxymoron* or *Ferdydurke* by Witold Gombrowicz; these are quite as different from traditional titles as the titles of certain modern works of music (e.g., Edgar Varèse's *Density 21.5*) or of non-objective and surrealist paintings are different from the more clearly descriptive titles of the past.

Very short titles (such as Zamyatin's *We*) and long circumstantial

---

1. Helmut Heissenbüttel has a poem, *Büchertitel sind magisch* (in *Kombinationen*). I am indebted for this reference as well as the Corneille statement to Harald Weinrich's article, "The Textual Function of the French Article," in *Literary Style*, edited by Seymour Chatman (New York: Oxford University Press, 1971), pp. 221–34. There are also some remarks, for what they are worth, on book titles in Nabokov's *Transparent Things*, Chapter 18, *ad fin.*

titles, such as modern imitations of those popular in the eighteenth century, are also strange. Nabokov likes to defamiliarize the names of other novels in his own novels by distorting titles: thus in *Pnin* a student is learning Russian so that she may read *Anna Karamazov* in the original; and in *Ada* Chekhov's *Four Sisters* is mentioned. Non-fiction titles, too, are often quite obviously chosen for their provocative effect—e.g., Lilli Palmer's autobiography, *Change Lobsters—and Dance*. We need hardly comment here on the defamiliarizing effect of pseudonyms and *noms de plume*.

Terms such as "protean" and "amorphous" are frequently used of the novel form.[2] There are incredibly long novels—*romans fleuves*—and very short novels ("novelettes"). There are novels in verse, in dialogue, in the form of letters, and "menippean" novels[3]; novels with varying modes of narration; novels about novelists writing novels; lipogrammatic and ring-form or "ouroboros" novels; cubist novels and boxed, looseleaf "shuffle" novels; historical novels and utopian (or dystopian) novels; "scientific" naturalistic novels reflecting an extreme realism and wildly fantastic novels; *romans-charognes*, avant-garde novels, anti-novels, and "roussans"[4]; experimental novels, "art" novels, and novels that are primarily vehicles for ideology; there are picaresque novels, *Bildungsromane*, *romans à clef*, symbolist novels, gothic novels, detective novels, pornographic novels . . . The forms and varieties are almost endless.

So far as prose narratives of less than novel length are concerned, there is great variety here as well. There are very long short stories as well as prose narratives of absurd brevity, such as this:

> The other day a man went to work, but on his way, he met another man, who had bought a loaf of Polish bread and was on his way home, to his own place.
> That's about all.[5]

2. "It [the novel] is most distinctly one of the moister areas of literature—irrigated by a hundred rills and occasionally degenerating into a swamp"— E. M. Forster, *Aspects of the Novel*.

3. See Mikhail Bakhtin, *Problems of Dostoevsky's Poetics*, translated by R. Rotsel (Ann Arbor: Ardis, 1973), Chapter IV.

4. This term was coined by E. M. de Vogüé in his *Le roman russe* (1886) to replace *romans* when applied to Russian novels.

5. *A Meeting* by Daniil Kharms from *Russia's Lost Literature of the Absurd*, translated and edited by George Gibian (Ithaca: Cornell University Press, 1971), p. 59. Such brevity is paralleled in verse by one-line poems (monostichs) and in music by compositions like Schönberg's *Canon for String Quartet* which lasts forty-two seconds.

Though such an eccentricity is no doubt a defamiliarization of what we generally assume to be a familiar feature of a prose narrative, i.e., that it be at least of significant length, and though certain other short prose and mixed forms, or adaptations of these, might be used in a similar way, the great variety of such forms reduces the possibilities of defamiliarization, at least in any formal, genre sense. In any literary system where there is a strict observance of separation of genres and where innovation is not officially tolerated, any novelty, distortion, or hybridization, when it does occur, more readily has a defamiliarizing effect. But in a system where there is a proliferation of many mixed, "impure," and hybrid forms, innovations will obviously be less striking. Still, there is ample opportunity for defamiliarization with respect to certain categories and particular features of narrative content. For example, the chronology may be tampered with—interrupted, suspended, protracted, curtailed, or even inverted.[6] The chronological scope of novels varies greatly: from the decades and centuries covered in some novels to the temporal brevity so noticeable in Dostoevsky (not to mention Joyce) and the quite amazing brevity in a novel such as Claude Mauriac's *L'Agrandissement* which involves *two minutes* of elapsed time.[7]

Excessive detail may defamiliarize: in Peacock's *Nightmare Abbey* the following passage occurs in Chapter 13:

> The whole party followed, with the exception of Scythrop, who threw himself into his armchair, crossed his left foot over his right knee, placed the hollow of his left hand on the interior ankle of his left leg, rested his right elbow on the elbow of the chair, placed the ball of his right thumb against his right temple, curved the forefinger along the upper part of his forehead, rested the point of the middle finger on the bridge of his nose, and the points of the two others on

6. Toying with chronology is often associated with Sterne: see, e.g., Jean-Jacques Mayoux, "Variations on the Time-sense in *Tristram Shandy*," in *The Winged Skull* (Kent State University Press, 1971). See also David Lodge, *Language of Fiction* (New York: Columbia University Press, 1967), pp. 39–40.

7. "The fact that a major part of *The Idiot* transpires in twenty-four hours, that the bulk of the incidents narrated in *The Possessed* covers only forty-eight hours, and that everything but the trial in *The Brothers Karamazov* comes to pass in five days is as central to Dostoevsky's vision and intent as is the terrifying brevity of time which separates King Oedipus from Oedipus the beggar," George Steiner, *Tolstoy or Dostoevsky* (New York: Random House, 1959), p. 151. See the interesting remarks on chronology in the *nouveau roman* in Vivian Mercier, *The New Novel from Queneau to Pinget* (New York: Farrar, Straus & Giroux, 1971), Introduction.

the lower part of the palm, fixed his eyes intently on the veins in the back of his left hand, and sat in this position like the immovable Theseus.[8]

There are similar passages in Sterne and Joyce, while Michel Butor's novel *Degrés* (1960) represents an extreme development in circumstantiality, as Maurice Nadeau's comments make clear:

> It consists of an exhaustive account, by a history and geography teacher, of one hour's lesson, on Tuesday, 12th October 1954. It contains not only an account of the lesson itself, but the entire life of the teacher, of the nephew to whom the account is addressed, of the school in which he teaches, of his family and his activities outside school, and of the actions and gestures of some of the thirty-two pupils in his class and of his colleagues. As the description grows, as detail is added to detail, the attempt to seize the whole of reality ends by effacing this reality.[9]

Defamiliarization may also result from the minute observation and description of things—the *chosiste* approach, for instance, of some of the new French novelists (Robbe-Grillet, Nathalie Sarraute, see p. 95). A somewhat different—but no less defamiliarizing—preoccupation with things is found, for example, in the novel *Auch Einer* (1879) by F. T. Vischer, where the concern is with the "malice of the inanimate object" (*die Tücke des Objektes*). There is a strange passage in Tolstoy's *The Death of Ivan Ilych* where the author seems to indicate a certain animate response on the part of a hassock (see above, p. 57). But the ascribing of malice to inanimate objects is but one aspect (as is the concept of the "pathetic fallacy") of lingering animistic beliefs which has a parallel in such things as the former statute on deodands in English law.

The absence of conventional punctuation, although encountered rather frequently in attempts to render verbally the "stream of consciousness," may still strike us as unfamiliar and strange. The effectiveness of the method is best represented by what has become a classical

8. Peacock, it should be noted, ends this passage ironically: "We hope the admirers of the *minutiae* in poetry and romance will appreciate this accurate description of a pensive attitude." On "close-ups," see above, pp. 19–20.

9. Maurice Nadeau, *The French Novel Since the War* (New York: Grove Press, 1969), p. 136.

instance—the lengthy monolog of Molly Bloom in *Ulysses*.[10] But the device has been used elsewhere of course: for example, there is a striking passage in the Russian writer Aleksey Remizov's *Savva Grudt-syn* (1949), the retelling of a seventeenth-century "demonological" tale.[11] A similar juxtapositional device is used in the fugue-like passages that occur in much modern prose fiction—e.g., *passim* in Goytisolo's *Count Julian* (see above, p. 53). There seems to be a foreshadowing of such extended fugal associations in the ancient and medieval accumulations of nouns in asyndetic groups.[12] Closely related to eccentric punctuation are other typographical devices (absence of capital letters, unusual paragraph indentations, Sternean diagrams, etc.) which, if structurally motivated, are effective but nevertheless unfamiliar. Stichomythia-like dialog passages in certain writers such as Dostoevsky also catch the eye.

As regards the defamiliarization of fictional characters, these latter may, for example, be described (in a sort of inversion of the *Entwicklunsroman* hero) as growing backwards, as in the case of the principal character in Gombrowicz' *Ferdydurke*. Or they may be insects (as in Kafka) or other absurd or grotesque creatures (such as the mad dwarf in Grass's *The Tin Drum*). These are amongst the anti-heroes so prevalent in modern Western fiction, whose presence the Soviet literary authorities point out as further evidence of decadence and "deheroization" (*degeroizatsija*), and whose origin is sometimes traced back to either Diderot's or Dostoevsky's "underground men." Or the hero may, in the *Doppelgänger* tradition, be "doubled," either in whole (Dostoevsky's *The Double*) or in part (Gogol's *The Nose*).[13] The narrator may be an animal (Tolstoy's *Kholstomer*), from another planet (Sinyavsky's *Pkhentz*), a pathic (John Rechy's *City of Night*), etc. Or some phenomena traditionally seen and described from the male viewpoint are defamiliarized by being seen from the woman's point of view, as in Tolstoy's *Family Happiness* in which the author, "feminizing" himself by using, for

10. On "stream of consciousness" authors and techniques, see Shiv Kumar, *Bergson and the Stream of Consciousness Novel* (New York: New York University Press, 1963).

11. This particular passage is about two pages long and may be found in *Besnovatye—Savva Grudtsyn i Solomonija* (Paris: "Opleshnik," 1951).

12. See Helmut Hatzfeld, *El "Quijote" Como Obra de Arte del Lenguaje* (Madrid: Aguirre, 1966), pp. 212 ff., on *acumulación* in Cervantes.

13. See the article by Dmitri Chizhevsky, "The Theme of the Double in Dostoevsky," in *Dostoevsky*, edited by René Wellek (Englewood Cliffs, N.J.: Prentice-Hall, 1962), pp. 112 ff.

example, the feminine forms of Russian verbs in the past,[14] describes the process of falling in love, courtship, and marriage.

The names of characters in much realistic fiction are "normal" names nominalistically oriented (*"nomen nomen"*); but symbolic names or charactonyms (or, as Lessing called them, *redende Namen*[15]) often appear in fiction that has a "realist" (i.e., Platonic) basis where a name "signifies" (*"nomen omen"*). The names of many of the characters in Dostoevsky (but *not* in Tolstoy[16]) are in this category, but examples may be found in the other literatures as well.[17] But of course a great many charactonyms are anything but defamiliarizing: they are rather, like the names in English Restoration comedy, familiarizing devices. Toponyms, either real or imaginary, may be made strange (such as those in Nabokov's fiction) and occasionally a cavalier attitude toward locale (unless it be an attempt to universalize) is noticeable: thus it is not until three-quarters of the way into *The Brothers Karamazov* that Dostoevsky mentions, in passing, the name of the locale—and then it is a symbolic one (Skotoprigonevsk, the "cattle pen"). Names may be replaced by numbers in science fiction and utopias.[18]

But since names have been traditionally a mark of individuality (Herodotus tells us of an African people, the Atarantes, "the only people in the world to do without names. Atarantes is the collective name—but individually they have none"), Nathalie Sarraute in particular amongst the new French novelists has broken radically with the onomastic as well as with the narrative conventions of the novel:

14. Something that Donne did not have to do when he wrote "Breake of Day," his only poem in which a woman speaks.

15. Aristotle called them *ou ta tuchonta onomata* ("purposeful names"), *Poetics*, 1451b. They are also referred to as aptronyms, significant names, figurative names, telling names, or name labels.

16. Occasionally the name Karenin is interpreted as a charactonym (Greek *karēnon*, "head") and very possibly Toporov in *Resurrection* (a parody of Pobedonostsev, the Procurator of the Holy Synod) is one (*topor* = "axe"); but one would be hard pressed to find others.

17. See the remarks on the naming of characters in the English novel in Ian Watt, *The Rise of the Novel* (Berkeley: University of California Press, 1967), pp. 18–21. See also the comments on polyonomasia in Dostoevsky and Cervantes in Leo Spitzer, *Linguistics and Literary History* (Princeton: Princeton University Press, 1967), note 14a, p. 77.

18. Such impersonal numbers instead of names add to the effect of coldness and alienation in Zamyatin's novel, *We*. See the remarks concerning names in utopias in Michael Holquist, "How to Play Utopia," in *Game, Play, Literature*, edited by Jacques Ehrmann (Boston: Beacon Press, 1971), p. 111.

Balzac gives the people in his novels names, occupations, houses, sets of personal possessions, a full complement of external signs intended to fix their individuality for the reader. In Nathalie Sarraute's vision this individuality is seen as no more than a flimsy envelope. . . . As few people as possible are given names in Nathalie Sarraute's novels, and there is an absolute minimum of particularizing action. . . . Realism lies not in the slavish representation of the surface world but in the rendering of the deeper world beneath it which gives it its structure. Nathalie Sarraute is fond of quoting Paul Klee's statement to the effect that art does not reproduce what can be seen, it makes things visible.[19]

Thus in Sarraute's *Martereau* (1953) the narrator (Martereau) is the only named character in the novel.

The novels of Nathalie Sarraute, of Robbe-Grillet, and the other new French novelists break with novelistic traditions in many ways. The radical re-working or "undoing" of the novel form as exemplified in Sarraute's *Portrait d'un inconnu* (1948), for instance, prompted Sartre to introduce the term "anti-roman," while the very title of such a study as Barthes' *Le Degré zéro de l'écriture* (1953) points up the nature of the sweeping changes that have occurred.[20] The essence of these changes may be summed up, I think, in stating that "contemporary realism is not to be cast in terms of the representation of things but in those of a knowledge of language, of a profound exploration of the 'réalité irréelle du langage.' This is not some call for 'irresponsible verbal pyrotechnics,' but, on the contrary, a recognition of the reality of language and of the writer's responsibility with respect to that reality, a responsibility the consciousness of which is the basis of the work of a Mallarmé or a Joyce."[21]

19. Stephen Heath, *The Nouveau Roman* (Philadelphia: Temple University Press, 1972), pp. 48–49. Cf. also the remarks of George Steiner on the anonymity of certain characters in Proust as compared with the polyonomasia of Tolstoy: *Tolstoy or Dostoevsky* (New York: Random House, 1961), pp. 101–102.

20. In a brief note Borges says of the Cabalists: "They thought that a work dictated by the Holy Spirit was an absolute text: in other words, a text in which the collaboration of chance was calculable as zero"—Appendix to *European Literary Theory and Practice*, edited by Vernon Gras (New York: Delta, 1973), p. 367. It is interesting that the movement in the direction of "absolute texts" (in the sense of Flaubert's dream of a purely structuralist novel) seems to return again, willy-nilly, to something like a mystical view of language.

21. Heath, *The Nouveau Roman*, p. 64. But, because of the emphasis on language, to turn over the study of literature to linguists would be comparable to turning over education to professional educators. We know the results here.

And Samuel Beckett, writing on Joyce, says: "Here form *is* content, content *is* form. You complain that this stuff is not written in English. It is not written at all. It is not to be read—or rather it is not only to be read. It is to be looked at and listened to. His writing is not *about something; it is that something itself.*"[22]

Whether or not we concur with Lucien Goldmann, who has claimed that Nathalie Sarraute's fiction represents the closing of an already established tradition (begun by such writers as Proust, Joyce, Woolf, or Stein) rather than the beginning of a new one,[23] we can agree with Stephen Heath when he refers (somewhat loosely, to be sure, but in a manner quite in accord with the present study) to Shklovsky and *ostranenie* in commenting on the "strangeness" of a Robbe-Grillet text:

> Is it not a strangeness (*ostranenie*) that is felt in the presence of a Robbe-Grillet text? . . . We are confronted with a *text*, something material, a construction that in its formality, its use of various elements which we recognize as elements of comforting sense and which we would like to relate as usual to achieve the satisfaction of meaning, and yet which here, in their variation and repetition, their exploration as forms, resist our recuperation, disrupts our expectations, forces us to *read* and not to recognize.[24]

Heath is referring to such passages as the following, quoted by Vivian Mercier in a study of the new French novel:

> The brush descends the length of the loose hair with a faint noise somewhere between the sound of a breath and a crackle. No sooner has it reached the bottom than it quickly rises again toward the head, where the whole surface of its bristles sinks in before gliding down over the black mass again. The brush is a bone-colored oval whose short handle disappears almost entirely in the hand firmly gripping it.[25]

22. Quoted in Mercier, *The New Novel*, p. 40.

23. Lucien Goldmann, "Nouveau roman et réalité" in *Pour une sociologie du roman* (Paris, 1964).

24. Heath, *The Nouveau Roman*, p. 151. He translates *ostranenie* as defamiliarization.

25. Mercier, *The New Novel*, p. 170. Mercier mentions neither Shklovsky nor defamiliarization.

The reference above to Gertrude Stein reminds us of the strangeness of her prose which also supplies many instances of defamiliarization:

> Helen Furr had quite a pleasant home. Mrs. Furr was quite a pleasant woman. Mr. Furr was quite a pleasant man. Helen Furr had quite a pleasant voice quite worth cultivating. She did not mind working. She worked to cultivate her voice. She did not find it gay living in the same place where she had always been living. She went to a place where some were cultivating something, voices and other things needing cultivating. She met Georgine Skeene there who was cultivating her voice which some thought was quite a pleasant one. Helen Furr and Georgine Skeene lived together then.[26]

In connection, too, with the mention above of Proust, aside from any particular features of his prose style, it is noteworthy that Frederic Jameson cites a passage in À la recherche du temps perdu where a character in the novel compares the impressionist techniques of the painter Elstir and the "Dostoevskian side of Madame de Sévigné's letters." Jameson writes:

> It is only fair to point out that the idea of art as a renewal of perception is not unique with the Russian Formalists, but can be found in one version or another everywhere in modern art and modern aesthetics . . . thus Proust resembles the Formalists . . . not only in what he says, but in his manner of saying it. It is already a defamiliarization to compare Madame de Sévigné with Dostoevsky; the very shock has the effect of making us see her style in a new and utterly unforeseen light, as though for the first time.[27]

2

In addition to the defamiliarization of such things as the category of time and the tradition of individuality as represented by the

26. From "Miss Furr and Miss Skeene" (1922). A longer excerpt is quoted in Wylie Sypher, Rococo to Cubism in Art and Literature (New York: Random House, 1963), p. 282.

27. Frederic Jameson, The Prison-House of Language (Princeton: Princeton University Press, 1974), pp. 54–55. Although Tolstoy is more often mentioned in loose graphic analogies as resembling the plein-airistes, the name of Dostoevsky very frequently occurs in various modernist associations. Thus Nathalie Sarraute has acknowledged her indebtedness to Dostoevsky, and Max Ernst has a painting of himself and a group of Surrealist artists in which the painter and Jean Paulhan are seated on Dostoevsky's lap.

frequent use of personal names, we may also have defamiliarization of nature. This began very early (and to a great extent continues) with the personification of aspects of nature and especially in the literary metonymic antonomasias: Poseidon-Neptune for the Sea, Artemis-Diana for the Moon, Aphrodite-Venus (or the Cyprian, the Cytherean, etc.) for Love, and so on. As these became, over the centuries, commonplaces, they lost their defamiliarizing effect; but in recent times, as more and more people know less and less about classical mythology, they are regaining this effect. I refer here, however, more to such a narrative device as that used by Gogol, for example, in (very likely) making fun of the romantic adulation of nature so prevalent amongst his immediate predecessors and contemporaries; Chichikov in *Dead Souls* is leaving a town in a carriage: "Hardly had they left the town behind when, as is usual in this land of ours, all sorts of stuff and nonsense [*chush' i dich'*] appeared on both sides of the road—hillocks, a fir grove, sparse, stumpy, scrubby young pines and the charred stumps of old ones, wild heather, and such rubbish [*vzdor*]."

Tolstoy, too, likes to deromanticize and debunk the traditional awe evoked in romantic minds by, for instance, mountains, even though (he might not have known this) it was his idol Rousseau who is often given the credit for introducing into literature the romanticism of mountains.[28] Thus, in *The Cossacks*, as Olenin, a young and already jaded officer from Moscow, is nearing his new military assignment in the Caucasus, he exclaims:

> "This is where it starts!" Olenin told himself, expecting at any time now to see the snow-capped mountains about which he'd heard so much. Then, one evening, the Nogay driver pointed his whip to where mountains could just be discerned among the clouds. Olenin looked intently, but the sky was overcast and the clouds concealed the mountains almost entirely. He made out something gray, white, fleecy and, try as he might, he couldn't discover anything attractive about the vista. And these were the mountains he'd read and heard so much about. He decided that they looked much like the clouds, and that all the talk about their peculiar beauty was just as false as admiration for Bach or as fictitious as the love of women.

28. "It was Rousseau who, with an extraordinary intensity and power of expression, created the emotion of the mountains. No doubt it existed before him, at least in elementary form; but it was he who molded these elements into a new shape and who forced the new emotion upon us."—E. de Bruyne, *Het aesthetisch beleven,* quoted in Herbert Kohl, *The Age of Complexity* (New York: Mentor, 1965), p. 206.

The oblique, impressionistic reference to the beauty of a person, place, or thing rather than a lengthy verbal repertory of details may defamiliarize both the object and the traditional descriptive approach. Perhaps the best example occurs in the *Iliad* (Book III) when the old men on the ramparts of Troy, who have been vilifying Helen as the cause of the war, suddenly see her as she comes out and, immediately forgetting their criticism as they contemplate her beauty, say, "No wonder the Greeks and the Trojans have been fighting all these years for such a woman!" Thus the beauty of Helen is effectively suggested by its effect not only on old men but also on men who hold a bitter grudge against the woman. But the point is that this illustrates, at a very early stage in European literature, something that we would consider even today as a rather sophisticated technique of treating a situation that might have lent itself most conveniently, one would suppose, to traditional verbal iconography.

Proust's descriptive method is also one that seeks a new vision. As Martin Turnell writes, "Proust's approach differs from all these writers or rather he combines a number of different approaches and produces a new standpoint and a new method. The classical novelists were convinced that in spite of his changing moods, man was essentially *one*. Proust was equally convinced that he was *many*."[29] Turnell quotes the following passage as a case in point:

> Suddenly Saint-Loup appeared, accompanied by his mistress, and then, in this woman who was for him all the love, every possible delight in life, whose personality, mysteriously enshrined in a body as in a tabernacle, was the object that still occupied incessantly the toiling imagination of my friend, whom he felt that he would never really know, as to whom he was perpetually asking himself what could be her secret self, behind the veil of eyes and flesh, in this woman I recognized at once "Rachel when from the lord," her who, but a few years since—women change their position so rapidly in that world, when they do change—used to say to the procuress: "Tomorrow evening, then, if you want me for anyone, you will send round, won't you."

A person, place, or object may thus be defamiliarized by being described as seen through neutral, uninvolved, or "rival" eyes or through the eyes of two or more characters with differing criteria and

---

29. Martin Turnell, "People in Proust" in *Literary Modernism*, edited by Irving Howe (New York: Fawcett, 1967), p. 249.

bases for judgment. Such devices have been used, of course, by many writers and they have been employed successfully in the cinema. But in novels similar methods of recording multiple vision are frequently encountered: in Leonid Leonov's *The Thief* (1927), for example, there is a kind of counterpoint set up between what Leonov himself writes in the novel and what a fictional novelist *within* the novel writes:

> Leonov has complicated and enriched his narrative by including the device of a novel within a novel. Firsov, the novelist-character, serves as a recording sensibility close to the center of events, and as a philosophizing voice that comments on the action as none of the other characters can. But it must not be thought that Firsov is simply a spokesman for Leonov. The "novel" that Firsov "writes" seriously distorts "real" events at important moments, and Leonov is able to deepen the reader's understanding by pointing to Firsov's misinterpretations and falsifications.[30]

However, the problem of "point of view" in fiction is discussed in numerous studies of the novel: Boris Uspensky, for instance, goes into considerable detail, treating point of view as a compositional problem and analyzing it on the ideological, phraseological, psychological, and spatio-temporal planes.[31] He includes several varieties of what he calls the "sequential survey" (the movement of the narrator's viewpoint sequentially from one character to another) and cites illustrative passages from Gogol and Tolstoy.

But one really need not concentrate on the more subtle or rarer narrative techniques in order to find examples of defamiliarization: the prose fiction of the world is filled with an almost limitless variety of descriptions (with and without metaphor) of quite ordinary aspects of life—but descriptions in which the author has managed, in one way or another, to view something afresh. I mean such things as Tolstoy's defamiliarization of the "profession-of-love" topos in "Family Happiness":

> Then I looked at the ground and saw a little frog which gave a jump and then stood still in front of me, while its tiny shadow was reflected on the shining clay of the path.

30. Rufus W. Mathewson in the Introduction to *The Thief* (New York: Vintage, 1960), pp. x–xi.

31. Boris Uspensky, *A Poetics of Composition* (Berkeley: University of California Press, 1973), Chapters 1–5.

"You're not afraid of frogs, are you?" he asked.

I turned and looked at him. Just where we were there was a gap of one tree in the lime-avenue, and I could see his face clearly—it was so handsome and so happy!

Though he had spoken of my fear of frogs, I knew that he meant to say, "I love you, my dear one!"

Or the illuminating manner in which Djuna Barnes describes a bachelor's room: "There is a certain belligerence in a room in which a woman has never set foot; every object seems to be battling its own compression—and there is a metallic odour, as of beaten iron in a smithy."[32] Or the sudden appearance of a Russian woman in the northern snow country of Japan:

He thought he would never tire of looking at the autumn flowers that spread a blanket of silver up the side of the mountain.

A White-Russian woman, a peddlar, was sitting in the hallway when he came out of the bath. So you find them even in these mountains—He went for a closer look.[33]

Or the "new twist" given by Italo Svevo to the description of a husband, on a honeymoon, being dragged through the art galleries:

But even on our honeymoon I did not always find it easy to live up to the model I had put before myself. Augusta wanted to see everything just as if she had been on a voyage of instruction. It was not enough to have been to the Pitti Palace, one had to go through all those innumerable galleries, stopping at least a few minutes in front of each work of art. I refused to go beyond the first room, and saw nothing else; but it was sufficient fatigue inventing excuses for my laziness. I spent a whole morning in front of the portraits of the founders of the Medici family, and made the discovery that they were like Carnegie and Vanderbilt. How very strange! Yet they belonged to my own race. Augusta did not share my surprise. She knew what Yankees were, but she did not yet quite know what I was.[34]

And the list might go on and on.

32. Djuna Barnes, *Nightwood* (New York: New Directions, 1961), p. 79.

33. Yasunari Kawabata, *Snow Country*, translated by Edward Seidensticker (New York: Berkeley, 1960), p. 78.

34. Italo Svevo, *Confessions of Zeno*, translated by Beryl de Zoete (New York: Vintage, 1958), p. 143.

Another device, that of pretending an inability to describe this or that scene, has marked rhetorical associations (paraleipsis, preterition); though it was used frequently in the past, its employment is rare today. There is apt to be something mechanical and affected—if not something amateurish—about its use. We can see this clearly in a passage in an early work by Dostoevsky, *The Double* (1846), although the passage may be interpreted as an attempt at defamiliarizing what had already become a commonplace in novels—the description of a ball. Here Dostoevsky, intervening in the first person, wishes he were a Pushkin or a Homer or had the secret of an elevated and forceful style in order to attempt a description; but of course he does, while regretting his incompetence, manage to describe the ball by telling us what he *would* say.

Bathos, both intentional and unintentional, provides another area of defamiliarization (essentially because of the *para prosdokian* or "contrary-to-expectation" effect). Longinus used the word (meaning "profundity" or "height" in Greek) as a synonym for *hypsos* (sublimity), but it was Alexander Pope who, in his parody of Longinus, *Peri Bathous or Martinus Scriblerus His Treatise of the Art of Sinking in Poetry* (1728), gave the word its modern meaning. We tend, in this connection, to think primarily of poetry, but the device is also used—or occurs—in prose. There are numerous examples of bathos used for humorous or ironic effect in, say, the parodies of Sir Max Beerbohm (e.g., *Zuleika Dobson*), including the employment of *parenthyrson* (misplaced or affected, bathetic enthusiasm), and in the writings of parodists and satirists in the other literatures. Thus in *What the Nightingale Sang* the Russian humorist and satirist, Mikhail Zoschchenko, begins by exclaiming how the people of the future will laugh at our present problems and foibles. But then he supposes that the people of the future will very likely have their own problems: for instance, someone may be spat upon from a dirigible. Or in another short work he begins by recording Soviet accomplishments: trade is flourishing, construction is booming, mountains are being scaled, and citizens spend their time in a cultured manner—they bathe frequently, for instance (Zoschenko was expelled from the Union of Soviet Writers in 1946). There is also, I think, an intentional effect of bathos in Turgenev's *Fathers and Sons* in the references to Bazarov's dissection of frogs; and (unfortunately) an unintentional bathetic effect in Steinbeck's *The Grapes of Wrath* when Casy prays over Grampa Joad's body:

This ol' man jus' lived a life an' jus' died out of it. I don't know whether he was good or bad, but that don't matter much. He was alive, an' that's what matters. An' now he's dead, an' that don't matter. Heard a fella tell a poem one time, an' he says: "All that lives is holy." Got to thinkin', and purty soon it means more than the words say."

3

The transformation of characters in fiction is by its very name defamiliarizing. In this area I would include almost everything from, at one extreme, the changes or modifications described as taking place in fictional characters that we see in the more particular types of *Bildungs-* and *Enwicklungsromane* as well as the changes described in a large mass of fiction and ascribed to such things as the impact of love or other emotions or the influence of other external forces on a character; and, at the other extreme, the more physical manifestations in narratives of the supernatural and grotesque (the *versipellis*, werewolf, and vampire themes). The defamiliarizing effect is less noticeable, to be sure, in works belonging to the former extreme, although we can see it rather clearly in a novel such as Dostoevsky's *Crime and Punishment* (in the person of Raskolnikov[35]) and even more clearly in Tolstoy's *Resurrection* (in the character of the "repentant nobleman," Prince Nekhlyudov). In works at the other extreme, however, the defamiliarization or metamorphosis comes—as it was meant to—as a real "shock": Doctor Jekyll becoming Mr. Hyde, for instance, or Count Dracula becoming a bat. We rightly consider the great majority of fictional works at this extreme as representing a low order of literature; but we do not consider Kafka's *Metamorphosis* as such, because the metamorphosis is presented as a simple fact and *fait accompli*, so to speak, and the author does not concern himself at all with the etiology of the transformation. There is no science-fiction–like account of drugs or rays or operations, or no family curses or other supernatural intervention. Thus, from one point of view, Kafka's work is also a defamiliarization of the very old tradition of metamorphosis in literature.

35. See the article by Alfred Kuhn, "A Note on Raskol'nikov's Hats," *The Slavic and East European Journal* (Winter 1971): 425–32, where parallels are drawn between Raskolnikov's changing states of mind and his changes of headgear.

Also on a somewhat higher level than mere science fiction is Bulgakov's short novel, *The Heart of a Dog*. Here the device of metamorphosis (a dog is operated on and transformed into a leather-jacketed Soviet commissar-like type, spouting Soviet jargon) is used for satirical effect. The metamorphosis of sex is another variety that is encountered from time to time in literature—from ancient Greek times (Tiresias) to Gore Vidal. The type of defamiliarization referred to earlier in Tolstoy's *Family Happiness*, in which the author sees and describes the action from the woman's point of view, is also encountered occasionally; and the plots in many works of fiction—especially plays—have turned on men masquerading as women (Bradon Thomas' *Charley's Aunt*) or vice versa (Shakespeare's *As You Like It*). The androgyne (or gynander) theme—without the Platonic overtones—most notably attracted a number of minor writers during the period of decadence at the end of the preceding century.[36]

The theme of madness or incipient insanity has always had an attraction for romantic writers,[37] and the personality changes described as occurring in this connection often produce startling defamiliarization: witness the ending of Ibsen's *Ghosts*. In Russian literature down to the present many of the major romantic writers (not to mention minor figures) have handled this theme, and numerous parallels may be found in the other European literatures. Though Pushkin (who once prayed in a poem that he not lose his mind) tacks on at the end of *The Queen of Spades* the information that Hermann lost his mind and was now confined in an institution, his eighteenth-century classical predilections generally militated against any further dalliance with psychotic states in fiction. But Gogol has, for example, *The Diary of a Madman*, a brief account by a minor official, Poprishchin, who suffers from delusions and who eventually ends up in a madhouse. The defamiliarization here is largely due to the very strange "canine correspondence," a detail borrowed from E. T. A. Hoffmann. Concerning Gogol's story, Setchkarev writes:

> T█ development of the mental disturbance into delusions of grande█ as a consequence of an inferiority complex resulting from an unhapp█love affair is described with realistic detail and considerable empathy. However, the hero writes his memoirs himself, and, in ad-

36. See Ma▒o Praz, *The Romantic Agony* (New York: Meridian, 1956).

37. See Dm▒y Chizhevsky, *On Romanticism in Slavic Literatures* (The Hague: Mouton, 1▒7), Chapter IV.

dition, in the madhouse—a complete impossibility. The letters of the dogs are represented as really existing and their contents are so *normal* (in contrast with the memoirs themselves), that in spite of the precision and detail of the description, one constantly feels one-self in a fantastic and unreal atmosphere.[38]

The principal character in Dostoevsky's *The Double*, Golyadkin, is also taken away to an asylum. The eccentricity of Golyadkin's speech is almost pathologically distinctive:

> Jedes Wort verbessert er oder ersetzt es durch ein anderes, noch ehe der Satz zu Ende ist. Immer wieder schaltet er einschränkende oder beschwichtigende Redensarten ein; manchmal besteht seine Rede nur aus Redensarten wie: "Ich hoffe, Sie verstehen mich wohl; ich meine; das heisst; ich wollte nur sagen . . ." Es ist die Redeweise eines Aphatikers, eines Menschen mit krankhaften Redehemmungen.[39]

One of Chekhov's best-known stories is *Ward Number Six* in which the author, while commenting ironically on Tolstoy's doctrine of non-resistance to evil, defamiliarizes the madness theme by describing how a doctor in an asylum ends up by himself becoming an inmate of the asylum. Amongst Chekhov's contemporaries in the neoromantic "decadent" movement which began in the 1880s the "diary-of-a-mad-man" topic was especially popular—e.g., Bryusov's *Now When I Have Awakened* ("Notes of a Psychopath") and Bely's *Adam* ("Notes found in an insane asylum")—but these are very poor things and not worth discussing.

Conrad Aiken has an impressive short story, "Silent Snow, Secret Snow," concerned with the appearance of schizophrenia in a young boy, the onset being accompanied by a growing and secret preoccu-pation with snow and a gradual loss of contact with reality:

> It was even what pleased him, what rewarded him: the thing was his own, belonged to no one else. No one else knew about it, not even his mother and father. There, outside, were the bare cobbles; and here, inside, was the snow. Snow growing heavier each day, muffling the world, hiding the ugly, and deadening increasingly—above all—the steps of the postman.

38. Vsevolod Setchkarev, *Gogol,* translated by Robert Kramer (New York: New York University Press, 1965), p. 133.

39. N. S. Trubetzkoy, *Dostoevskij als Künstler* (The Hague: Mouton, 1964), p. 47.

The defamiliarization here involves not only the description of the changing appearance of the world as seen through the boy's eyes but also the fact that it is the dementia of a child and not of an adult that is the subject of the story. So far as young children are concerned, it has been traditional in literature to describe them as innocent, cute, inquisitive, naughty, or—at the most—cruel; to treat them as the victims of schizophrenia or to point out (and to emphasize the point), as Tolstoy does in *The Death of Ivan Ilych,* that they sometimes indulge in onanism as their fathers lie dying is to defamiliarize this tradition. This is also done by associating them in some way with the forces of evil, as Henry James does in *The Turn of the Screw:* here the author (according to H. P. Lovecraft)

> triumphs over his inevitable pomposity and prolixity sufficiently well to create a truly potent air of sinister menace; depicting the hideous influence of two dead and evil servants, Peter Quint and the governess, Miss Jessel, over a small boy and girl who had been under their care. James is perhaps too diffuse, too unctuously urbane, and too much addicted to subtleties of speech to realise fully all the wild and devastating horror in his situations; but for all that there is a rare and mounting tide of fright, culminating in the death of the little boy, which gives the novelette a permanent place in its special class.[40]

On the other hand, the marked preoccupation with cruelties inflicted on children that we find, for example, in Dickens and Dostoevsky is hardly defamiliarization; such authors only describe something that is more prevalent than most genteel folk care to admit. And, given our traditional views of children, it is a facile form of defamiliarization to write, as the Russian Futurist Mayakovsky does, "I love to watch children dying"; this has the shock effect of the kind of statements that some of the Decadents liked to make in public *pour épater le bourgeois* ("Have you tried children's brains lately?").

If writers have occasionally found it effective to defamiliarize our picture of children, they have also, throughout the history of literature and to a much greater extent, found it rewarding, for one reason or another, to defamiliarize women. This is particularly true in the West since the advent of Christianity and in the so-called Christian cultures. Here, for instance, is St. John Chrysostom:

40. H. P. Lovecraft, *Supernatural Horror in Literature* (New York: Dover, 1973), p. 70.

If you consider what is stored up inside those beautiful eyes, and that straight nose, and the mouth and the cheeks, you will affirm the well-shaped body to be nothing else than a whited sepulchre; the parts within are full of so much uncleanness. Moreover, when you see a rag with any of these things on it, such as phlegm, or spittle you cannot bear to touch it with even the tips of your fingers, nay you cannot even endure looking at it; and yet are you in a flutter of excitement about the storehouses and depositories of these things?[41]

There is a vehement malevolence here, as there is to only a slightly lesser degree in Swift (the narrator is among the Brobdingnags):

I must confess no object ever disgusted me so much as the sight of her monstrous breast, which I cannot tell you what to compare with, so as to give the curious reader an idea of its bulk, shape and colour. It stood prominent six foot, and could not be less than sixteen in circumference. The nipple was about half the bigness of my head, and the hue both of that and the dug so varified with spots, pimples and freckles, that nothing could appear more nauseous. . . . This made me reflect upon the fair skins of our English ladies, who appear so beautiful to us, only because they are of our own size, and their defects not to be seen but through a magnifying glass, where we find by experiment that the smoothest and whitest skins look rough and coarse, and ill coloured.

In *The English Rogue* (1665) Richard Head describes a visit to a bawdy-house run by "Mother Cresswell" and defamiliarizes the girls in culinary terms: "up came one of Venus her chief darlings. Excellent flesh! and she herself the cook that dressed it, spending most of her day-time about it, that she might with the better appetite be tasted at night."[42]

Schopenhauer's opinion of woman is well known: in a letter he once wrote: "Wait until you have reached my age and see what you will then think of these short-legged, long-torsoed, narrow-shouldered, broad-hipped, teat-bedecked creatures."[43]

And there is more than one kind of defamiliarization in that

41. Quoted in Katherine M. Rogers, *The Troublesome Helpmate: A History of Misogyny in Literature* (Seattle: University of Washington Press, 1966), p. 18.

42. Quoted in H. Greenwald and A. Krich, eds., *The Prostitute in Literature* (New York: Ballantine, 1960), p. 81.

43. Quoted in Karl Stern, *The Flight From Woman* (New York: Farrar, Straus & Giroux, 1965), p. 113.

strange work by Kierkegaard, *The Diary of a Seducer* (1849). Karl Stern writes:

> *The Diary of a Seducer* is a horrid book; there is no other word for it. There is a peculiar air of cold, diabolical cynicism about it. It could easily be, without changing a word, a chapter in Dostoievsky's *The Possessed*, right next to Stavrogin's confession. It belongs to those books that give you the sense of a haunting presence, and you are glad to put it aside once you are through. One finds it hard to believe that it comes, even as a fictitious story, from a soul as sensitive and gentle as Kierkegaard's.[44]

But there is a vast range of variety in the defamiliarization of women in literature, not all derogatory, to be sure; yet the varieties we find both in major writers (Lawrence, Faulkner) and on the lower levels of literature (in the kind of things treated, for example, by Praz in *The Romantic Agony*) or even in pornography are interesting from the technical and aesthetic as well as the sociological and psychological points of view.[45]

The traditional figure of the mother, with its almost sacrosanct associations, has tempted many writers to defamiliarize, from Euripides and his treatment of Medea to the present, when the cult of "momism" has frequently (especially in the works of Philip Wylie) received rather rough handling.[46] As for the figure of the mother-in-law, this has had, from the earliest times, pejorative associations, and the word for mother-in-law in many languages is practically synonymous with cruelty. Thus a writer may defamiliarize this image and tradition by portraying a mother-in-law as loving, kind, and gentle.

We frequently encounter in fiction the portrayal—and very often the defamiliarization—of figures from real life—e.g., the lampooning, in the form of Menippean satire, of the recently deceased Emperor Claudius in the *Apocolocyntosis* ("Pumpkinification"—a parody of "apotheosis") traditionally ascribed to Seneca the Philosopher. The historical figure of Marko Kraljević, who actually fought *for* the Turks in the fourteenth century, is portrayed in South Slavic and Bulgarian epic poetry as a Slavic hero fighting *against* the Turks. Or, in more recent times we have, for example, Tolstoy's idealization of General

---

44. *Ibid.*, p. 213.

45. See Peter Michelson, *The Aesthetics of Pornography* (New York: Herder & Herder, 1971). There are also many interesting aspects of defamiliarization in Jeannette Foster, *Sex Variant Women in Literature* (New York: Vantage, 1956).

46. See Rogers, *The Troublesome Helpmate*, Chapter VII.

Kutuzov and "deheroization" of Napoleon in *War and Peace,* or his treatment of Tsar Nicholas I in *Hadji Murat.* Gaining popularity today are novels which assume the guise of non-fiction, and much nonfiction that assumes the guise of novels. Especially noteworthy in this respect is such a work as E. L. Doctorow's *Ragtime,* in which there is a striking mingling of the real and the imaginary, in the sense that the lives of certain real-life figures of the past are intertwined with imaginary characters, and in which historical personages are treated as fictional characters. For instance, the Archduke Franz Ferdinand is driving through Germany and stops his car when he sees Houdini circling above in an aircraft; when Houdini lands, he is introduced to the Archduke who congratulates the magician as the inventor of the flying machine. In a review of this "novel," Jonathan Raban (defamiliarizing the language of novel criticism in terms of illicit relationships) writes the following:

> Exogamy is the most basic of all principles for maintaining vitality within the tribe, and the novel has been marrying-out for as long as it has been a distinct literary form. Nineteenth-century realism copulated fruitfully, and sometimes fatally, with social sciences: prose fiction was justified as "a valid mode of social research," a phrase which goes rather better in French than it does in English. More recently, a novel by Christine Brooke-Rose, *Thru,* climbed into bed with, and expired struggling in the arms of, structural linguistics. John Berger's *G* was full of bits of old art criticism which he had once published as essays in *New Society.* And so on.
>
> But the longest-lasting and most incestuous of the novel's many marriages and affairs has been with journalism. In Dickens, journalism and fiction lie uneasily side by side: *Martin Chuzzlewit,* for instance, is fiction proper for its first third, and savage journalism thereafter. Wells, fighting a losing battle in his correspondence with Henry James, tried to justify the novel as a form of journalism. In America, a whole school of novelists who had trained as newspapermen— Dreiser, Hemingway, Steinbeck, Farrell—treated the novel as if it were an on-the-spot report of imaginary events. The "New Journalism" of Tom Wolfe, Gay Talese, and Hunter Thompson has taken to treating real events with the verbal licence (though without the moral involvement) of fiction. More impressively, Norman Mailer found a latent novel plot in the actions of the undisguised characters who make up *The Armies of the Night.*[47]

47. *Encounter* (February 1976): 71. The reference to journalism suggests the names of Dostoevsky and Solzhenitsyn as well as a large bulk of Russian novelistic fiction; see D. S. Mirsky, *A History of Russian Literature* (New York: Knopf, 1949), p. 172.

A recent novel by Gore Vidal, *1876,* is also representative of this tendency to (as one review puts it) breathe "movement and laughter into the historical past" by stirring historical figures in a fictional sauce. Nor should we forget the novels of Alexander Solzhenitsyn—*The First Circle* or *August 1914,* for example—with their intermingling of the real and the imaginary. In this connection, one cannot help mentioning the fact that it is in official Soviet literature from the thirties on that we see what is perhaps the greatest assortment and most flagrant examples of the defamiliarization of real-life figures—such as Lenin and Stalin, Churchill and Roosevelt—or of other Americans; this is an accomplishment matched only by the now classical instances of the distortion of history that one finds in the Soviet Russian historians.[48]

4

It has occasionally been observed that the great writers have been satisfied with commonplace themes and that the significance of their art lies in the skillful manipulation of language; that the *fabula* or raw material of a work is secondary in importance to the linguistic treatment of this material. This seems to be true in some cases but is certainly not true of a very large body of prose and poetry in which the theme or subject-matter itself is some strange or unusual facet of reality or involves a view of reality seen from an eccentric vantage point. As examples of such defamiliarized content I would cite at random fictional works like Balzac's *Sarrasine,* Tynyanov's *Lieutenant Kije (Podporuchik Kizhe),* Yukio Mishima's *Onnagata,* Isaac Singer's *Blood,* Thomas Mann's *Der schwarze Schwan,* or Thornton Wilder's *The Bridge of San Luis Rey.*[49] If we move into the domain of the grotesque and supernatural, we have a vast body of prose fiction exemplified by such things as Quevedo's *Visita de los Chistes,* Hoffmann's *Der goldene Topf,* Gogol's *Midsummer Night,* Maupassant's *Le Horla,* Poe's *The Black Cat,* Meyrink's *Der Golem.*[50] On a some-

48. See C. E. Black, ed., *Rewriting Russian History: Soviet Interpretations of Russia's Past* (New York: Praeger, 1955).

49. On *Sarrasine,* see Roland Barthes' structuralist study, S/Z (New York: Hill & Wang, 1974). On Tynyanov's story, see above, Chapter III, note 26.

50. A number of the works cited here are discussed in Kayser's *The Grotesque in Art and Literature.* The references in Kayser to "estrangement" in connection with Poe and to the "alienation of familiar forms" in connection with Lewis Carroll are noteworthy. Kayser also quotes Heine on the comparative

what lower level is the equally vast body of gothic novels and *Schauerliteratur,* including many of the works discussed briefly but deftly in H. P. Lovecraft's *Supernatural Horror in Literature* (e.g., Arthur Machen's *The Great God Pan,* F. Marion Crawford's *The Upper Berth,* Leonard Cline's *The Dark Chamber*), as well as innumerable works of science fiction. And I think we should include here also the Surrealist novel.[51]

On balance, however, it appears that the works of those writers who, without defamiliarizing their language (in the sense discussed above, p. 11), utilize some unusual, strange, esoteric, or grotesque situation as their *fabula,* suffer in stature when a "unity of effect" is sought that relies upon defamiliarization alone (in the sense that detective stories and pornographic works, for example, rely upon mystification and excitement alone). This is especially true of short works. On the other hand, short-story writers who avoid defamiliarization and who prefer the description of "simple folk" and everyday, ordinary life situations also run the risk of producing banal effects. I think this is true of, say, a great number of Italian short stories—in the manner of Giorgieri-Contri's *The Man's Heart,* for example. We seem to feel that there is somewhere a middle ground, when the writer who employs an eccentric vision or even bizarre situations and effects is still able to inject, verbally and conceptually, an element of the "concrete universal," as, for example, Gogol manages somehow to do in *The Overcoat.* There have been numerous successful attempts to explain the effects of this and similar works, and some brave attempts to explain *how* these effects are gained (there is even a study by the Russian Formalist, Boris Eykhenbaum, entitled "How Gogol's *The Overcoat* Was Made"), but none of these are satisfactory. Here, for example, is what Vladimir Nabokov writes of Gogol's famous story:

> Great literature skirts the irrational. *Hamlet* is the wild dream of a neurotic scholar. Gogol's *The Overcoat* is a grotesque and grim nightmare making black holes in the dim pattern of life . . . [the

---

scarcity of good tales of horror in French literature (p. 82). Cf. E. M. Cioran: "The sublime, the horrible, blasphemy or cry are approached by French only to be denatured in rhetoric," quoted in Claude Mauriac, *The New Literature* (New York: Braziller, 1959), p. 214.

51. See Kingsley Amis, *New Maps of Hell* (New York: Ballantine, 1960), and J. H. Matthews, *Surrealism and the Novel* (Ann Arbor: University of Michigan Press, 1966).

intelligent reader] will find in *The Overcoat* shadows linking our state
of existence to those other states and modes which we dimly appre-
hend in our rare moments of irrational perception.[52]

This is delightful and perhaps the best one can do in suggesting what
Gogol is about; yet one cannot help but hope that linguistic, structuralist, and stylistic studies beyond the "intersentence" stage may possibly tell us even more.[53]

Even if we leave aside significant and major works of fiction in
which there is gross defamiliarization (i.e., fiction in the manner of
Kafka or Mann's *Dr. Faustus*,[54] utopian and dystopian novels, surrealist novels, etc.), we still find that the authors of major realistic
novels of the past and present have very often been strongly tempted
to introduce defamiliarizing incidents and details. These inserts vary
from manifestly "tall story" passages, such as the one in Rabelais concerning words frozen in winter that "thaw" and are heard in the
spring,[55] to *incredibilia* introduced in the guise of dreams and hallu-
cinations (the dialogue between Ivan and the Devil in *The Brothers
Karamazov*) or the retelling of ancient legends in an "updated" or
modernized version (e.g., the "Traitor Prince" chapter in Solzhenitsyn's *The First Circle*) or the use of ancient myth as a structural basis
(as in *Ulysses* or Sartre's *Les Mouches*). I would also include here
such things as the passing reference, in Tolstoy's *Resurrection*, to
homosexual marriages, the "spontaneous combustion" of human beings
(in Gogol and Dickens), the chromatic treatment of Russian phonol-
ogy and the crescent revolver in the first chapter of Nabokov's *The
Gift*.

Perhaps it is appropriate to mention here a particular type of
narrative defamiliarization which occurs in many literatures but which
has come to be called in Russian literature Aesopian (or Aesopic)
language. This refers to the use of what appears to be a politically or

52. *Nikolai Gogol* (New York: New Directions, 1944), pp. 140 and 145.

53. See the long bibliographical note on such studies at the end of Nils Erik
Enkvist's paper, "On the Place of Style in Some Linguistic Theories," in *Literary
Style*, edited by Seymour Chatman (New York: Oxford University Press, 1971),
p. 61.

54. See Kayser's comments on *Dr. Faustus* in *The Grotesque in Art and
Literature*, Chapter V, section 4.

55. See above, Chapter III, note 57. The original form of this story occurs
in Antiphanes of Berge's *Apista*. In Greek there is a verb, *bergaizein*, which
means "to lie unblushingly." See W. W. Tarn, *Hellenistic Civilisation* (Cleveland:
Meridian, 1961), p. 291.

otherwise innocent language in a piece of fiction or non-fiction that is, however, a cleverly allusive and camouflaged satire or commentary. The term in Russian usage also connotes the use of such a language, often long-winded, circuitous, and allegorical, especially contrived to slip illicit criticism or oppositional political discussion past the censor. There are many examples of Aesopian language in the writings of the Russian satirist, Saltykov-Shchedrin, who in fact first introduced the phrase, and many more in the works of both pre- and post-revolutionary Russian writers, most notably in the fiction of Mikhail Zoshchenko and Mikhail Bulgakov. For example, the latter has a story entitled "The Fatal Eggs" in which a ray, developed by Soviet scientists, is used to accelerate the hatching and growth of eggs. But, through an error, reptilian eggs are supplied for the pilot experiments instead of chicken eggs; and the monsters which result ravage the countryside until they are killed by a frost.[56] The story may easily be read (and was so read by Soviet critics) as an attack, under the guise of science fiction, on state interference both in scientific experimentation and poultry breeding. But the term "Aesopian language" may readily be applied (without, however, the connotations of circumventing censorship) to such notable works of satire as Swift's *Gulliver's Travels,* Montesquieu's *Persian Letters,* Orwell's *Animal Farm,* or Evelyn Waugh's *The Loved One.*

5

Another rather important area of defamiliarization in prose fiction, especially in connection with the novel, is the defamiliarization of traditions and conventions, several instances of which have already been cited. I would include here such significant and well-known examples as Cervantes' defamiliarization (or burlesque) of the romances of chivalry or Fielding's defamiliarization of the sentimental tradition as represented by the novels of Samuel Richardson, as well as many other examples of deviations or divergences, in form and language,[57] from accepted conventions: the important role, for in-

56. The events of Bulgakov's story seem to have been reported as true by a New York newspaper in the twenties. See Bulgakov's *Diaboliad and Other Stories,* edited by E. and C. Proffer (Bloomington: Indiana University Press, 1972), p. 48.

57. The late Leo Spitzer was especially interested in linguistic features which deviated from the norm. See above, p. 41, on *Differenzqualität;* also David Lodge, *Language of Fiction* (New York: Columbia University Press, 1967), Chapter II.

stance, that Richardson's novels played, along with their striking emphasis on domestic details, in establishing a new linguistic sensitivity and the adjustment of the language of the novel to a new feminine code[58]; or the shift (to some extent, at least, under the influence of Dostoevsky's novels) from the Spanish woman as the typical *femme fatale* to the Russian woman ("It was Mérimée who localized in Spain the type of the Fatal Woman which towards the end of the century came to be placed more generally in Russia"[59]); or Jane Austen's influence in delimiting the scope and size of—and, in this sense, defamiliarizing—the usual three-volume English novel.

We encounter further instances of defamiliarization—in the form of innovations—amongst the many claims made by and in behalf of certain writers (or literatures) for having been the first to do this or that: thus Quintilian was proud to claim *satura tota nostra est;* Hoffmann is credited with having introduced the city of Berlin into German literature; and Marinetti boasted (ignoring the priority of D'Annunzio) of having been the first to introduce the "beauty of speed" into literature.[60] Of such claims asserted throughout the histories of all the major literatures, some have been substantiated and are valid, while others are disputed; and they vary from quite important and influential "firsts" to rather insignificant ones (the Russian poet Baratynsky, for example, claimed that he first used the conjunction *odnako*, "however," in Russian poetry). And they have a long history: the Athenian tragedian Phrynichus wrote a tragedy on a theme not associated with the legends of Dionysus and the audience, we are told, noting the innovation, asked, "What have these matters to do with Dionysus?"[61]

Discussions of "interior monologue" and "stream of conscious-

58. Ian Watt uses the term "decarnalisation" in connection with Richardson's achievements; see *The Rise of the Novel* (Berkeley: University of California Press, 1967), Chapter V. Watt also quotes Diderot's remark to the effect that Richardson's works of fiction required a new term, something other than *romans* (p. 299).

59. Mario Praz, *The Romantic Agony*, p. 197. See also pp. 322 ff. and 336 ff. for numerous examples of Russian women in fiction. There is another amazing group of Russian women cited in Jeannette Foster's study (see above, note 45). On a higher level we have a good example of the Russian woman in Madame Chauchat in Mann's *The Magic Mountain*.

60. Renato Poggioli, *The Theory of the Avant-Garde* (New York: Harper & Row, 1971), p. 29.

61. Plutarch, *Symposiaca*, 615A, quoted in Gilbert Norwood, *Greek Tragedy* (New York: Hill & Wang, n.d., p. 2). Hence the Greek word *aprosdionyson* = *mal à propos.*

ness," the stylistic devices which these terms stand for being frequently employed in (especially modern) fiction, are very often concerned with terminological priorities. Was the Russian critic Nikolay Cherny-shevsky the first to use the former phrase (*vnutrennij monolog*) in his 1856 article on Tolstoy or is it fairer to assign the credit to Edouard Dujardin, who made extensive use of the term but at a later date? Or does the credit rather go to Valéry Larbaud (to whom Dujardin him-self attributed priority) or to Victor Egger, who published in 1881 a scholarly treatise entitled *La parole intérieure?*[62] So far as the relations between the method of interior monologue and defamiliarization are concerned, however, this device, though not so syntactically unusual as most "stream of consciousness" passages are apt to be, is significant; and, in the sense that such a descriptive device causes us to see some phenomena anew and in a fresh light, it is defamiliarizing. Cherny-shevsky writes the following on Tolstoy's use of interior monologue:

> Monologues almost invariably differ from dialogues only ex-ternally even if they contain more than simple anatomizing of a stable feeling: Hamlet seems to be divided into two and to argue with him-self in his famous meditations; his monologues really belong to the same sort of scene as that between Faust and Mephistopheles or the Marquis Posa's arguments with Don Carlos. The particularity of Count Tolstoy's talent consists in that he does not limit himself to depicting the results of the psychic process. The process itself in-terests him, and Count Tolstoy masterfully depicts the evanescent manifestations of that inner life that replace each other extremely rapidly and with an inexhaustible variety. There are painters who are noted for their art of capturing the flickering reflection of a ray on the quickly rolling waves, the shimmer of light on rustling leaves, its cast on the changeable outlines of clouds. . . . Count Tolstoy does some-thing similar in respect to the mysterious movements of psychic life.[63]

But Chernyshevsky claims that it was Lermontov who, more than any other Russian prose writer, developed this device; this is an important point, since we now credit Lermontov with having pioneered the Russian psychological novel, particularly in the "Princess Mary" sec-

62. Kumar, *Bergson and the Stream of Consciousness Novel*, p. 7, blithely gives priority to Egger for the term *monologue intérieur*. On Chernyshevsky, see Gleb Struve, "*Monologue intérieur:* The Origins of the Formula and the First Statement of its Possibilities," *PMLA* 69 (1954): 1101–11.

63. Translated by Ralph Matlaw in *Belinsky, Chernyshevsky and Dobrolyu-bov* (New York: Dutton, 1962), pp. 100–101.

tion of *A Hero of Our Time*.[64] In an article on interior monologue in Mikhail Sholokhov's *Virgin Soil Upturned* (1931), Gunter Schaarschmidt clearly points out the defamiliarizing effect of this device:

> It may be assumed that the linguistic structure of IM [interior monologue] will be very close to, perhaps even identical with, that of dialogue in a literary text. The main difference between the two can be seen to lie in their function and semantic features. Not being determined for an auditor, IM is non-communicative and inward-directed, and its semantic information is largely redundant. This feature explains its linguistic structure and external functioning which are in striking contrast with the underlying structure of the narrative. IM can thus be conceived of as an aesthetic device par excellence in the sense of Wittgenstein's formula: "All that aesthetics does is 'to draw your attention to a thing,' to 'place things side by side.'"[65]

Though most often mentioned in connection with the major fiction of writers like Joyce, Proust, Dorothy Richardson, and Virginia Woolf, the device of interior monologue (of whatever variety and by whatever name we call it—*erlebte Rede, nesobstvenno-prjamaja rech', style indirect libre*, etc.) is a notable feature of much modern fiction in other literatures—e.g., Italo Svevo's *La Coscienza di Zeno*, the works of Broch and Döblin, the prose of Bely, etc. But the "stream of consciousness" technique (it was William James who first used the metaphor in 1890), if we distinguish it clearly from interior monologue (with which it is sometimes identical), usually has a more manifest defamiliarizing effect: the familiar syntax of narrative, descriptive prose is made strange through the employment of "imitative form." That is to say, a wide assortment of verbal and syntactical devices (including anacoluthon and parataxis) is used to suggest the uninhibited flux and flow of perceptions and thoughts in a character's mind, as illustrated by a brief excerpt from what is perhaps the most famous example in modern literature, Mrs. Bloom's *film de conscience* in *Ulysses*:

64. See John Mersereau, *Mikhail Lermontov* (Carbondale: Southern Illinois University Press, 1962), p. 122.

65. Gunter Schaarschmidt, "Interior Monologue in Sholokhov's *Podnjataja celina*," *The Slavic and East European Journal* (Fall 1967): 259. Schaarschmidt gives some interesting details on the changing views of Soviet critics concerning interior monologue.

> . . . she gave me the Moonstone to read that was the first I read of
> Wilkie Collins East Lynne I read and the shadow of Ashlydyat Mrs
> Henry Wood Dunbar by that other woman I lent him afterwards with
> Mulveys photo in it so as he see I wasnt without and Lord Lytton
> Eugene Aram Molly bawn she gave me by Mrs Hungerford on account
> of the name I don't like books with a Molly in them. . . .

There are many similar passages, however, in other writers and in
other literatures, including the less familiar ones—in the Argentinian
Julio Cortázar's *Rayuela* (1963), for example, or the Hungarian Magda
Szabó's *Az Oz* (*The Fawn*, 1962)—some such passages being less and
some more radically defamiliarized than others.

A similar practice occurs in prose narratives which do not purport
to reflect or imitate the stream of thoughts within a specific character's
consciousness but which rather are themselves a defamiliarized vision
of reality as seen through the consciousness of the writer. I refer here
not to such "classical" instances of defamiliarization (in the Chizhev-
skian "negative allegory" sense) as those in Tolstoy and the other
writers mentioned at the beginning of Chapter I, but rather to works
of prose fiction in which the writers, affiliated perhaps with futurist,
expressionist, surrealist and other avant-garde movements, give us an
impressionistic, often radically disjunct and fragmented, and occasionally typographically patterned prose. But the varieties encountered
may vary from the quaint "newsreel" and "camera eye" effects in Dos
Passos and the cinema-inspired montage techniques in other writers,
to the more extreme—but comprehensible—forms we find, for instance,
in Goytisolo:

> . . . muy fino el tipo, así dientefrío y tó, con su bigotico así ensima
> de su jeta gaita, too decolorío el blanco, así que viene y me dise que
> no, que no se debe, asimimmo, que no se debe desil luse, dise, posque
> eso quiere desil que yostoy hablando de la lujelétrica y que lo que
> tengo que desil, dise él, e. ej. . . .[66]

Beyond this, there is the *outré* "cut-up" style of William Burroughs
and other similar experiments (including "reified language"[67]); and,

66. *Reivindicación del Conde don Julian* (Mexico City: Joaquín Mortiz,
1970), p. 195.

67. See, e.g., *Experiments in Prose*, edited by Eugene Wildman (Chicago:
Swallow Press, 1969), p. 122 ff.

beyond this, the relinquishing of verbal language altogether in the manner of Christian Morgenstern's *Des Fisches Nachtgesang* (consisting of macrons and breves).

The differences between, on the one hand, the appearance of a typical passage of avant-garde prose with its profusion of inconcinnities, juxtapositions, ellipses, distortions and numerous other defamiliarizing devices and, on the other, the appearance of some more-or-less conventional, "correctly"—even exquisitely—ordered realistic passage of prose fiction (from, say, Flaubert's *Madame Bovary*) are as striking as the comparable differences that have been noted in the other arts during, especially, the last century. One of the features of avant-garde painting (and we include here the works of the Impressionists who, to be sure, hardly defamiliarized reality to the extent of their non-figurative successors) that was particularly irritating to the critics and the academic establishment (not to mention the public) was what clearly appeared to be the "unfinished" aspect of the new canvases: they no longer had the familiar *fini* quality or the *facture* of traditional representational art. Rather one's attention was attracted more and more, as the movements proliferated, to the surface of the painting, to the *matière* itself. The public, most critics, and many painters saw the changes as a threat to the traditional art of illusion and to the venerated principle of the transparency of art. Ingres, for example, wrote: "The brushstroke, as accomplished as it may be, should not be visible: otherwise it prevents the illusion, immobilizes everything. Instead of the object represented, it calls attention to the process: instead of the thought, it betrays the hand."[68] Ruskin, however, saw that there was in fact a relationship between "realism" and the concept of the artificiality of the work of art:

> So that although the perfection of art will always consist in the utmost *acceptable* completion, yet, as every added idea will increase the difficulty of apprehension, and every added touch advance the dangerous realism which makes the imagination languid, the difference between a noble and ignoble painter is in nothing more sharply defined than in this,—that the first wishes to put into his work as much truth as possible, and yet to keep it looking *un*-real; the second wishes to get through his work lazily, with as little truth as possible, and yet to make it look real.[69]

68. Quoted by Charles Rosen and Henri Zerner in "The Revival of Official Art," *The New York Review of Books* (March 18, 1976): 36.
69. *Ibid.*

But it was not only the apparent disparagement and upsetting of the view of the "painting as window" that disturbed viewers and critics; the content itself of avant-garde art was in many cases even more disturbing to genteel hearts. What Herbert Read wrote of Expressionism not too long ago in our own enlightened age echoes many similar remarks made earlier, albeit in much more unpleasant terms, concerning other movements in the arts: "Expressionism must not be confused with realism. Realism is sober, factual, precise; expressionism is frenzied, intense, fantastic. Its purpose is not to present, but to move, to give the observer an emotional shock."[70]

Avant-garde criticism, too, turned in new directions and defamiliarized in several ways the traditional functions and modes of critical language and theory. As Poggioli remarks, for example, American New Criticism, "in its struggle against the commonplaces of traditional aesthetics, does not restrict itself to refuting them simply as errors but condemns them as fallacies and seals them as heresies."[71] And the same author expatiates at length on modern criticism that often seems more recondite and occult than the creative works themselves; he speaks of critical hermeticism, the "Byzantinism" of contemporary literary journalism, and the "mandarins of criticism" whose writings veil rather than elucidate the literature under discussion.

6

The term "idiolect" (occasionally misspelled "ideolect") has come to be used in two somewhat different—but etymologically related— meanings: occasionally it refers to the language of an individual within a larger language community or an individual style or idiom.[72] More often it means the employment in literature (as a characterizing device) of the lexicon, grammar, syntax, and pronunciation peculiar to a certain group, profession or stratum of society. In this latter sense the word is frequently used in studies of Russian literature to translate the Russian term *skaz*, sometimes rendered oral "yarn" or dialect-

70. Herbert Read, *Art and Alienation: the Role of the Artist in Society* (New York: Horizon, 1967), p. 60. Read is not using "alienation" in the Shklovskian sense of *ostranenie* nor does he refer to Shklovsky and defamiliarization.

71. Renato Poggioli, *The Theory of the Avant-Garde*, p. 33. See his Chapter 8 on "Avant-Garde Criticism." See also above, p. 9.

72. E.g., by Harry Levin in "The American Voice in English Poetry," in *Refractions* (New York: Oxford University Press, 1968), p. 182.

story technique.[73] So far as defamiliarization is concerned, idiolect represents a borderline situation: to supplement fictional characterization with specific and recognizable linguistic features is, after all, a way of familiarizing the reader even more intimately with a character and adding verisimilitude to the narrative. But there seems little doubt that in many cases (other, that is, than passages in which a broad, approximate, and often crude imitation of dialect or cant is employed) something more is involved and that we have in such instances various forms of what can in fact be called defamiliarization. That is to say, idiolect provides the writer with a means of intensifying the individuality of a character, of describing the character as a representative of a certain calling or social class from a different and unconventional point of view, of enriching and varying the lexical and stylistic spectrum of his narrative, and—last but not least—of displaying his erudition and virtuosity. For example, Spitzer points out several instances of what he calls "linguistic perspectivism" in *Don Quijote*. He cites the Spanish narrative of the Captive (I, 37 ff.), embellished with words from Arabic and Turkish, thus "offering a linguistic mosaic that adds to the local color of his story," and shows how Cervantes effectively contrasts in the idiolect passage the Arabic words, which are almost always related to religious—specifically Christian—matters, with the Turkish words which are purely descriptive and without transcendental connotations.[74]

Other examples are found in Pérez Galdós' *Aita Tettauen* (in *Episodios Nacionales*) in which the author uses Sephardic words and phrases, which he went to considerable length to research (in, for instance, the anonymous *Orden de Ros Asanah y Kypur*), to specify more accurately the speech of his Sephardic characters.[75] The defamiliarizing effect of the idiolect passages in the Spanish text is quite apparent. The MHG passages in Mann's *Doktor Faustus* are familiar examples of idiolect and I think we may also include the French ("language of love") passages in the conversations between Castorp and Mme Chauchat in the same author's *Der Zauberberg*. In Russian literature the name of Nikolay Leskov (d. 1895) is most frequently associated with *skaz* (see Chapter III, note 8), although the speech

73. See the note in Uspensky, *A Poetics of Composition*, p. 19, on *skaz*. Cf. also Jameson, *The Prison-House of Language*, pp. 83–84.

74. "Linguistic Perspectivism in the *Don Quijote*," in *Linguistics and Literary History*, p. 63.

75. See Vernon Chamberlin, "Galdós' Sephardic Types," *Symposium* 17 (1963): 85–99.

characterization or idiolect in Dostoevsky is often noted and discussed. There is an extensive lexicon of *blatnoj jazyk* (*Gaunersprache* or thieves' cant) in Leonov's novel *Vor* (*The Thief*) and another Soviet writer, P. Bazhov, is known for his *skaz* stories (in the collection *Malakhitovaja shkatulka*) which use the language and idiom of the Ural mine and metallurgical workers. The language of Raymond Queneau's novels is frequently idiolectic. Thus the first word in his novel *Zazie* is "Doukipudonktan" ("D'où qu'ils puent donc tant?"), rendered "Howcanaystinkso" in an English version. The idiolect is especially characteristic of the "philosophical" passages in all his novels where one can find a sort of phonetic transcription of the French colloquial language and argot. Queneau has evinced a marked interest in certain statements that Vendryès made in *Language*, most notably the comparison drawn there between the syntax of spoken French and that of certain American Indian languages, e.g., Chinook. Vivian Mercier writes the following concerning this:

> Vendryès pointed out that the syntax of spoken French often resembles that of certain American-Indian languages: the first part of the sentence "contains all the grammatical indications (that is to say, the 'morphemes') and the second all the concrete data (the 'semantemes')." Thus, in spoken French one doesn't say, "Your cousin hasn't yet traveled in Africa" but "She hasn't yet there traveled, your cousin, in Africa." The opening sentence of *Le Dimanche de la vie* could be translated literally: "He didn't suspect that every time he passed in front of her store, she was watching him, the storekeeper the soldier Brû." Because this construction sounds so unfamiliar in English, an intelligent translator might not render it literally, but in French it manages to be both familiar and unfamiliar—familiar to the ear, unfamiliar to the eye.[76]

The difference between simple "dialect stories" and idiolect as stylization is further made clear, for example, in Maurice Nadeau's comments on Céline:

> Céline is too good a writer to be satisfied with a "phonographic" language. He submits the spoken language as such to a treatment that breaks it up, sweeps away its fossilized associations and clichés,

76. Mercier, *The New Novel*, p. 52. See also her comments on Robert Pinget, p. 363 ff.

and when he does not find a phrase ready-made he invents one. He is not a mouthpiece of the man in the street, but Louis-Ferdinand Céline, who follows his own rhythm.[77]

And Richard Bridgman, discussing the "colloquial style" in Stephen Crane and demonstrating how in *Maggie* the author subjects a speech to three degrees of stylization, adds: "Crane's technical subtlety demonstrates the heightened awareness achieved at the end of the century, not only of the psychological nuances of the situation being described, but also of the technical means by which these nuances might be reproduced."[78]

Tolstoy, like many other writers, was wont to supplement his lexicon with neologistic onomatopoetic words and phrases, such as *ozhig-zhig-zhig* (the sound of a sword being sharpened); but later novelists have gone further and have strongly colored their style with idiosyncratic forms—some even going so far as to develop a kind of paralanguage (e.g., the *glíglico* of Julio Cortázar). Writers may develop an idiolect by drawing almost solely on their imaginations or they may exploit the resources of already available patois and jargons: thus in his *La Vie généreuse des Gueux, Mercelots at Boesmiens* (1596?)—one of the progenitors of picaresque literature in France—Jean Jullieron ("Pechon de Ruby") made use of an extensive vocabulary of *bleschien* or *blesche,* a pedlars' and thieves' argot.[79] Italian writers have, for example, *baccaglio* to draw upon, German writers *Rotwelsch,* and Russian writers the *blatnoj jazyk* (referred to above) or, in the case of Solzhenitsyn, the rather amazing language of the Soviet prison camps.[80] There is also a distinct type of idiolect used by writers to characterize more accurately and with technical verisimilitude the language of fictional lawyers, physicians, politicians or—as in the case of Gayev in Chekhov's *The Cherry Orchard*—a billiard player.[81]

77. Nadeau, *The French Novel Since the War,* p. 44.

78. Richard Bridgman, *The Colloquial Style in America* (New York: Oxford University Press, 1968), p. 52.

79. See Jean-Paul Clébert, *The Gypsies* (Harmondsworth: Penguin, 1967), p. 63.

80. The works of Solzhenitsyn served as the source for many of the entries in M. Galler and H. Marquess, *Soviet Prison Camp Speech: A Survivor's Glossary* (Madison: University of Wisconsin Press, 1972).

81. Chekhov had played billiards but had never mastered the jargon: he asked Alexander Vishnevsky to listen to people playing the game and to note down as many terms as possible. On idiolect in Chekhov; see Thomas Winner, *Chekhov and His Prose* (New York: Holt, Rinehart and Winston, 1966) and the literature cited in note 13, p. 246.

I think we may also consider as a special type of idiolect those passages in texts which rely, quite forthrightly if occasionally in a subtle fashion, on the effect or symbolism of quotations. We see this, for instance, throughout Mann's *Doktor Faustus*, but especially in the brothel scene which was taken almost verbatim from Deussen's *Recollections of Nietzsche*. Commenting on this aspect of Mann's novel, Erich Heller writers:

> In transferring the encounter with the prostitute from Nietzsche's life to Leverkühn's, Thomas Mann not only points once again to the relatedness of his composer to that philosopher, but also, by translating Deussen's report about Nietzsche into Leverkühn's parodistic style, sounds one of the most intriguing themes of the book: for Adrian adopts, for the purpose of this letter, the German of the sixteenth century, the Lutheran Devil's own language.[82]

And the French novelist Michel Butor has himself remarked that the surprisingly large number of quotations in his *Degrés* gives body and stylistic color to what might otherwise have been too "monochromatic" a text.[83]

7

Devices of defamiliarization in drama and the theater are, by the very nature of the medium, frequent and apparent. Although what has been said earlier about various devices in prose fiction and poetry applies as well, in many cases, to certain dramatic works, I should like now to consider a number of instances of more specifically dramatic defamiliarization. Just above we cited Plutarch's story about Phrynichus' tragedy and the question it elicited from the Athenian audience; other technical innovations in the ancient Greek theater were also defamiliarizing: the introduction of a second actor by Aeschylus and of a third by Sophocles, the introduction of scene painting by the

82. Eric Heller, *Thomas Mann: The Ironic German* (Cleveland: Meridian Books, 1961), p. 258.

83. See Mercier, *The New Novel*, p. 260 ff. On the use of quotations in narratives, see Hermann Meyer, *Das Zitat in der Erzählkunst* (Stuttgart, 1962); English version by T. and J. Ziolkowski, *The Poetics of Quotation* (Princeton: Princeton University Press, 1968). See also William York Tindall, *The Literary Symbol* (Bloomington: Indiana University Press, 1960), pp. 191 ff.

latter, the realism, feminist leanings, and defiance of the conventions of stage costume by Euripides, the reduction of the choral songs to mere musical interludes in post-Euripidean tragedy, etc. In the sea-changes that occurred in drama with Seneca and his notorious but influential theater (a strange product of Roman rhetoric and Stoicism), in the insoluble conflict that was inherent and manifest—but seldom faced up to—in attempts to combine the notions of tragedy and Christianity, and in the rise of the neoclassical practice of expressing everything, including the most violent emotions, in controlled rhetorical forms— in all these we see various modes of defamiliarization. But we can discern even more clearly the familiar made strange in the often artificial application, in dramatic works of the seventeenth century and thereafter, of certain ancient devices—e.g., the use of *antilabē* (the division of an iambic recitative line between two or more persons), the introduction of "recognition" (*anagnorisis*) scenes, the continued employment of a climactic peripety-element, and the use of *periaktoi* and other machines, supplemented by such modern innovations as the "lycopodium flask."[84]

With the appearance of bourgeois drama as represented, say, by Lessing's *Miss Sara Sampson* and *Minna von Barnhelm* and, later, by Ibsen's plays, there was a shift of accent away from the great and the public to the domestic and the private and a concomitant defamiliarization of what had once been conceived of as tragic. George Steiner writes:

> Where the causes of disaster are temporal, where the conflict can be resolved through technical or social means, we may have serious drama, but not tragedy. More pliant divorce laws could not alter the fate of Agamemnon; social psychiatry is no answer to *Oedipus*. But saner economic relations or better plumbing can resolve some of the grave crises in the dramas of Ibsen.[85]

And certainly the French have, with few exceptions, seen in Shakespeare a defamiliarization—repugnant, in this case—of the familiar proprieties and *bienséances* of the neoclassical stage. It was likewise

---

84. There is a good example of *antilabē* in the Russian classic, Griboedov's *Gore ot uma*, Act I, line 153. Chekhov was tempted to retain a recognition scene in *The Sea Gull* but eventually cut it out; he retained marked peripeties in his four major plays, however. See David Magarshack, *Chekhov the Dramatist* (New York: Hill & Wang, 1960), pp. 189–93, 207, 235, 276.

85. George Steiner, *The Death of Tragedy* (New York: Knopf, 1961), p. 8.

the violation of these conventions (Hugo's use, for instance, of *enjambement*) that caused the furor surrounding the premiere of *Hernani* in 1830. How strange, too, must have seemed the opening line of Hugo's *Cromwell*, "Demain, vingt-cinq juin mil six cent cinquante-sept," against the background of pseudoclassicism and the lofty associations of the *alexandrin*, used here merely to express a precise chronological datum.

The traditional "action" of drama was itself defamiliarized with the development of a new markedly static theater, exemplified in Russia by the plays of Chekhov (who had a notable forerunner in Turgenev). The static quality of Chekhov's plays, the frequency of the sometimes almost embarrassing pauses, and the "phatic" dialogue were later carried to extremes in the works of Beckett and avant-garde theater in France. Concerning Beckett's *Waiting for Godot*, Pronko writes:

> Beckett's genius has been to present this so-called static play, where "nothing happens" in such a way that it sustains our interest from one end to the other. When destructive critics claim that absolutely nothing happens in this play, we might answer, says the brilliant young Spanish playwright Alfonso Sastre, "Does this seem no small achievement to you? This is precisely the fascinating thing about *Waiting for Godot:* nothing happens. It is, in this sense, a lucid testimony of nothingness. And it cannot be denied that, while many dramas of intrigue in which a great deal happens leave us cold, this 'nothing happening' of *Godot* keeps us in suspense."[86]

The fame of Chekhov is closely associated with the accomplishments of the Moscow Art Theater and the director, Konstantin Stanislavsky. The latter's emphasis on emotional authenticity and his theory of *perezhivanie* ("reliving" a part), his scrupulous attention to realistic details in stage settings and stage business (although this often ran counter to Chekhov's intentions), and his advocacy of "ensemble" acting—all, in their separate ways, had a defamiliarizing and lasting effect on theatrical practice. It might be added here that great actors may also defamiliarize: here, for example, is what Marc Slonim writes of Mikhail Chekhov's performance (under Stanislavsky's direction) as Khlestakov in Gogol's *The Inspector General:*

86. Leonard C. Pronko, *Avant-Garde: the Experimental Theater in France* (Berkeley: University of California Press, 1964), p. 30.

The Inspector General was staged by Stanislavsky as a satire without any stress on a definite historical period, and Chekhov used this general framework to create of Khlestakov a symbol of emptiness and evil, an embodiment of that very "void" Gogol always identified with the Devil. It was a grotesque acted with an open use of hyperbole in gestures and intonations but with such subtle shadings and such psychological refinement that the effect of the performance was stunning. Chekhov made Khlestakov frightening, abnormal, and universal. The spiritual tension and depth of this interpretation were carried over to the spectators with such hypnotic power that they remained spellbound and shivering. On opening night Vakhtangov whispered in amazement: "And this is the same man we meet every day?"[87]

Though we can see a certain amount of defamiliarization in the plays of Pinero (in the sense that *The Second Mrs. Tanqueray*, for example, suggested to the average playgoer that he might get something more out of the theater than idle amusement) or of Synge with the inimitable magic of his language, more startling effects are apparent in areas of experimentation. I refer especially to such things as the Symbolist theater (Maeterlinck, Yeats, Strindberg, von Hoffmannsthal, Andreev, Lorca, Claudel) as well as symbolist production (the "New Stagecraft") and various antirealistic movements. In England William Poel was influential in demonstrating the aesthetic advantages of reduced and simplified settings for Shakespeare's plays; and Gordon Craig directed the production by the Moscow Art Theater of a version of *Hamlet* with reduced and stylized settings.

Familiar and traditional features of drama were most radically defamiliarized in Expressionist, Futurist, and Surrealist plays. German dramatic expressionism, which had its roots in the theater of Büchner, is characterized, both in the plays themselves and in the stagecraft, by the same fondness for violent visual imagery and distortion of forms that is seen in the graphic art of the movement.[88] In Sorge's *Der Bettler* (1917) the characters are universalized and the play is developed along symphonic lines, with variations and repetitions of mood, rather than on the basis of cause and effect. Georg Kaiser's *Hölle Weg Erde* (1919) contains highly stylized and, in some pas-

87. *Russian Theater from the Empire to the Soviets* (New York: Collier, 1962), p. 297.

88. See John Willett, *Expressionism* (New York: McGraw-Hill, 1970) and especially pp. 117 ff., "Expressionism in the Theater."

sages, "Joycean" dialogue. There was also an expressionist acting technique (mainly German) with intense, angular, and explosive mannerisms that was defamiliarizing in its own way.

The principles of Italian Futurist theater are outlined in Marinetti's "The Futurist Synthetic Theater" (1915): such theater would "symphonize the audience's sensibility by exploring it, stirring up its laziest layers with every means possible; eliminate the preconception of the footlights by throwing nets of sensations between the stage and the audience."[89] An outstanding example of Russian Futurist drama (actually a rollicking comedy) is Mayakovsky's *Klop* (*The Bedbug*, 1929) with incidental music (now lost) by Dmitry Shostakovich.[90] Surrealist (or dadaist) theater may be represented by Tristan Tzara's *Le Coeur à gaz* (1921) in which the *dramatis personae* are parts of the body; the dialogue is nonsensical, and the development may best be described as aleatory.

So far as modern "ritual" drama is concerned, there are two very different approaches: the one represented by Eliot's *Murder in the Cathedral* (1935) and the other by the plays of Jean Genêt. In both cases there is marked formal defamiliarization of traditional theater. Eliot is trying to emulate or recreate ancient religious drama, complete with working chorus, but with Christianity substituted for paganism and, in this sense, it is also what Spengler would call a "pseudomorphosis." Genêt, on the other hand, has turned religion upside down—evil is good and good evil; and his plays, if likened to ritual, are suggestive of the Black Mass. This is especially true of *Les Nègres* (1959) which includes the ritual murder of a white woman.[91] Antonin Artaud, who saw the archetype of ritual theater in the Eleusinian mysteries, was the leading spokesman of the Genêt-type ritual drama, and his views are set forth in *Le Théâtre et son double* (1938).[92] Artaud might well have made use of such Shklovskian terminology as defamiliarization and disautomatization in urging that it is the function of theater to rouse the audience from torpor and to stimulate its creative powers, deadened by bourgeois drama. Artaud revives, by the

89. Quoted in *Marinetti: Selected Writings*, edited by R. W. Flint (New York: Farrar, Straus and Giroux, 1971), p. 128.

90. English translation in *The Bedbug and Selected Poetry*, edited by Patricia Blake (New York: Meridian, 1960).

91. See the fine review of *The Blacks* by Robert Brustein in *Seasons of Discontent* (New York: Simon and Schuster, 1967), p. 49 ff.

92. English translation by Mary Richards: *The Theater and Its Double* (New York: Grove Press, 1958).

way, the Aristotelian notion of catharsis when he says, for example, that the spectator's taste for crime, his erotic obsessions, and his savagery—even his cannibalism—can be vicariously satisfied in the presence of scenes of ritual cruelty.

It hardly seems necessary to comment here on the even more bizarre aspects of the "theater of the absurd"; rather we should consider another area of modern drama that is particularly significant with regard to defamiliarization, viz., theatricalism. In brief, the theory and practice of theatricalism holds that a stage performance is simply *that*, with no attempt being made to create an illusion of real life; indeed, various devices are employed specifically to dispel and violate such an illusion. There is good reason to believe that theatricalism as such (although foreshadowed in Greek drama, in Shakespeare, Calderón, Racine, Schiller, and others) began in Russia just prior to and following the Revolution in dramatic works produced under the direction of Vsevolod Meyerhold, Nikolay Evreinov, Aleksandr Tairov, and Evgeny Vakhtangov.[93] But the name that comes to mind immediately in this connection is that of Luigi Pirandello, the author of the very well-known play, *Sei personaggi in cerca d'autore* (1921). Pirandello was the most accomplished writer within a group of Italian playwrights (Chiarelli, Antonelli, Cavacchioli), active between 1915 and 1925, known collectively as the *teatro del grottesco*. The general outlook of these playwrights, strongly colored by the anti-logical and anti-rational philosophy of the period and influenced no doubt by the popular appeal of irony and symbolism, may be summed up in the words of Professor Adriano Tilgher: "The absolute conviction that everything is vain and hollow and that man is only a puppet in the hands of fate. Man's pains and pleasures as well as his deeds are unsubstantial dreams in a world of ominous darkness that is ruled by blind fortune."[94] Tilgher's reference to puppets reminds us that such terms as "puppetization" are frequently applied to the mechanical, mannikin-like manner of performance of the characters in most of the *teatro del grottesco* plays.[95]

Another important name is that of Bertolt Brecht whose "V-effect" (*Verfremdungseffekt*), referred to earlier, is quite familiar.

93. See Barnard Hewitt, *History of the Theater from 1800 to the Present* (New York: Random House, 1970), Chapter VI.

94. Quoted in Kayser, *The Grotesque in Art and Literature*, p. 135.

95. See, e.g., Walter Starkie, *Luigi Pirandello* (New York: Dutton, 1926), p. 22.

Brecht felt that the dramatist—especially the "epic" dramatist—should alienate or estrange (*verfremden*) the action and characters on the stage so that the spectators might view these objectively and not merely react to them. He deliberately widens the distance between his play and the audience; he thus makes a sharp distinction (as George Steiner puts it) between "realness" and "realism" and, in this sense, defamiliarizes the concept and practice of theatrical realism. It is interesting, by the way, that Brecht particularly liked the manner in which Charles Laughton interpreted the part of Galileo in the play of the same name. Brecht "physicalizes" Galileo's intelligence in this play and Laughton's acting emphasized this; Brecht commented: "And the movements of his hands in his trouser pockets when he was planning new researches were all but scandalous. Whenever Galileo was being creative, Laughton revealed a contradictory mixture of aggressiveness and defenseless softness and sensitivity."[96]

These various concepts of the drama, the great variety of modernist and avant-garde plays, and the proliferation of experimental theater in the West all stand (fortunately) in marked contrast to the situation in Soviet Russia where, with rather few exceptions, the theater has deteriorated under the *Gleichschaltung*-effect of the doctrine of "socialist realism." (It should be pointed out that this doctrine is itself a form of defamiliarization, something that can be clearly seen in most of the attempts—e.g., Gorky's—to define the notion.[97]) The blandness—even insipidity—of Soviet theater may be explained to some extent by claiming (as M. Yenkovsky, a manager of the Leningrad Comedy Theater once did) that Soviet Russia no longer has those sharp contradictions so characteristic of the pluralistic, democratic societies which are reflected in Western theater. Indeed, at one time there was a heated controversy as to whether in fact, in view of the imminent appearance of a classless society, conflict on the Soviet stage should any longer be tolerated, and a theory of "conflictless drama" was advanced (true, with tongue in cheek by Nikolay Virta) and seriously argued down to the present time. But, as I say, there are exceptions. Several years ago (in 1972) Mikhail Shatrov's *Przheval-*

96. Quoted in Lionel Abel, *Metatheatre* (New York: Hill & Wang, 1963), p. 100. See also the remarks by Wylie Sypher in *Literature and Technology: the Alien Vision* (New York: Random House, 1971), pp. 97 ff.

97. Gorky's definition is quoted, for instance, in the "Proletarian Literature" chapter of Empson's *Some Versions of Pastoral*. The defamiliarizing aspect of socialist realism is even more apparent in Andrey Sinyavsky's ("Abram Tertz's") *On Socialist Realism*.

sky's Horse opened at the Leningrad Komsomol Theater; it criticized unscrupulous careerism and pointed up the tendency for higher-ups to overlook dishonesty in subordinates when any unfavorable report might cause embarrassment. The play contained a daring (in Soviet terms) scene between a Komsomol brigade leader and a scantily clad lady doctor. In another play, Roshchin's *Valentin and Valentina* (a modernized version of *Romeo and Juliet*) shown at the Gorky Moscow Art Theater in 1971 there was a nude tableau, and Hedrick Smith reported in the *New York Times,* December 31, 1972, that Premier Kosygin walked out after seeing this. The scene was later removed.

8

Defamiliarization in poetry only begins with those grammatical, syntactical, and metaphorical devices noted in Chapter III. There are also devices of prosodical or metrical defamiliarization, one of the most obvious being the use of scazons or choliambics (*"Hinkiambus"*), i.e., an iambic (hexameter) line with a spondee or trochee in the last foot. The meter was first used by Hipponax for his invectives and later by Herodas in his *mimiambi* and imitated by Catullus: "Miser Catulle desinas ineptire."[98] Occasionally verses with a similar "limping" or "halting" effect are called choliambic, e.g., Tsvetaeva's "V ogromnom gorode moem—noch'."[99] The much used dactylic hexameter line could also be defamiliarized with a *versus miurus* (an iamb or pyrrhic in the last foot) or a *versus dolichurus* (an extra syllable in the last foot); and in late and medieval Latin verse there is a great fondness for experimenting with any unusual linguistic, syntactic, and prosodic mannerism—anything, in short, that was strange in appearance or sound and that would surprise or puzzle (tmesis, asyndeton, *versus rapportati*, leonine verse, pangrammatic verse, etc.). In modern versification something like G. M. Hopkins' "sprung rhythm" was and still is an effective means of defamiliarization:

Not, I'll not, carrion comfort, Despair, not feast on thee;
But ah, but O thou terrible, why wouldst thou rude on me
O in turns of tempest, me heaped there; me frantic to avoid thee and flee?

98. When the fifth foot is also a spondee, the line is called ischiorrhogic ("with broken hip").
99. See A. Kvjatkovskij, *Poèticheskij slovar'* (Moscow, 1966), s.v. *kholijamb.*

Yvor Winters expresses the novelty and impact of this rhythm when he writes (discussing another poem by Hopkins):

> The poem, then, is not written in syllabic meter, for the number of syllables varies from line to line; if it is an attempt at accentual meter, it is irregular, for two lines contain extra accents. But it can be described, and without undue trouble, as a variant on standard English meter, a variant both learned and perverse, but in which the rhythm is successfully maintained, in which the perversity is equalled by the skill.[100]

We also have prosodic defamiliarization in those few and poor attempts by modern poets (Jodelle, Baïf, Gessner, Milton) to revive— or at least experiment with—classical quantitative verse; or in the experiments of, say, the Russian poet Bryusov with syllabic verse long after the establishment in Russian poetry of syllabic-accentual prosody. I think, too, that there is defamiliarization of standard Russian metrics in Balmont's translation of Blake's *The Tiger* when, in the first line, "Tigr, tigr, zhguchij strakh," the monosyllable *tigr* is treated as a trochee. But, as we shall see, such things are insignificant in comparison with the much more striking effects involved in the adaptation by many modern poets of various unusual verse forms drawn not only from antiquity but also from the Near and Far East.

Auxiliary devices such as alliteration and assonance may serve not only to supplement structurally the content of a poem but may also disautomatize and defacilitate. Assonance (vocalic rhyme) is an essential feature of much good poetry and especially of Symbolist practice: "La blême lune allume en la mare qui luit"; even when it is somewhat overdone it is not offensive:

> U nashikh ushki na makushke,
> Chut' utro osvetilo pushki
> I lesa sinie verkhushki—
> Frantsuzy tut kak tut.

But alliteration, unless handled with taste, is apt to distract as much as defamiliarize (as in this example from Balmont):

> Landyshi, lyutiki. Laski ljubovnye,
> Lastochki lepet. Lobzan'e luchej.

100. Quoted in Hans-Werner Ludwig, *Barbarous in Beauty* (München: Wilhelm Fink, 1972), p. 62. This is an elaborate study of Hopkins' versification.

The seventh-century Indian poet Magha has an *ekāksara* stanza (using only one consonant) which, by using rare and obscure words, he has managed to render meaningful:

> Dādado dudda-dud-dādī
> dādādo duda-dī-da-doh
> dud-dādam dadade dudde
> dad'-ādada-dado 'da-dah.[101]

Popular in the Latin Middle Ages, along with many other metrical trifles, were wholly alliterative poems, such as Hucbald's *Ecloga de Calvis*, every word in its one hundred and forty-six lines beginning with the letter c (for *calvus*, "bald"), appropriately dedicated to Charles the Bald.

Onomatopoeia is another device used widely in poetry: the first poem in the *Book of Poetry* (Shih Ching), the earliest known anthology of Chinese poetry (12th–7th cent. B.C.), begins "Kuan, kuan chü chiu" ("*Kuan, kuan,* cry the ospreys"). Used in moderation, onomatopoeia is as effective as assonance and alliteration; joined with neologisms, as in the poetry of a master craftsman like Mayakovsky, it is quite defamiliarizing:

> Tintidlikal
> mandolinoj,
> dundudel violonchel'ju.

A further step may be taken from the use of the aural effects of "echo-words" to that of the visual effects of certain letters, words, and groups of words which provide relevant associations. For example, Hungarians like to point out the resemblance in their language between the *word* for "scissors" and the *thing: olló*.[102] A better example is this "monostich" by (I believe) Richard Lebovitz:

HANDSAWWWWWWWWWWWWWWWW.

101. The -h breathing (*visarga*) at the end of two lines is not counted as a consonant. For the meaning of this stanza, see A. L. Basham, *The Wonder That Was India* (New York: Hawthorn, 1963), p. 425.

102. It is interesting that Tennyson once remarked that he knew the quantity of all English vowels except those in the word "scissors." On Tristan Tzara's "scissors technique" for producing "original" poetry, see Poggioli, *The Theory of the Avant-Garde*, p. 190.

Beyond this lie the *carmina figurata* which have been popular, especially in baroque periods, since Hellenistic times and which appear from time to time today as "concrete poems." Then there are the "comma" poems of the Philippine-American poet, José Garcia Villa, with each word followed by a comma (supposedly in imitation of Seurat's *pointillisme*); Aragon's *Sérénade,* consisting of the letters of the alphabet (one of the most "universal" of poems, according to Henri Peyre, and "accessible to all persons literate in the Latin alphabet"[103]):

a b c d e f
g h i j k l
m n o p q r
s t u v w
x y z;

and finally the *"Schwindstufe"*—Gnedov's "Poem of the End."

Unusual rhymes or rhyme-schemes may have a defamiliarizing effect—e.g., the Spanish *versos de cabo roto* ("nipped" or "cropped" verses) which rhyme only when the last syllable of each line is cut off (as in the verses ascribed to Urganda following the Prologue to *Don Quijote*). In most of the literatures in which rhyme is used there are certain poets known for their bravura performance with rhyme; in Russian poetry such a figure is Mayakovsky—the "supreme virtuoso," according to Boris Unbegaun.[104] Gumilev's technical skill is also apparent in this humorous eight-syllable rhyme:

Slysha svist i voj lokomobilja
Dver' lingvisty vojlokom obili,

although other poets have done better, e.g., Victor Hugo with his "holorhyme":

Gal, amant de la reine, alla, tour magnanime
Galamment de l'arène a la Tour Magne, a Nîmes.

103. Henri Peyre, *The Failures of Criticism* (Ithaca: Cornell University Press, 1967), p. 212.
104. *Russian Versification* (Oxford: Oxford University Press, 1956), p. 148. See also the story of the rhyme, *triomphe/monogomphe,* in C. Bombaugh, *Oddities and Curiosities of Words and Literature* (New York: Dover, 1961), in the "Refractory Rhyming" section.

Poets may specifically call attention to the difficulty, the ingenuity, or the necessity of using a certain rhyme, as Pushkin does (in the manner of Byron) in *Eugene Onegin* (VI, 44):

Mechty, mechty! gde vasha sladost'?
Gde, vechnaja k nej rifma, mladost'?

And there are many varieties of irregular rhymes (approximate, broken, eye, truncated, etc.) as well as such things as *rime brisée* or "jesuitical verses":

Who calls you shy,   he tells the truth,
He's a lying youth   who says you're sly.

Rather unusual are those rhyme-schemes adopted along with exotic verse-forms from other literatures, such as the monorhyme in the ghazal (of Persian origin); here are two couplets by K. A. von Platen-Hallermünde:

Der Strom, der neben mir verrauschte, wo ist er nun?
Der Vogel, dessen Lied ich lauschte, wo ist er nun?

Wo ist die Rose, die die Freundin am Herzen trug,
Und jener Kuss, der mich berauschte, wo ist er nun?[105]

As noted earlier in the case of prose works, the titles of poems or collections of poems may also defamiliarize: Browning's *Pippa Passes*, Govoni's *Poesie elettriche*, Cendrars' *Poésies élastiques*, Voznesensky's *Parabolicheskaja ballada* and *Treugol'naja grusha* ("The Triangular Pear"), Günter Grass's *Gleisdreieck*, Neruda's *Ritual de mis piernas*, etc. It is obvious, however, that such titles with their very odd and surprising juxtapositions of words ("parabolic" + "ballad") match the poetry they represent quite as faithfully as the less startling titles of traditional bodies of poetry ("To a Skylark").[106]

105. I quote this from my article, "The Russian Ghazal," *Symposium* 18 (4) (Winter 1964): 342–51.

106. There are some comments on the titles of modern poems in Poggioli, *op. cit.*, pp. 138, 142, and in Hugo Friedrich, *The Structure of Modern Poetry* (Evanston: Northwestern University Press, 1974), p. 124.

Poetry may include variations in form from perfectly regular metrical units arranged in lines and strophes, verses with resolutions and substitutions (which often appear "irregular"[107]), logaoedic measures and "free verse"; rhyme and all the traditional supporting devices—even metaphor and imagery—may disappear until we have various types of astichic poems or "poems in prose." Words may be replaced by letters and symbols in titles (as in Ardengo Soffici's "Bif&zf + 18") or in the poems themselves (as in the Morgenstern opus mentioned above in section 5). Or poems may be reduced to two- or three-line fragments (see Ezra Pound's *Papyrus*) or to monostichs:

> O zakroj svoi blednye nogi.
> ("O cover thy pale legs"—Bryusov)

Poems may be "verbless" (or almost so) over lengthy stretches, as in the first stanza of Gottfried Benn's *Nacht* which consists only of nouns; the Russian poet Vyacheslav Ivanov was called the "poet of nouns," while another Russian poet, Valery Bryusov, has been called the "poet of adjectives."[108]

Although macaronic poetry as such (in the manner, say, of Teofilo Folengo) is no longer popular, a good deal of modernist verse has been, especially since the symbolists, quite learned and often generously sprinkled with tags of ancient and foreign languages. Some of this polyglotry simply reflects the erudition of the *doctus poeta* but some no doubt symbolically reflects the cosmopolitanism or, rather, the hybridization of certain contemporary cultures: Eliot's *The Waste Land* and Pound's *Cantos* suggest themselves in this respect. Or the works of certain poets show the profound influence of another culture: it has been remarked, for example, that in his *Poemi conviviali* Giovanni Pascoli "contrives to speak Greek with Italian words."[109] The use by some poets of a less familiar language or dialect may defacilitate, as in the case of Hugh MacDiarmid (C. M. Grieve) who

107. Thus Turgenev (who was something of a poet), in editing some of Tyutchev's poems, "corrected" the amphibrachic substitutions which he took to be irregularities.

108. See Georgette Donchin, *The Influence of French Symbolism on Russian Poetry* (The Hague: Mouton, 1958), pp. 166–67. The term *bezglagol'nost'* ("verblessness") is often used of Balmont's poetry.

109. J. H. Whitfield, *A Short History of Italian Literature* (Harmondsworth: Penguin, 1960), pp. 263–64.

prefers Lallans or "synthetic Scots" and for this reason "He at first seems a very special kind of acquired taste, writing as he does in a half-foreign tongue that requires a sympathetic ear and, often, a glossary to be understood."[110] And some poetries are, more than others, defamiliarized through the regular use of an alien linguistic content: thus Urdu poetry, because of the traditional "scattering" in it of Persian words, is called *Rekhta*.

But we see more striking defamiliarization in the adaptation by poets of ancient and foreign—especially oriental—verse forms: Swinburne's Sapphic strophes, Cowley's "Pindaric odes," Delvig's dithyrambs, René Ghil's use of the Malayan *pantoum* form, the appeal of the Japanese *haiku* and *tanka*, the Persian ghazal, the Spanish *glosa*.[111] There are some especially interesting examples in Russian poetry of the imitation of the older *byliny* or folk epics, Lermontov's *The Song of the Merchant Kalashnikov* being one of the best. Here the traditional *zachin* or prooemium is present as well as the characteristic dactylic clausulae, *troekratnost'* (or triplicity), and polyprotheticism. Quite different are actual attempts by poets to deceive or perpetrate hoaxes—as in the case of Thomas Chatterton's *Rowley Poems*, Mérimée's *La Guzla*, or Pierre Louÿs' *Les Chansons de Bilitis*. In the latter case, the French writer claimed to have translated (into *faisandé* French) a hitherto unknown Greek text of prose poems glorifying Sapphic love, but the eminent classical scholar, Wilamowitz-Möllendorff, easily demonstrated that the poems could not have been of ancient provenance.

Modifications of traditional verse forms are defamiliarizing; this is especially true of shorter, well-established forms such as the sonnet. As Tindall notes, the inversion of octaves and sestets in Dylan Thomas' sonnet-sequence, "Altarwise by owl-light," is a formal anticipation of further inversions. There are also the *sonetto doppio* (or *rinterzato*— an example may be found in the *Vita Nuova*, vii), the *sonetto caudato*, the acephalous sonnet (with the first octave missing), the limping sonnet, etc. Perhaps even more noticeable effects may result from the employment of traditional forms for untraditional content: the sonnet form, for example, to trace the history of the sonnet (Pushkin) or elegiac distichs to elaborate on slops (Radimov quoted above, p.

---

110. M. L. Rosenthal, *The Modern Poets* (New York: Oxford University Press, 1965), p. 132.

111. The *glosa* (or gloss) is a *rara avis* outside of Spain; but I know of one example by the Russian poet, Vyacheslav Ivanov (in his *Cor Ardens*).

10). We might include here, too, not only a great mass of poor, pedestrian verse (such as the numerous specimens in *The Stuffed Owl*) but also *Dinggedichte*—e.g., the modern Polish poet Tymoteusz Karpowicz's *Sen ołówka* ("The Pencil's Dream")[112]—or such amazing things as Raymond Roussel's *La Vue,* concerning which Rayner Heppenstall writes:

> The title-piece in the volume *La Vue* is a poem of some two thousand lines. The volume contains two further poems, *Le Concert* and *La Source,* of about half that length. Each describes, in far more detail than it is possible to imagine being physically visible, a miniature view. In *La Vue* it is a sea-side prospect engraved on a lens set into a penholder. In *Le Concert,* it is the heading of a sheet of hotel writing paper, showing the hotel itself, an omnibus standing before it, the lake beyond and public gardens with a bandstand. In *La Source,* the label on a bottle of mineral water shows the spring itself and a girl in peasant costume serving customers.[113]

But poems about things—especially small things—are not new: there are ancient examples (Martial's *Xenia*), and the practice has been popular in later—notably baroque—ages (cf. the French *blasons*). We also think of the *chosiste* approach in general and of Ponge's *Le Parti-pris des choses*.[114]

Finally, it is strange to see poetry employed for criticism of genius, but this is what the Soviet poet Nikolay Aseev does in his *Antigenial'naja poèma* ("Anti-Genius Poem") in which the collective genius of the masses is vaunted and individual genius disparaged. But this "poem" (which one might—did we not know it to exist in fact—believe to be a figment of some anti-Soviet guile) reflects the same absurd Leninist mentality that tried to establish collectively conducted symphonic orchestras and proletarian training schools for writers.[115]

112. Polish and English text in Czeslaw Milosz, *The History of Polish Literature* (New York: Macmillan, 1969), p. 480.

113. Rayner Heppenstall, *Raymond Roussel* (Berkeley: University of California Press, 1967), p. 24.

114. Ponge's work is available in English: *The Voice of Things,* translated by Beth Archer (New York: McGraw-Hill Paperback, 1974). There was a short-lived Russian *veshchizm* (*chosisme*) movement in connection with LEF; see Mihajlo Mihajlov, *Russian Themes,* translated by Marija Mihajlov (New York: Farrar, Straus & Giroux, 1968), p. 299.

115. See also another strange work by A. Toporov, *Krest'jane o pisateljakh* (Moscow & Leningrad, 1930), which records the reactions of Russian peasants to various works of literature, reactions which anticipate those of Khrushchev and other members of the Soviet elite.

9

For both prose and poetry—and including, of course, drama—the most generally defamiliarizing procedure, especially since the beginning of the twentieth century, has involved those discontinuities and juxtapositional devices which have already been referred to both explicitly and implicitly in the preceding chapters. Indeed, *all* the most representative art forms of the present century have, to a greater or lesser degree, been characterized by a rather rapid diminution and frequently complete disappearance of the transitional devices which, with relatively few exceptions, had been for centuries familiar features of works of art; devices which, as part of the text, had provided the reader, the listener, or the viewer with a syntaxis of elements by which he might constantly orient himself and in which he could find an easy gradation from beginning to end and from part to part. The overwhelming bulk of literatures in the Indo-European languages since ancient times has not only been, to use Peirce's philosophical term, a synechism or continuum; it also seems to reflect, especially since the Renaissance, the view of reality as an ordered hierarchy that we find classically stated, for example, in Leibniz:

> In all the visible corporeal world we see no chasms or gaps. All quite down from us the descent is by easy steps, and a continued series that in each remove differ very little one from the other. . . . There are animals so near of kin both to birds and beasts that they are in the middle between both. . . . And when we consider the infinite power and wisdom of the Maker, we have reason to think, that it is suitable to the magnificent harmony of the universe, and the great design and infinite goodness of the architect that the species of creatures should also, by gentle degrees, ascend upwards from us towards his infinite perfection, as we see they gradually descend from us downwards.[116]

But noticeable at first about 1870 and thereafter (especially following the turn of the century) appearing with ever greater frequency and in ever more multifarious forms, the technique of juxtaposition has now become a regular feature of all the arts. Seeing essentially this very change but from a slightly different point of view (his emphasis is on the word), George Steiner writes:

116. Quoted in Arthur Lovejoy, *The Great Chain of Being* (New York: Harper, 1960), p. 184.

The principal division in the history of Western literature occurs between the early 1870's and the turn of the century. It divides a literature essentially housed in language from one for which language has become a prison. Compared to this division all preceding historical and stylistic rubrics or movements—Hellenism, the medieval, the Baroque, Neo-classicism, Romanticism—are only subgroups or variants. From the beginnings of Western literature until Rimbaud and Mallarmé (Hölderlin and Nerval are decisive but isolated forerunners), poetry and prose were in organic accord with language. Vocabulary and grammar could be expanded, distorted, driven to the limits of comprehension. There are deliberate obscurities and subversions of the logic of common discourse throughout Western poetry, in Pindar, in the medieval lyric, in European amorous and philosophic verse of the sixteenth and seventeenth centuries. But even where it is most explicit, the act of invention, of individuation in Dante's *stile nuovo*, in the semantic cosmography of Rabelais, moves with the grain of speech. . . . With them [i.e., Rimbaud and Mallarmé] Western literature and speech-consciousness enter a new phase. The poet no longer has or aspires to native tenure in the house of words. The languages waiting for him as an individual born into history, into society, into the expressive conventions of his particular culture and milieu, are no longer a natural skin. Established language is the enemy. The poet finds it sordid with lies. Daily currency has made it stale. The ancient metaphors are inert and the numinous energies bone-dry. It is the writer's compelling task, as Mallarmé said of Poe, "to purify the language of the tribe." He will seek to resuscitate the magic of the word by dislocating traditional bonds of grammar and of ordered space. . . . He will endeavour to rescind or at least weaken the classic continuities of reason and syntax, of conscious direction and verbal form . . . Because it has become calcified, impermeable to new life, the public crust of language must be riven.[117]

If, in discussing transition versus juxtaposition, we limit ourselves to poetry, we may distinguish between external and internal nexus. By external nexus I mean, of course, all syntactical transitional and articulating devices, especially conjunctions; by internal nexus I mean primarily imagistic transition. In Pound's *Papyrus* there is (as in other, longer poems) a complete absence of external nexus:

>Spring . . .
>Too late . . .
>Gongula . . .

117. George Steiner *After Babel* (New York: Oxford University Press, 1976), pp. 176–78. On defamiliarization as deformation, semioclastics, *brisure*, etc., see above, p. 43ff.

But there *is* an internal, imagistic nexus, not readily apparent, to be sure, that unifies the words and the lines as effectively as any verbal conjunctions. Ordinarily, however, any art—in this case, poetry—is quite obviously defamiliarized when traditional external nexus is abandoned; it is even further defacilitated when there appears to be no or minimum internal nexus, as in these verses by Hart Crane:

> Witness now this trust! the rain
> That steals softly direction
> And the key, ready to hand—sifting
> One moment in sacrifice (the direst)
> Through a thousand nights the flesh
> Assaults outright for bolts that linger
> Hidden,—O undirected as the sky
> That through its black foam has no eyes
> For this fixed stone of lust . . .[118]

And similar, even more enigmatic passages might be cited from Mallarmé.

But disjunctions, discontinuities, and juxtapositions in modern poetry, defamiliarizing as they are, are often employed to reflect structurally the discontinuities in reality as perceived by the modern mind:

> Nightingales, Anangke, a sunset or the meanest flower
> Were formerly the potentialities of poetry,
> But now what have they to do with one another,
> With Dionysus or with me?

These lines (and more) by Ronald Bottrall are quoted by John Press and contrasted with some verses by Herrick: "It is instructive to compare Herrick's introductory lines with a poem by Ronald Bottrall, 'The Thyrsus Retipped,' to notice how the older poet walks in a world that has not entirely lost the glory and the wholeness of Eden, whereas the poet of our day looks blankly at an indifferent, neutral world of unrelated objects."[119] The technique of juxtaposition is, of

118. Crane himself could not explain this poem ("Possessions") and said that it had to rely on its organic impact on the imagination. See Philip Horton, *Hart Crane* (New York: Viking, 1957), p. 172.

119. John Press, *The Chequer'd Shade* (London: Oxford University Press, 1963), p. 118.

course, a symbolist device (as well as a form of metaphor) widely
used in the modern arts where it is often referred to as "montage."

10

Before ending this chapter, I would like to comment on one other
area in which we have a kind of defamiliarization. Many readers will
recall having had a vague sense of *déja vu* during the reading of a
poem or a piece of fiction. In some cases this merely amounts to the
remembrance of a roughly similar incident, metaphor, description, or
plot. In other cases research will disclose that in fact some other work
or portion of a work has been adapted (as in Shakespeare or Pushkin)
with very essential modifications by the writer in question and that
this information is available in standard literary histories. In still other
cases the resemblances noted amount, in modern terms, to something
close to—or actual—plagiarism. In the past, actual literary borrowings
were, until the recognition of auctorial rights and the appearance of
copyright legislation, looked upon rather liberally (e.g., the *furta
Virgiliana*, Spenser's borrowings in his *Faerie Queene*). But I refer
more specifically to situations such as the following. In 1844 Nathaniel
Hawthorne published a story, "Rappaccini's Daughter" (later included in *Mosses from an Old Manse*), which was an expansion and
embellishment of a brief passage in Sir Thomas Browne which Hawthorne copied into his *American Notebook;* this was the story of an
Indian king who sent to Alexander the Great a young girl who had
been nurtured with poisons in such a way that, while she herself was
immune, she was in effect lethal to any man who embraced her. Now
if one reads the story, "The Poison Garden," by the Russian writer
Fedor Teternikov ("Fedor Sologub"),[120] he will notice immediately
striking parallels and similarities. Hawthorne's story is set in Italy
(although the Indian tale is alluded to), Sologub's in Russia. The girl
in Hawthorne's story (Beatrice) is the daughter of a sinister physician,
Doctor Rappaccini, who tends a garden of poison plants and who has
used his daughter for experiments; she has been so nurtured on poison
that she has become immune but lethal. In Sologub the girl is simply
"the Beauty" and is the daughter of an equally sinister and mad

120. "Otravlennyj sad" is in the collection, *Kniga ocharovanij* (1909). There
is an English translation by Samuel Cioran in *The Silver Age of Russian Culture*,
edited by C. and E. Proffer (Ann Arbor: Ardis, 1975).

botanist, Professor Botanik, who also tends a poison garden and has "treated" his daughter in the same way. In both stories a young student rents an upper-storey room overlooking the poison garden; in both stories there is an old landlady who converses with the student; in both stories the student first sees the girl in the garden from his window and falls in love with her; and in both stories the student learns more of the girl's father from another professor. In Hawthorne's version this professor gives the student an antidote that is supposed to cure the girl, but she dies after this is administered. In Sologub, after a night of love, both student and girl die. Although each of the stories is embellished with (to use Tomashevsky's term) different "free motifs," what essentially has happened is that a story by Hawthorne, well known in America (but of course not *too* familiar in Russia) has been, to put the matter delicately, defamiliarized by Sologub.[121]

Since a significant amount of structural elements in the Hawthorne story was retained by Sologub, we can see clearly what has been omitted, added, or otherwise altered. In other cases, when there are numerous intermediate versions between what we assume to be the original story and a very distant and later version, the relationships are much less distinct and defamiliarization is more radical. Such a situation may be seen especially well, for example, in studies of the diffusion down through the centuries via numerous languages and literatures of the Indian collection of tales, the *Panchatantra,* and of the Pali *jatakas.*[122]

121. Carola Hansson in her *Fedor Sologub as a Short-Story Writer* (Stockholm: Almqvist & Wiksell, 1975) briefly mentions the story as "a fantastic, morbid story very reminiscent" of earlier works (p. 14). Mario Praz mentions the Hawthorne version in *The Romantic Agony* in a note on de Sade.

122. See the Introduction to Franklin Edgerton's translation, *The Panchatantra* (London: Allen & Unwin, 1965).

LITERARY HISTORY

1

IN THE FOLLOWING FOUR SECTIONS I should like to review briefly some of those periods in a number of world literatures during which de-familiarization has been used with noticeable frequency and intensity. Although many and various devices of defamiliarization were used in Greek literature of the Hellenic and earlier ages, there is an increased employment of such devices during the Hellenistic or Alexandrian period (c. 323–30 B.C.) and it is with this that we shall begin. That the works of Hellenistic literature are, aside from their philological interest, on a considerably lower level than the earlier classical Greek literature cannot be denied. Indeed, the term "Alexandrian" is always somewhat pejorative and suggests poetry, for example, that is learned but uninspired, technically brilliant but essentially frigid; thus Mirsky quite correctly employs the term (as well as "Byzantine") of the verse of the Russian Symbolist poet, Vyacheslav Ivanov. As a matter of fact, the names of almost all the periods, movements, and schools to be mentioned below bear, in varying degrees, somewhat disparaging connotations. They suggest bodies of literature which represent a "Silver" Age (or something even less than this) rather than a "Golden" Age of greatness—bodies of literature in which excessive attention has been paid to formal embellishment and to *labor limae* and in which we note especially the clever—very often amazing—attempts to render the familiar unfamiliar.

Though Lycophron's *Alexandra* is, in this sense, the crowning glory of Hellenistic or Alexandrian poetry, one can open, say, Couat's *La poésie alexandrine sous les trois premiers Ptolémées* almost at random and find statements such as the following:

The Alexandrian poets like to have their meaning guessed at rather than understood; they do not surrender the key to their erudite language at first reading; occasionally we recognize them by the very fact they are unintelligible. . . .

Each poet in turn writes ingenious verses in which the exquisiteness of the subtle language and versification makes us forget how improbable and banal the subject is, and in which the reminiscences of antiquity, the forgotten proper names of towns and heroes, mingling with the audacities of the modern language, create a charm of even more piquant novelty.[1]

One of the major figures of Alexandrian poetry is Theocritus, the author (and very likely the inventor) of pastoral idylls (*eidullia*) which of all ancient genres had, after the epic, the greatest influence on subsequent literatures. Curtius' remark, that this popularity of the pastoral is due to the fact that "the shepherd's life is found everywhere and at all periods,"[2] is quite wrong: the appeal of the pastoral is precisely its artificiality and its atmosphere of Arcadian quiet and escapism. "That habit of retrospect," writes Gilbert Murray, "that yearning over the past, which pervades all the poetry, though not the scientific work, of Alexandria, is peculiarly marked in Theocritus."[3] And William Empson points up pastoral defamiliarization when he writes: "The essential trick of the old pastoral, which was felt to imply a beautiful relation between rich and poor, was to make simple people express strong feelings . . . in learned and fashionable language."[4]

The Alexandrian aversion to the commonplace, the trite, and the conventional is concisely expressed in some verses by Callimachus (directed, very possibly, at Apollonius Rhodius) which begin, "I hate the poems of the epic cycle and I do not care for a road that carries many to and fro."[5] Callimachus himself liked especially to defamiliarize ancient legends by elaborating on details neglected by his predecessors; nor was he reluctant about embellishing the stories of the gods with clever rhetorical *mots*:

1. *Alexandrian Poetry Under the First Three Ptolemies*, transl. James Loeb (London: Heinemann, 1931), pp. 103, 136.

2. Curtius, *European Literature and the Latin Middle Ages*, p. 187. See Congleton's article on "Pastoral" in the *Princeton Encyclopedia of Poetry and Poetics*.

3. Gilbert Murray, *The Literature of Ancient Greece* (Chicago: University of Chicago Press, 1956), p. 383.

4. William Empson, *Some Versions of Pastoral*, p. 11.

5. *Anthol. Palat.*, xii.43, quoted in *The Penguin Book of Greek Verse*, p. 323. On Callimachus, see above, p. 85.

Like the preachers of the sixteenth century, he endows the gods, whom it is his mission to praise, with his own cleverness. . . . We must add that the poet as well as those who read his works was conscious of these literary incongruities. It was a deliberate piece of self-deception: they knew that these commonplaces of mythology would not touch anyone unless they were modified to suit the taste of the age, and that only thus could the poet be sure of not displeasing.[6]

It was during the Alexandrian and subsequent Greco-Roman periods that early forms of extended prose narratives, the so-called "Greek romances," appeared and proliferated. These had their origin in school rhetorical exercises—in the contrived situations, the set speeches and apostrophes, the formal descriptions of works of art and landscapes that were easily expanded and embellished. Tarn seems excessively severe on the Greek rhetorical tradition when he writes: "For some reason rhetoric intoxicated Greeks; it took the place filled today by cheap journalism and the cinema; men flocked to rhetorical displays as to a theatre. It debased everything it touched. Petronius said it taught people much about pirates and so forth but little about life."[7] One must admit, however, that the romances do contain striking examples of the defamiliarization of reality—particularly those "shrieking implausibilities" which Professor Moses Hadas notes as being most objectionable to the modern reader.[8]

With rather few exceptions (e.g., Apollonius Rhodius' *Argonautica* with 5835 lines), the Alexandrians preferred and exhibited themselves best in short forms: the epigram, mime, diatribes (especially of the Cynics), meliambics (those of Cercidas are the most familiar), the *silloi* of Timon of Phlius, as well as a large assortment of *paignia* (trifles) and *technopaignia* or *carmina figurata*. There was also, as in later *fin de siècle* periods, a good deal of indecency: e.g., the verses of Sotades, renowned for the foulness of his language, the *kinaidoi* of Timon, and other cinaedological poems.[9] But on the subject-matter of Alexandrian poetry in general Couat remarks that the

6. Couat, *Alexandrian Poetry*, pp. 291–92.

7. W. W. Tarn, *Hellenistic Civilisation* (Cleveland: Meridian, 1961), p. 281. The still unsurplanted study of the Greek romances is Erwin Rohde's *Der griechische Roman und seine Vorläufer* (1876).

8. See his Introduction to *Three Greek Romances* (Garden City: Doubleday, 1953).

9. The decadent aspect of Alexandria led Pierre Louÿs to use the ancient city as a setting for his erotic novel *Aphrodite* (1896).

poets tended to choose whatever was morbid in human passions and that they "made improper use of a violent and subtle psychology which is ill suited for poetry."[10] Women played a considerable role in Hellenistic history and women and the emotions of women are treated frequently in Alexandrian literature—but always, of course, from the male point of view: the *Adoniazusae* of Theocritus, the ballad-like "Alexandrian Erotic Fragment," the mimes of Herodas, etc.

In connection with Gilbert Murray's reference above to Alexandrian science (and Hellenistic contributions here were quite significant), we must mention the *Phaenomena* of Aratus of Soli. As pointed out by Couat, this poem of 1154 hexameters is the "first manual in verse of a truly scientific kind that Greek literature produced." We would hardly refer to Aratus' work today as "truly scientific," but the *Phaenomena* represents a marked defamiliarization of poetic content. At a time when the poets felt that the subject matter of verse had been exhausted, an exposition of astronomical knowledge might, even in the traditional form of hexameters, afford a new vision and fresh material for poetic embellishment. Couat comments: "His [i.e., Aratus'] task was to express ideas little suited to poetry—ideas of distance, measure, height, of celestial revolutions; to draw parallels, circles, divisions of these circles; to introduce into his hexameters technical terms about the poles, the tropics, the Equator, the Zodiac, the full moon."[11] The influence of Aratus (via Cicero's Latin translation) is seen in Lucretius' much greater poem; his popularity and appeal are indicated by the fact that, along with Menander and Epimenides, he is quoted by St. Paul (Acts 17:28).

There are affiliations between the Alexandrian tradition and both the Latin neoteric poets (Cicero's *cantores Euphorionis*) and Byzantine art and literature.[12] But there is nothing decadent about Catullus and no exceptional defamiliarization; we find this rather in the late Silver Age literature. As for Byzantine literature, it is difficult—if not impossible—to characterize in any cursory way a literature that covers a period of more than a millennium. But the term "Byzantine," like "Alexandrian," is also frequently used in a loosely pejorative sense, suggesting—as applied to literature, for example—a static, hieratic, and highly formalized system. And in general summaries and evaluations

10. Couat, *Alexandrian Poetry,* p. 547.

11. *Ibid.,* p. 504.

12. On Byzantine art, see D. V. Ainalov, *The Hellenistic Origins of Byzantine Art* (New Brunswick: Rutgers University Press, 1961).

of Byzantine literature by persons other than Byzantologists harsh terms are often employed: thus Professor Rose in his *Handbook of Greek Literature* speaks of "Byzantine rubbish" and "such repositories of muddled learning as Tzetzes." Even F. H. Marshall begins an article on Byzantine literature with the words, "Byzantine literature as a whole is not a great literature," while Steven Runciman writes: "Byzantine literature had something of the same limitations as Byzantine learning. It lacked a certain creative spontaneity."[13]

Though one has no difficulty finding in profusion throughout the course of Byzantine literature specific examples of almost all the devices of defamiliarization mentioned in the preceding chapters, from the lipogrammatic *Odyssey* of Tryphiodorus (fourth century) to the long-winded and hardly intelligible didactic poem (*Stichoi autoschedioi eis koinēn akoēn*) by Georgios Lapithes in the fourteenth century, we might also point to such things as the *Tale of Barlaam and Josaphat,* a seventh-century defamiliarized—i.e., Christianized—version of a sixth-century Indian *jātaka* or birth-story of Gautama Buddha. We see similar defamiliarization in the later *Christos Paschōn* (*Christus Patiens*), a purely literary religious drama of the Passion of Christ that is actually a cento of passages from Euripides, Aeschylus, Lycophron, and the Bible. Krumbacher comments:

> Wir empfinden die Ausstattung der heiligen Personen mit den übel zugerichteten Lappen der attischen Bühne als eine wüste Profanierung. Das mumienhaft erstarrte Gewand der alten Tragödie passt den auf einem ganz anderen Boden erwachsenen Gestalten nicht; ihre Bewegungen erscheinen darin ungereimt, und wir haben beim Anblick der so bunt aufgeputzten Figuren mehr mit der Heiterkeit als mit den Thränen zu kämpfen.[14]

There is still another kind of defamiliarization (an obvious exaltation of form over content, of grammar over literature) in the Byzantine love of minute grammatical analysis of brief passages; such analysis was called schedography, and the polymath Michael Psellus in the eleventh century claimed that he had revived this as a science. There

---

13. F. H. Marshall, *Byzantium: An Introduction to East Roman Civilization,* edited by N. H. Baynes and H. St. L. B. Moss (Oxford: Oxford University Press, 1961), Chapter VIII; Steven Runciman, *Byzantine Civilization* (New York: Meridian, 1958), Chapter X.

14. Karl Krumbacher, *Geschichte der Byzantinischen Litteratur* (Munich, 1897, reprinted New York: Burt Franklin, 1958), vol. II, pp. 746–47.

are numerous Byzantine beast fables but what is unusual is the vegetable fable, represented by the *Pōrikologos* (i.e., "poricology" or
vegetable book) of the twelfth century. Queen Quince assembles her
notables—the Lord High Steward Pomegranate, the Protonotary Pear,
the Logothete Apple, the Protovestiary Orange, the Protostator Peach,
and the Grand Drungariū́s Lemon; the Grape accuses certain officials
of conspiracy and treason, the Abbess Olive appears as a witness, and
so on. As in many such fables there is parody—in this case, of the
notorious Byzantine bureaucracy of titles and offices.

There is good reason, finally, to apply the concept of defamiliarization to Byzantine culture as a whole: certainly this is often defined
in terms such as "Hellenized Orientalism" or "Orientalized Hellenism."[15] We might even regard the Eastern Orthodox Church as a defamiliarized form of Christianity—something, indeed, that Fedotov
comes close to doing. This is a controversial area, to be sure, and one
somewhat removed from purely literary study; yet one is strongly
tempted to include here such a work as John Allegro's *The Sacred
Mushroom and the Cross* which, in a very real sense, defamiliarizes
both Judaism and Christianity. Granted that all systems, whether
imaginary (fictional) or real (historical), may be defamiliarized, i.e.,
seen from a fresh, new, different point of view, still, one is suspicious
of a study that (as Allegro's does) derives the Hebrew form of Joshua
from a (hypothetical) Sumerian IA-U-ShU-A, which is supposed to
mean "semen which saves."[16]

2

Beginning with the Silver Age of Latin literature (A.D. 14–180)
and especially during the following very extensive periods of Late
(180–529) and Medieval (529–1500) Latin, we note many of the same
features which characterize—and discredit—Alexandrian and Byzantine
literary works. There is, most notably, the pervasive and corrosive influence of rhetoric and a concomitant artificiality which, as H. J. Rose
puts it, eventually swallows both prose and poetry "and leaves them
equally unlike any human speech." With significant exceptions (e.g.,

15. G. P. Fedotov, *The Russian Religious Mind* (New York: Harper, 1960),
p. 24.
16. John Allegro, *The Sacred Mushroom and the Cross* (New York: Doubleday, 1970), p. 35.

Tacitus), the Latin prose and poetry of these late periods assume, as more and more efforts are expended on rhetorical and formal embellishment, a striking superficiality; we see this clearly in the writings of Lucius Annaeus Seneca (the Philosopher): "It is not," writes Professor Rose, "until after reading him for some time that it becomes apparent how wearisome a writer grows who has nothing else, neither depth of thought, real originality, nor the power to become perfectly plain and simple."[17] Similar statements—often much harsher—by scholars and critics concerning both periods and individual authors occur regularly in literary histories of post-classical Latin literature. A good deal—perhaps all—of the artificiality and superficiality of late Latin literature is due to attempts by writers who have nothing significantly new to say to treat anew traditional commonplaces; and the rise and spread of Christianity provided a vast, fresh area of defamiliarization. But let us look at a number of examples.

In the closet tragedies of Seneca, which had an almost notorious influence on Elizabethan drama, we can see quite clearly—aside from the rhetoric—a defamiliarization of traditional theater and dramatic matter. Take, for instance, the *Medea:* Seneca has sensationalized and exaggerated the Euripidean version, turning it into a "blood-and-thunder" melodrama of revenge. And in the *Phaedra* the heroine of Euripides' *Hippolytus* is no longer a naturally chaste woman struggling, tragically, with an overpowering emotion but a wanton, intent on seduction. Professor Beare writes:

> Seneca's plays differ from anything bequeathed to us by the stage of earlier times, whether Greek or Roman; and one reason for the difference is that his plays were designed not for the stage but for reading. . . . The pervading atmosphere is not that of a stage-play, in which the dramatist must visualize every scene and every movement, but that of a *recitatio.* . . . The grand object seems to be to startle the audience into applause by novel excesses in emotion or expression.[18]

The historical writings of Tacitus are works of lasting, impressive, and significant content; but the inimitable epigrammatic Tacitean language with its concision of expression and rejection of Ciceronian periods as well as the inconcinnity and periphrasis ("spades" are re-

---

17. H. J. Rose, *A Handbook of Latin Literature* (New York: Dutton, 1960), pp. 347, 370.

18. *The Oxford Companion to the Theatre* (London: Oxford University Press, 1964), s.v. "Seneca."

ferred to as "things by which earth is extracted") and such characteristic features as the single-word ablative absolute all represent a unique
defamiliarization of traditional Latin historical prose. This language
in fact anticipates the merely affected verbiage of a mass of later prose
stylists in much the same way the extraordinary language of Persius'
satires foreshadows the almost purely baroque and trifling verse of
later poets writing in Latin (see above, p. 82).

The *Satyrica* of Petronius, though both a parody—or defamiliarization—of the bombastic but innocent eroticism of the Greek romances
and a satire of various facets of Roman society, has appealed to
modern readers merely as a salacious and decadent tale (Fellini's film
version exploited this aspect of Petronius). Strangely, the *Satyrica* is
rarely mentioned during the Middle Ages and the Renaissance, but
one part, the story of the Widow of Ephesus, seems to have been continuously known (the *Cena Trimalchionis* portion was only found in
the seventeenth century) and the Petronian phrase applied to Horace,
curiosa felicitas, has always been one of the best known of such pithy
expressions in the whole of criticism. The bawdiness of the *Satyrica*
was quite popular in the eighteenth century, although Pope was criticized by Johnson and others for the reference to Petronius in the
Essay on Criticism. So far as language is concerned, however, the
Metamorphoses (or *The Golden Ass*), a picaresque romance by
Apuleius at a later date (second century), is somewhat more significant: here the style is a "gorgeous barocco" (Rose) and also prefigures
the linguistic anomalies of later ages—it is no wonder that the *Hisperica Famina* (see below) drew upon Apuleius' lexicon. As Seneca
defamiliarized Roman theater, Apuleius defamiliarized certain literary
traditions of the romance (he seems to have used as his *Kernquelle*
a much shorter work in Greek); Ker comments:

> Apuleius, with all his rhetorical tastes, was at home in a fanciful
> world utterly remote from the "hypocritical and hackneyed course of
> literature" as practised in the schools. He leaves modern authors of
> Romance very little to invent in addition to his discoveries. He gives
> up the accepted Olympian tradition, the deities of the professional
> epic, and goes to look for new fancies in local superstitions, in old
> wives' tales, in a strange country, full of terror and laughter, the
> Thessaly of the Classical *Walpurgisnacht.*[19]

19. W. P. Ker, *The Dark Ages* (New York: Mentor, 1958), p. 35. Cf. also
Auerbach's remark (in *Mimesis*) concerning Apuleius' "predilection for a haunt-
ing and gruesome distortion of reality" and the comparison with Kafka.

Incidentally, the allegorical side of the *Metamorphoses* inspired what is perhaps the first Christian novel—the so-called *Clementine Recognitions,* a work translated by Rufinus from a Greek original.

The African Latinity of the Christian apologist, Tertullian (also second century), difficult and obscure, is replete with every rhetorical device imaginable. With a trained legal mind, of great technical cleverness, Tertullian also shows the theologian's cavalier attitude towards commonsense truths and the familiar world as we know it; indeed, he was instrumental in developing the language and style of Christian theology and is responsible in no small measure for the rigidly dogmatic theology of Western Christianity. He was, as rhetorician and theologian, a lover of paradox, and later minds of a similar cast (Miguel de Unamuno, Lev Shestov) have loved to quote him (*et sepultus resurrexit, certum est quia impossibile est*), while rationalists have had a frank contempt for both his style and his matter (Voltaire called him "that African madman"). There is something definitely baroque—even decadent—about Tertullian's Latin, reminding one of those Jesuit churches of Belgium which Baudelaire called the "boudoirs of religion." But he reminds us of something else as well: "We are but of yesterday, and we have filled everything you have—cities, islands, forts, towns, exchanges, yes! and camps, tribes, decuries, palace, senate, forum. All we have left to you is the temples."

Claudian, the "last of the Roman poets," makes a brief but impressive appearance at the end of the fourth century. Born in Alexandria, his native language was Greek and he seems to have remained a pagan (although perhaps nominally a Christian) at the court of Honorius; but his Latin poetry (epigrams, political encomia and invectives, and especially the unfinished *De Raptu Proserpinae*) shows considerable technical skill and, for the most part, good taste. Gibbon thought highly of Claudian, as did Coleridge who viewed him as a transitional figure between the Classic and Gothic modes of thought. It is interesting, too, that Walter Pater was another admirer. We can understand Gibbon's and Pater's positions but Coleridge's is puzzling; I would agree with Sir C. A. Elton (*Specimens of the Classic Poets,* 1814) to the effect that in all Claudian's verse "it would be difficult to point to a single natural, unaffected sentiment." Claudian's language, though admittedly not quite so rhetorical as that of the great mass of his predecessors and successors, is very rich in simile (he has more than any of his predecessors[20]), allegory, allusion, and peri-

20. Statistics in Alan Cameron, *Claudian: Poetry and Propaganda at the Court of Honorius* (Oxford: Oxford University Press, 1970), p. 297.

phrasis—e.g., ". . . quos Smyrna dedit, quos Mantua libros Percurrens."[21]

One of the very important names in the fifth century is that of Martianus Capella whose "prosimetric" *De Nuptiis Philologiae et Mercurii* ("The Marriage of Learning and Business") became one of the essential textbooks for the entire Middle Ages. But this work was also largely responsible for the marked medieval predilection for allegory (which is a type of defamiliarization), while the author's Latin is, according to Helen Waddell, "thoroughly vicious." As Ker and other scholars point out, the medieval taste in Latin was in fact derived from writers like Apuleius and Martianus Capella.

Juvencus, a fourth-century Spanish priest, had written a metrical harmony of the Gospels, the first in what was to be a long series of Christian epics down to Milton. In the following century Sedulius, "poeta Christianissimus," wrote the famous *Carmen Paschale* (or "Easter Poem"), a type of Messiad or epic of the life of Christ, together with a prose version, the *Opus Paschale*. Here Sedulius has taken over a major genre of the pagan culture and has adapted the epic form and language to Christian ends (he uses Virgil's description of the Elysian Fields to describe the Christian paradise). The *Carmen Paschale* is thus doubly defamiliarizing—it defamiliarizes the epic form as well as the Christian Message. Curtius is rather critical:

> He [i.e., Sedulius] demonstrates that even a recent convert could take over the frippery of the pagan school rhetor . . . for Sedulius, literary form, whether in poetry or prose, is mere playing with forms. . . . Sedulius had a large measure of literary ambition, but he had nothing to say. So he hit upon the device of saying something over again in a different form.
>
> Throughout its existence—from Juvencus to Klopstock—the Biblical epic was a hybrid with an inner lack of truth, a *genre faux*. The Christian story of salvation, as the Bible presents it, admits no transformation into pseudo-antique form.[22]

Apollinaris Sidonius, a Gallic noble born at Lyons and later Bishop of Clermont, is known for his poetry and his letters, a prime source on the declining culture and imminent barbarism of the fifth century. In one of the letters Sidonius cannot refrain from elaborating

21. Quoted by Curtius in *European Literature and the Latin Middle Ages*, chapter on Mannerism, p. 276.

22. *Ibid.*, pp. 460, 462.

a palindromic sentence, something indicative of the pervasive influence of the mannerism of the age. Sidonius' Latin is strange but his stylistic eccentricities—the *mos sidonianus*—exerted considerable influence during the later Middle Ages. One precept of his (in a letter) might in fact serve, Curtius notes, as a guiding principle of literary mannerism: *Natura comparatum est ut ni omnibus artibus hoc sit scientiae pretiosior pompa quo rarior.*

Otherwise quite a minor figure, Fulgentius the grammarian, a native of Africa, represents the "late African style" and shows the continued tendency to defamiliarize reality and *realia* through rhetorical embellishment. His Latin is appalling, "decadent, involved, littered with wasteful connectives and rhetorical extravagances, pompous, inflated, pretentious, prolix, infested with Asianic exaggeration."[23] Among his works of special significance are the *Mythologiarum libri*, replete with rote learning, amazing errors, and naive etymologizing; Fulgentius explains—or rather freely interprets—classical myths and ruthlessly imposes on them fantastic allegorical interpretations:

> Perhaps one can concede a certain grudging admiration for the persistent, if not remorseless, allegorical searching, equally part of his age, and for the endlessly optimistic assertion of hidden morality; one soon feels that however unpromising the particular name of a legend, Fulgentius will not fail to find some curious gem in the soil, and his most congenial association is with those medieval interpreters of Scripture who uncovered endless jewels of allegory.[24]

3

Traditionally the Middle Ages begin with the founding of Monte Cassino in 529 by Benedict of Nursia. As medievalists point out, the sixth century stands out distinctly for several reasons: it is greatly superior to the fifth and it contrasts almost brilliantly with the following and very dark seventh century; and it is exceptionally well represented by a group of rather important poets (Venantius Fortunatus), scholars (Cassiodorus), and historians (Gregory of Tours), not to mention the imposing figures of Pope Gregory the Great ("the spiritual father of the Middle Ages") and, of course, Boethius. Though For-

23. L. G. Whitbread, *Fulgentius the Mythographer* (Columbus: Ohio State University Press, 1971), p. ix.
24. *Ibid.*, p. 18.

tunatus has his defects as a poet, Cassiodorus his shortcomings as a scholar, and though both Gregories had notorious difficulties with their Latin, the century is not especially rich in examples of defamiliarization, unless we rummage amongst the numerous lesser figures. But it was probably during the sixth century that the very odd work known as the *Hisperica Famina* was produced. The title means "Western Sayings" and, although the text "is a bantling no nation is anxious to claim" (Helen Waddell), it may have originated at the school of Llantwit Major in Wales where Gildas, the earliest of the British historians, was educated. It may in fact have been a student exercise—or even a joke. In any case, it is the most extreme specimen of defamiliarization in Latin (even perhaps in any other literary language) of any period; a farrago of rare and unusual words drawn from such writers as Apuleius and Martianus Capella with an admixture of Greek and Hebrew in transliteration, its "hisperic" lexicon is as strange as its syntax (one of the rules seems to have been always to insert the verb between a noun and its adjective). The Latin of Aldhelm is outlandish enough; and Wright and Sinclair, after quoting a passage from Aldhelm, remark, "It is very nearly as bad as the *Hisperica Famina*."[25] If one cannot consult Stowasser's learned edition (Vienna, 1887), a short but typical passage will be found in Ker.

As one may easily ascertain by paging through Curtius' compendious *European Literature and the Latin Middle Ages,* throughout the long medieval period there is no dearth of examples of defamiliarization in prose and poetry, in genres, conventions, and traditions. This holds true down through the Carolingian and Ottonian renascences, while in the twelfth century we find, according to Eduard Norden (quoted in Curtius), the "craziest of all stylists" in the person of Alan of Lille. With the rise, too, of scholasticism in the twelfth century we encounter another area of defamiliarization—a new way of seeing the world, especially in terms of particulars and universals, as well as new metaphor: thus Jean de Jandun writes that to live in Paris is to exist *simpliciter* (absolutely), to live elsewhere is to exist *secundum quid* (relatively).

But particularly significant, from the eighth century on, is the prominence of the North. Henri Pirenne writes:

> Before the 8th century what existed was the continuation of the ancient Mediterranean economy. After the 8th century there was a

25. F. Wright and T. A. Sinclair, *A History of Later Latin Literature* (New York: Macmillan, 1931), p. 125.

complete break with this economy. The sea was closed. Commerce had disappeared. We perceive an Empire whose only wealth was the soil, and in which the circulation of merchandise was reduced to the minimum. So far from perceiving any progress, we see that there was a regression. Those parts of Gaul which had been the busiest were now the poorest. The South had been the bustling and progressive region; now it was the North which impressed its character upon the period.[26]

The fame of medieval Irish scholarship is well known, as are the numerous and illustrious centers of learning founded by Irish monks (Luxeuil, Bobbio, St. Gall) and such important figures as the poet Sedulius (Śiadal) of Liége and Johannes Scotus (Erigena). "That fierce and restless quality," writes Helen Waddell, "which had made the pagan Irish the terror of Western Europe, seems to have emptied itself into the love of learning and the love of God"[27]; and Frank O'Connor, commenting on the elegance and urbanity of the poem *Meisse ocus Pangur Bán* ("Pangur Ban my cat and I") attributed to Sedulius, says that "it was written by a Latinist who probably came of a family of headhunters."[28] Though it is generally recognized that the Latin influence on early Irish literature was profound (more profound than, say, on German literature) and though Irish verse was based almost entirely on Latin metrics, there is a very apparent Celtic predilection for the fantastic and the strange, reminding one of the lush ornateness of Irish manuscript illuminations. Also manifest are two extremes—of book learning and of primitiveness: Ker says, "the wildest story will begin with a calm recital of the four requisites of story telling"—i.e., of school formulas. While medieval Irish court poetry is very difficult, with its enigmatic defamiliarizing periphrases (a piece of eel is called "a piece of the female race," since it was believed there were no male eels), early Irish ornamental prose frequently reaches extreme limits of defamiliarization.

The conventions of Welsh prose and poetry are even more difficult, although the obscurity of the poetry is often due simply to the

26. Henri Pirenne, *Mohammed and Charlemagne* (New York: Meridian, 1957), p. 236.

27. Helen Waddell, *The Wandering Scholars* (Garden City: Doubleday, 1961), p. 30.

28. Frank O'Connor, *A Short History of Irish Literature* (New York: Putnam's, 1967), p. 52.

obscurity of the myths employed. Ker remarks that the Welsh refused even more stubbornly than the Irish to write intelligible poetry and that certain works, such as the *Gododin*, have still not been fully translated. It is interesting, too, that Ker likens the difficulties of Welsh verse to those—even more notorious—of Icelandic court poetry.

But of course not all poetic obscurity was limited to the North. Beginning in the twelfth century the troubadours of southern France developed the *trobar clus*, another intentionally difficult, obscure, and hermetic style. Of all such defamiliarizing techniques in the West, the *trobar clus* has perhaps the most aristocratic and elitist tradition: the great majority of the famous troubadours were noblemen (such as Guiraut de Borneil, *lo maestre dels trobadors*) and more than twenty were reigning princes. As the system of chivalry may well be viewed as a form of defamiliarization ("The conception of chivalry as a sublime form of secular life might be defined as an aesthetic ideal assuming the appearance of an ethical ideal"—Huizinga), so the whole convention of courtly love may also be seen as a kind of fiction or defamiliarization of the erotic. French authors, Huizinga remarks, like to oppose *l'esprit gaulois* to the conventions of courtly love and to consider the former as "natural," the latter as artificial:

> Now the former is no less a fiction than the latter. Erotic thought never acquires literary value save by some process of transfiguration of complex and painful reality into illusionary forms. The whole genre of *Les Cent Nouvelles Nouvelles* and the loose song, with its wilful neglect of all the natural and social complications of love, with its indulgence towards the lies and egotism of sexual life, and its vision of a never-ending lust, implies, no less than the screwed-up [!] system of courtly love, an attempt to substitute for reality the dream of a happier life.[29]

What has been said of the troubadours and courtly love also applies to the minnesingers and *Frauendienst*. And it might also apply to the Arabic poets who celebrated what is known as *'udrī*-love—i.e., platonic love or *amor de lonh*. There is in fact good reason to believe that the medieval convention of *domnei* or *amour courtois* derives, in part at least, from Muslim Spain and the Middle East (it is possible,

29. J. Huizinga, *The Waning of the Middle Ages* (Garden City: Doubleday, 1956), p. 112.

too, that *trobar* is from the Arabic *tarraba,* to sing or make music[30]).
Gerald Brenan writes:

> I think therefore that one must conclude that the notion of
> courtly or platonic love (*amor de lonh,* love at a distance, as one of
> the early troubadours called it), which was the driving force behind
> most lyric poetry down to the time of Donne, had an Eastern origin
> and in fact reached the feudal courts of Southern France from Moslem
> Spain.[31]

So far as the Renaissance is concerned, since the rhetorical tradition continued unabated here, one may also find numerous instances
of defamiliarization. And before we move on to the seventeenth
century, which is richer (for our purposes) in striking examples, some
brief remarks on the Renaissance are in order. This was an age during
which the study and imitation of Cicero's Latin were of central
importance and there was a strong tendency (true, amongst a very
small elite) to rephrase the familiar—though vulgar—Latin of the
Church and the Middle Ages on the basis of Ciceronian models—
witness Cardinal Bembo's preference for the classical *divinae mentis
aura* over *spiritus sanctus.* There were also new opportunities to see
and consider many familiar aspects of reality or traditional concepts
through alien eyes—e.g., Pico della Mirandola's preoccupation with
Arabic and Hebrew language and thought; or Nicholas of Cusa's
method of speculation, under the influence of Augustine's writings, by
means of *docta ignorantia;* or the daringly new critical approach to
sacred scripture of men like Johann Reuchlin. Finally, the Renaissance
itself—or at least some facets of it—may be viewed as defamiliarization:

> It was not realism which the Renaissance achieved, only a differ-
> ent and more fruitful fantasy. Botticelli's maidens at springtime, the
> Venus upon the shell and waves, the Madonna who sits within her
> circular frame above a Gospel open to the Magnificat, are far too
> lovely for human verisimilitude, and they are engaged upon enter-
> prises which the purest human deeds can only approximate. They are,
> that is to say, idealized—cast forth by his brush as visual signs of
> perfection, which, once seen, would live (as indeed they do) in

30. J. B. Trend, "Spain and Portugal," in *The Legacy of Islam* (Oxford:
Oxford University Press, 1931), p. 17.

31. Gerald Brenan, *The Literature of the Spanish People* (New York:
Meridian, 1957), p. 26. See also H. A. R. Gibb in *The Legacy of Islam,* p. 184
ff. Gibb also cites K. Burdach, "Ueber den Ursprung der mittelälterlichen Min-
nesangs," on the Arabic background.

imagination forever. This much, to be sure, ecclesiastical art had always done. The difference was that perfection now ceased to be exclusively divine; it became human and therefore attainable within our world.[32]

4

The literary baroque of the seventeenth century manifests itself in several particular, national forms—French preciosity, Italian marinism, Spanish gongorism, etc., these terms themselves occasionally being generalized and applied to characteristic features of the age as a whole. Of these various baroque periods or movements, French *préciosité* is, due largely to Molière's comedy, perhaps the most familiar. The notorious periphrases or, rather, periphrastic formulas—which constitute what is essentially an idiolect and cant—are the most noticeable components of the style: *les trônes de la pudeur* (cheeks), *le supplément du soleil* (candle), *le mémoire de l'avenir* (almanac), *les commodités de la conversation* (chairs), etc. These examples, taken from Somaize's *Dictionnaire des Précieuses* (1660), quite obviously represent the defamiliarization of familiar objects; and this "precious" tendency to defamiliarize everyday actions and things quickly became, even in Russia, the subject of jokes and parody: thus Pushkin (in a letter, 1824) writes: "Send me some writing paper and some plain paper, some wine, some cheese, and do not forget (as Delille would say) 'the twisted steel that pierces the bepitched bottle-neck'—that is, a corkscrew."[33]

The comparable Italian tendency, *marinismo*, is named after the poet Giambattista Marino (d. 1625). The poetry of Marino (as well as of other Italian baroque poets) is a thesaurus of far-fetched simile, metaphor, oxymoron, hyperbaton, and of course periphrasis:

> Chi crederà . . .
> O ch'altro sia che la liev'aura mossa
> Una voce pennuta, un suon volante?
> E vestito di penne un vivo fiato,
> Una piuma canora, un canto alato?[34]

32. Barrows Dunham, *Heroes and Heretics: A Social History of Dissent* (New York: Delta, 1968), p. 267.

33. For a compendious study of preciosity, see R. Lathuillère, *La Préciosité* (Geneva, 1966).

34. From *L'Adone* (vii, 37ff.). For a study of Marino's style, see James Mirollo, *The Poet of the Marvelous, Giambattista Marino* (New York: Columbia University Press, 1963).

All of these resources are used with the utmost skill to produce the effect of what is called *ingegno* ("ingenuity," "wit") in accordance with the marinistic principle that the language of poetry depends not at all upon logic but rather upon a kind of metamorphosis (or defamiliarization) of ordinary reality:

> The metaphor, in effect, in the use which Baroque writers made of it, does not seem reducible to a plain and extrinsic rhetorical fact, rather it appears to respond to the expressive necessity of a mode of feeling and of manifesting things, as an element of a complex game of allusions and illusions, as an ideal possibility for the translation of all terms of the knowable into a vision of reality in which things seem to lose their static and well-defined nature to wander carried away in a universal transport which alters outlines and significances. The metaphor, rather than a rhetorical fact, seems in the Baroque age a vision of life; [whence] for this culture one could speak positively of a universal "metaphorism" and a "metamorphism" as of essential modes of noting and expressing reality.[35]

The *ingegno* of Marino is paralleled by the *ingenio* or *agudeza* of the Spanish baroque poets, especially of Luis de Góngora (d. 1627)—whence the term gongorism, often equated with marinism. A number of references have already been made to Góngora's periphrases and other stylistic devices but I should like to quote here a comment by Damaso Alonso:

> Todo el arte de Góngora consiste en un doble juego: esquivar los elementos de la realidad cotidiana, para sustituirlos por otros que corresponden, de hecho, a realidades distintas del mundo físico o del espiritual, y que sólo mediante el prodigioso puente de la intuición poética pueden ser referidos a los reemplazados. Es éste un doble juego en el que tanto se pierde como se gana. Se pierde en variedad: el mundo sufre una poda de cualidades físicas no interesantes estéticamente; pero las cualidades conservadas adquieren—con el aislamiento— nitidez, realce, intensidad, notas elevadas ahora a términos absolutos, perdidas antés—del lado real—en una confusión de contingencias.[36]

35. Giovanni Getto, quoted in Harold Priest, *Adonis: Selections from L'Adone of Giambattista Marino* (Ithaca: Cornell University Press, 1967), Introduction, p. xxxvi.

36. *Estudios y Ensayos Gongorinos* (Madrid: Editorial Gredos, 1955), p. 92. See also Elisha Kane, *Gongorism and the Golden Age* (Chapel Hill: University of North Carolina Press, 1928).

But it is not at all unusual, as we have seen, to encounter similar comments on other baroque-type poets of various eras; and one cannot but suspect that the respective scholars and critics, had they been acquainted with Shklovsky's concept of *ostranenie,* might well have used some equivalent of defamiliarization.

The name usually associated with baroque and mannerist excesses in Germany is that of Christian Hoffmann von Hoffmannswaldau (d. 1679) of the "Second Silesian School" (or High Baroque). There is no exact equivalent in German to *marinismo* or *gongorismo,* although occasionally the term *"die liebliche Schreibart"* is used of Hoffmannswaldau, and of course there is the word *Schwulst* (bombast, grandiloquence) often applied to extreme forms of the German baroque. Hoffmannswaldau is known particularly for his eroticism and his erotic periphrases: he likes to employ quaint expressions such as *dein rein altar* to refer to the *pudenda muliebria,* while his preoccupation with female breasts is frequently elaborated in *outré* metaphors: *ein seecompass / der hurtig rudern heisset / Eh man in hafen der vergnügung wird gebracht.* Elsewhere breasts are likened to skeleton keys, a pair of bellows, a coffin, cliffs, a garden, a pond, towers, a lighthouse, a julep, sisters sleeping in the same bed, hunters, a mine, rooms, unmeltable snowballs. In the case of Hoffmannswaldau the devices of defamiliarization worked almost too well: I think most readers would agree with Robert M. Browning:

> Hoffmannswaldau's [women] are almost automatons, concatenations of stylized physical details no one could possibly imagine as living beings. All this can, however, be interpreted meaningfully. If our thesis concerning the basic configuration of his work is correct, this is precisely the effect he was striving for. In spite of the metaphoric material fetched from every corner of the earth, the anti-heaven of lust is a narrow room, peopled by monomaniac automatons, mechanical, atomistic.[37]

In English literature John Lyly's euphuism is frequently cited as a slightly earlier counterpart to marinism and gongorism. Though Lyly was mainly a prose writer, we do find in his work many of the stylistic devices that we find in other, more typically baroque authors. But even closer parallels may be found in the verse of poets like Richard

37. Quoted in Robert M. Browning, *German Baroque Poetry, 1618–1723* (University Park: Pennsylvania State University Press, 1971), p. 169.

Crashaw (d. 1650), who has been called the most baroque of the English Metaphysicals.[38]

The penetration of baroque motifs and practices into Russia towards the middle of the seventeenth century did not add too much that was new to an already strong Muscovite rhetorical tradition which, throughout the sixteenth century, preferred the ornate, the obscure, and the allegorical. This pre-baroque is well represented by the chronicle prose of Ivan Timofeev, whose style Mirsky has called "the *reductio ad absurdum* of Muscovite rhetoric." Although Slavic scholars frequently refer to certain baroque elements in writers of the eighteenth century (e.g., the "baroque poetics" of Lomonosov's *Rhetoric*), the fact is that Russian literature of the seventeenth century can offer nothing at all comparable to Marino, Góngora, or von Hoffmannswaldau; nor can it match the wit of the Polish baroque poets—men like Jan Morsztyn (d. 1693) who, incidentally, translated Marino.[39]

Amongst the minor literatures (often unfortunately but necessarily omitted in surveys such as this) there are also poets and prose writers who represent the baroque movement and manner. In Hungarian literature, for instance, we have the works—such as the *Murányi Vénusz* ("Venus of Muranyi")—of István Gyöngyösi (d. 1704) with their highly metaphorical and "conceited" style. And in the literatures of the Near and Far East there are, of course, vast bodies of prose and poetry replete with devices of defamiliarization. In Arabic literature, although there is no exact equivalent of our seventeenth-century baroque, we might mention the names of two important writers, al-Mutanabbi and al-Hariri. The former (whom we quoted earlier, p. 83) lived in the tenth century and is regarded by many Arabs as their greatest poet. Arab critics have heaped fulsome praise upon him and his *Diwan* over the centuries, while Nicholson, referring to his "verbal legerdemain," concedes that he is not often to our Western taste because of his incredibly pinguid style that makes our most rococo baroque look like the severest classicism.[40] The philological interests of al-Hariri (d. 1122), not at all uncommon among Arabic poets, are shown by the fact that, in addition to his elegant *Maqamat* ("Assem-

38. See George Williamson, *The Donne Tradition* (Cambridge, Mass.: Harvard University Press, 1930), p. 116, and Mario Praz, *Secentismo e Marinismo in Inghilterra* (Florence, 1925), for a study of Crashaw and the baroque.

39. See Czeslaw Milosz, *The History of Polish Literature* (New York: Macmillan, 1969), p. 132 ff.

40. Reynold Nicholson, *A Literary History of the Arabs* (Cambridge: At the University Press, 1956), p. 304 ff.

blies"), he wrote *The Pearl of the Diver,* a study of grammatical errors committed by educated Arabs. In Persian and Tajik literature there is something quite similar to our baroque in the "Indian style" (*sabki hind*), best represented by the works of Bedil (seventeenth–eighteenth centuries) and in the "Bedilism" of other poets.[41]

The literatures of India constitute a vast body of works of special interest for this study, but I shall limit myself here to a few comments on classical Sanskrit literature (approximately 90 percent of all such extant literature belongs to the period after about A.D. 1200). Of particular relevance is the concept developed by the critic Bhamaha in the fifth century of our era of *vakrata* or "curvature." The term refers both to metaphor and obliquity of expression (or periphrasis) and clearly suggests defamiliarization through artistic distortion. Several centuries later another critic, Anandavardhana, elaborated a theory of "revealed" and "expressed" meanings, with the implication that the former might in fact be the opposite of the latter. These and other devices of defamiliarization, along with the effects of the austere restrictions that had been placed upon the rules of inflexion by the grammarian Panini (which led to the building up of compound nouns to replace clauses and to a preference for inordinately long sentences), produced some strange and technically complex works. For example, in Subhandu's novel *Vasavadatta,* a good specimen of the florid "Bengali" style, almost every sentence has a double meaning. This trick of *dvyasrayakavya* (relating two stories concurrently by exploiting the ambiguity of words) is seen in Dhananjaya's *Dvisandhana* (ninth century), which *simultaneously* narrates the *Mahabharata* and the *Ramayana,* and culminates in the *Ramacarita* of Sandhyakara (twelfth century), which may be read either as concerning the legendary Rama or the real King Ramapala of Bengal (the poet's patron). Bhosa accomplished an equally incredible *tour de force* by illustrating, in exact order, the whole of Panini's grammar in his *Ravanarjuniya.*[42]

(I shall not attempt to survey here the neoromantic period or the age of symbolism in the modern European literatures, since in the preceding chapters a very large number of representative types of defamiliarization was drawn from works of prose, poetry, and drama pro-

41. See Jan Rypka, *History of Iranian Literature* (Dordrecht: D. Reidel, 1968), pp. 496–97, 515 ff.

42. See the excellent survey by A. K. Warder, "Classical Literature," in *A Cultural History of India,* edited by A. L. Basham (Oxford: Oxford University Press, 1975), pp. 170–96.

duced in the period loosely referred to as modernism, and I have cited numerous studies dealing specifically with the literature and arts of this period.)

5

In the preceding chapters and sections the term "defamiliarization" has been used not only to cover a very broad range of linguistic and literary phenomena, but it has also been applied to various other human activities. It has been used with reference to almost everything in literature, from simile to metaphor, from polyptoton to allegory, from technopaegnia to juxtaposition, from choliambics to hyperbaton; it has been used of chivalry and scholasticism, of Alexandrianism and Senecan tragedy, of *chosisme* and anti-novels; and we have mentioned in connection with defamiliarization the language of politics and business, of medicine and the law, as well as defamiliarization in such widely diverse areas as cooking and religion, cosmetics and music. The objection might now be raised—if indeed it has not already been—that the significance of this term, here so broadly applied, has been stretched beyond the breaking point. The first and most obvious answer to such an objection would be, of course, simply to refer to similar criticism which has been leveled against, for instance, the term "romanticism." Whereas Arthur Lovejoy, among others, feels that the term "romantic" has come to mean so many things that it means nothing, René Wellek has argued quite convincingly that the term is both meaningful and useful.[43] But we must remember that the meanings and applications of the term "romantic" have multiplied and ramified during the two centuries or so that have elapsed since it was first used in a rather limited sense; in the case of *ostranenie*, however, the term was, from its very inception, seen and meant to be of broad significance. Thus Shklovsky writes: *Ja lichno schitaju, chto ostranenie est' pochti vezde, gde est' obraz.* Scholars such as G. Dorflès have suggested that the concept of defamiliarization be applied not only in poetry but in the other arts as well, and various critics down through the ages have expressed the opinion that language itself, in a very broad sense, involves something very close to defamiliarization. George Steiner, for example, writes that "Language is the main instrument of man's refusal to accept the world as it is."[44]

43. René Wellek, "The Concept of Romanticism in Literary History," in *Concepts of Criticism* (New Haven: Yale University Press, 1963).
44. George Steiner, *After Babel* (New York: Oxford University Press, 1976), pp. 217–18.

Furthermore, while it is difficult to put one's finger on what constitutes the essence of romanticism, it is not at all difficult to point out the common denominator in all cases of defamiliarization—it is simply this: the familiar is made unfamiliar. This holds true, whether we refer to a cook preparing a piece of pastry in the shape of a fish, whether we have in mind something like P. T. Barnum's "THIS WAY TO THE EGRESS" ploy, or whether we are considering, say, Annensky's allusion to suicide in the lines *bezdonnye prudy,/ Davno gotovye dlja spelogo stradan'ja* ("Bottomless ponds,/ long ready for ripe suffering"). It goes without saying that not every phenomenon, literary or other, invites or involves defamiliarization; Shklovsky, it will be noted, modifies his statement by adding *pochti,* and I have earlier cited a number of areas in which defamiliarization is *usually* not found. To be sure, there are situations in which it may not at first be clear whether we have defamiliarization or familiarization. For example, at certain cultural stages, following the introduction of pottery, clay vessels are occasionally decorated with a basket-weave design: is this done primarily to make the new objects resemble the former actual baskets, i.e., to familiarize the new artifacts, or is it done rather to make the clay vessels—these having become "familiar"—appear different, i.e., to defamiliarize them? The former is more likely the case.[45]

Though one or two examples of defamiliarization (or something analogous to this) in nature, as well as instances of accidental or unintentional defamiliarization in certain human activities were mentioned in Chapter I, this study has for the most part concerned itself with types of intentional—or what appears to be intentional—defamiliarization in literature and in several of the other arts. While the great majority of grammatical, syntactical, rhetorical, stylistic, metrical, and critical terms in common use are (or have become) neutral and passive technical terms which merely describe certain phenomena, the term defamiliarization is dynamic. It is dynamic because we may picture here an object (i.e., a tradition, a commonplace, an image, a word or phrase, a name, a place, chronology, an event, a quotation, a fact, etc.) being in some way manipulated or distorted—turned upside down or inside out, enlarged, reduced, or simply held up to be viewed from a different angle or in a new light. The term "defamiliarization" also injects elements of both intent and effect, the latter being the aspect of art that mainly interests us. So far as the artist's intent is con-

---

45. Cf. the roughly similar situation during and after the Renaissance when certain French words "were remodeled into closer resemblance with their Latin originals" (e.g., *dette* and *doute* altered to "debt" and "doubt"), Jespersen, *Growth and Structure of the English Language*, section 116.

cerned, we more often than not lack precise and valid evidence (and even when we have this at first hand, it is frequently suspect—"Never trust the artist, trust the tale"). There can be little doubt concerning Tolstoy's intent in the *loci classici* of defamiliarization in his novels: yet one often wonders, after reading an elaborate interpretation of the meaning of a text, whether in fact the author intentionally wove into this text the particular design—or meaning—that the critic (who may be of immense erudition) has found there. Especially problematical is a work such as Bruno Bettelheim's *The Uses of Enchantment: The Meaning and Importance of Fairy Tales* (1976), in which, like a Church Father hunting allegory in Scripture, the author searches for sexual allusion in such familiar fairy tales as "Little Red Riding Hood," "Cinderella," and "The Three Little Pigs." According to Bettelheim, the tale of Little Red Riding Hood involves rebirth into sexual maturity; Cinderella seeks to be accepted by the Prince in her natural state of dirtiness and inserts her penile foot into his vaginal slipper (!); while in the tale of the Three Little Pigs a child is supposed to understand "subconsciously that we have to shed earlier forms of experience if we wish to move on to higher ones" (i.e., the two pigs that die are discarded developmental stages of the third, surviving pig). If such interpretations are correct, then we have in these fairy tales—as we have perhaps in myths—the fictional defamiliarization of various human concepts, aspirations, or beliefs; if, however, Bettelheim is reading into these tales meanings of his own (as a Marxist might find in them *his* particular meanings), we have in his book the defamiliarization of familiar and—possibly—insignificant tales of fancy.

As the term "metaphor," for example, may be used in either a very general or very particular sense, so defamiliarization may have either a very broad and general meaning, referring to any situation in which the familiar is rendered unfamiliar, or it may be used in literature and the other arts for various specific purposes. Although I have not given any textbook classification of these different functions of defamiliarization, the variety of employment is evident in the numerous quotations and references cited. If, however, I were to attempt a classification, I should begin by first distinguishing between defamiliarization of form and defamiliarization of content (see p. 42). I would also be strongly tempted to consider defamiliarization not generically but, like symbolism, as a species of irony—irony here being taken in its broadest sense ("Commonly . . . the term is applied in the conventional sense to a contrast between what is spoken and what is meant"[46]). This extensive meaning of irony is not, of course, anything new; the German romantic critics interpreted the word in rather cavalier fashion, and the German esthetician K. W. F. Solger all but equated irony with art itself.[47] Hegel wrote of irony: "It works through the wit and play of wholly personal points of view, and if carried to an extreme amounts to the triumph of the creative power of the artist's soul over every content and every form.[48]

In more recent years I. A. Richards considered irony as characteristic of the highest poetry, and American New Criticism has developed the view of the poem as ironic structure. Cleanth Brooks, while admitting the inadequacy of the term, writes:

> Irony is the most general term we have for the kind of qualification which the various elements in a context receive from the context. This kind of qualification . . . is of tremendous importance in any poem. Moreover, irony is our most general term for indicating that recognition of incongruities—which . . . pervades all poetry to a degree far beyond what our conventional criticism has been heretofore willing to admit.[49]

The etymology of the word "irony" was mentioned early in the first chapter of this book in connection with Tolstoy's essentially ironic employment of defamiliarization, and the word is very frequently used in discussions not only of defamiliarization but also of other Shklovskian and Formalist concepts.[50] It is, in fact, remarkable that Shklovsky himself did not specifically relate—if not equate—*ostranenie* and *ironija*.

In sorting out and enumerating, for the purpose of classification, the various functions or effects of defamiliarization, although there would be no difficulty with the comic and the burlesque effects, there

46. Charles Glicksberg, *The Ironic Vision in Modern Literature* (The Hague: M. Nijhoff, 1969), p. 14.

47. See M. Boucher, *K. W. F. Solger, Esthétique et philosophie de la présence* (Paris, 1934), pp. 107–10.

48. Quoted in W. Wimsatt and C. Brooks, *Literary Criticism: A Short History* (New York: Knopf, 1962), p. 380.

49. Cleanth Brooks, *The Well Wrought Urn* (New York: Harcourt, Brace & World, 1947), pp. 209–10. See also Erlich, *Russian Formalism*, p. 275. It is interesting that Erlich writes: "As if in order to prove that 'the device of making strange' (*priem ostranenija*) was not merely a slogan of the literary avant-garde, but an omnipresent principle of imaginative literature, Shklovskij drew his most telling examples from the master of the 'realistic' novel, Lev Tolstoj" (p. 177).

50. E.g., in Jameson's *The Prison-House of Language*, pp. 79–81.

might at first appear to be a problem with parody. How, some-one might ask, can parody be related to defamiliarization? The answer is that parody, whether verbal, formal, or thematic, *is* also an instance of defamiliarization. If one consults the index of the 1929 edition of Shklovsky's *O teorii prozy*, he will find *"parodirovanie (= priem ostranenija)"* and page references to, for example, Fielding's parody of Richardson's novels as well as Sterne's parody of the form of the novel itself. But we may also see the relationship through the medium of irony (or its congener, satire). Parody, then, makes the familiar un-familiar in this way: the writer takes some familiar or characteristic feature of another writer and, by exaggerating it, abusing it, inverting it, or otherwise altering or distorting it, renders it ridiculous; that is, he causes us to see something we are familiar with in a new, strange, absurd, or grotesque light. This is exactly what Max Beerbohm does in his brilliant parody of Henry James, "A Mote in the Middle Dis-tance," or, for that matter, what a caricaturist does, for example, with Richard Nixon's nose or with Jimmy Carter's toothy smile. Though there is a range of parody from bold and humorous caricature to subtle but ironic imitation, it is always necessary that whatever is being parodied be familiar; otherwise we have the situation outlined by Tynyanov at the end of his essay on Gogol and Dostoevsky.[51]

But much more important than classification is the critical evalua-tion of how well or how ill the device of defamiliarization and its variety of effects are employed. It has already been noted that types of defamiliarization are especially prominent in certain post-classical, Alexandrian, baroque, decadent, or silver ages of literature, i.e., dur-ing periods when writers rely chiefly upon a *réchauffage* and fore-grounding of those devices formerly used by greater artists, but used by them as secondary elements, as means to an end and not as ends in themselves. It is not that the great writer makes less use of defa-miliarization than the mannerist but rather that he has more to say to us; his significance lies more in the flesh than in the skeleton. In the work of a fleshless writer—the novelist, for example, who bases his narrative on a series of *fiches* containing rare words and punning phrases—the bones rather than the flesh are more prominent. We phi-lologists sometimes enjoy frequenting the charnel houses of literature where the bones are more easily accessible for purposes of study; but this does not mean that we do not also enjoy—and recognize the aes-thetic superiority of—living gardens.

51. See the English version in *Twentieth-Century Russian Literary Criticism*, edited by Victor Erlich (New Haven: Yale University Press, 1975), pp. 102–16.

Without setting forth any elaborate theory of evaluation, I would simply suggest that our criteria for judging how well or effectively de-familiarization is used should be: discretion, moderation, consistency, and—most important of all—appropriateness (since even indiscretion, immoderation, and inconsistency are at times appropriate). And we need only turn to Horace's *Ars Poetica* for classical statements of these criteria:

> Amphora coepit
> institui, currente rota cur urceus exit?
> Denique sit quod vis, simplex dumtaxat et unum. (21–23)

> qui variare cupit rem prodigialiter unam,
> delphinum silvis appingit, fluctibus aprum.
> In vitium ducit culpae fuga, si caret arte. (29–31)

> In verbis etiam tenuis cautusque serendis
> hoc amet, hoc spernat promissi carminis auctor.
> Dixeris egregie, notum si callida verbum
> reddiderit iunctura novum. Si forte necesse est
> indiciis monstrare recentibus abdita rerum,
> fingere cinctutis non exaudita Cethegis
> continget, dabiturque licentia sumpta pudenter. (45–51)

Thus Lycophron's frigid concatenation of periphrases and metalepses, his lack of discretion and his immoderation in defamiliarizing the minutiae of his ancestors' mythology inevitably condemned the *Alexandra*, regardless of contemporary admiration on the part of fellow librarians and scholars, to the wax-works museum of literary oddities. Much the same may be said of Crashaw's poem, "Saint Mary Magdalene, or The Weeper," which begins:

> Hail, sister springs!
> Parents of silver-footed rills!
> Ever bubbling things!
> Thawing crystal! snowy hills,
> Still spending, never spent! I mean
> Thy fair eyes, sweet Magdalene!

These verses, with their tasteless and grotesquely obtrusive moving-water imagery, invite publication in something like *The Stuffed Owl* anthology. On the other hand, if a poet chooses to write a sonnet about a beautiful woman who is also an epileptic, as Claudio Achillini did, the poet is free, aside from certain restrictions within the sonnet form, to resort to somewhat more violent but nevertheless appropriate imagery. Indeed, one is surprised at Achillini's restraint in these lines from his *Bellissima Spiritata:*

> Là nel mezzo del Tempio a l'improvviso
> Lidia traluna gli occhi, e tiengli immoti,
> E mirano i miei lumi a lei devoti
> Fatto albergo di furie un sì bel viso.

But a general lack of taste and inappropriateness in matching language to theme, either when the former does not measure up to the latter or when—which is more frequent—it noticeably outweighs and overbalances the content, are more than common in all the literatures of the world.

In conclusion I would repeat that the extensiveness of the term defamiliarization is one of its virtues, allowing us to generalize and see a common element in many phenomena. One need not, in order to recognize the applicability of the term and the concept, believe that man has always been ready in all of his activities to deceive himself and others, although a sympathy with this idea helps. But certainly man seems always to have longed for a new and different vision of things and the world. The theologian who attempts to invest man's pitiful and precarious condition with transcendental significance is defamiliarizing reality as surely as the housewife does so when from time to time, and often to the chagrin of her husband, she rearranges the furniture or the garden, although of course the orders of value— not to mention the effects—may be quite different. The theories of Galileo, Harvey, Darwin, Freud, and Einstein defamiliarized and ultimately replaced traditional views, their motivation being essentially the same as that of the writer who likens a dam to a comb smoothing a Russian river, even though, again, there may be major differences on a scale of values. Defamiliarization, then, may be used for many purposes and it does many things: it amuses, saddens, angers, astonishes, ridicules, enchants, puzzles, and in some cases heralds discoveries that change our lives and alter history. And it may also wreak havoc, one of the most pernicious forms of defamiliarization being the deification of the state, an entity no more suitable (as Toynbee suggests) for being turned into a focus of emotion or an object of worship than a gas- or water-works.

INDEX

DEFAMILIARIZATION
IN LANGUAGE AND LITERATURE

was composed in 10-point linotype Caledonia and leaded two points
with display type in foundry Bulmer and printed letterpress by
Joe Mann Associates, Inc.;
Smyth-sewn and bound over boards in Columbia Bayside Linen by
Vail-Ballou Press, Inc.;
and published by

SYRACUSE UNIVERSITY PRESS
Syracuse, New York 13210